Jennifer Fellows was edu .ge,
University of London, sne studied English
Language and Literature. She then went on to
Newnham College, Cambridge and was awarded a
Ph.D. in 1980. In 1982–4, she was Leverhulme
Research Fellow, preparing an edition of *The Par-
lement of Foules* for the Variorum Edition of the
Works of Geoffrey Chaucer. Since then she has
worked as an editor for various academic pub-
lications, including the journal of medieval studies,
Medium Ævum. Her own published work includes
'Editing Middle English romances', in *Romance in
Medieval England*, ed. Mills, Fellows and Meale
(Cambridge, 1991) and 'Mothers in Middle English
romance' in *Women and Literature in Britain, c. 1100–
1500*, ed. Meale (Cambridge University Press, forthcoming).

OF LOVE
AND CHIVALRY

An Anthology of Middle English Romance

Edited by
JENNIFER FELLOWS

Consultant Editor
MALCOLM ANDREW
Professor of English Language and Literature
The Queen's University of Belfast

J M Dent & Sons
London
Charles E. Tuttle Co. Inc
Rutland, Vermont
EVERYMAN'S LIBRARY

Textual editing, introduction and commentary
© J M Dent 1993

This edition first published in Everyman by J M Dent
1993

Typeset at The Spartan Press Ltd
Lymington, Hants

Printed in Great Britain by
The Guernsey Press Co. Ltd
Guernsey, C.I.

for
J M Dent
Orion Publishing Group
Orion House
5 Upper St Martin's Lane
London WC2H 9EA

and
Charles E. Tuttle Co. Inc
28 South Main Street
Rutland, Vermont
05701 – USA

ISBN 0 460 87237 0

CONTENTS

FOR JUDY

et in memoriam G. F.

INTRODUCTION

Romance, like most literary genres, is notoriously difficult to define; many have been the attempts to establish the corpus of Middle English romance and to classify its components.[1] Common to all works normally accepted as part of that corpus, however, is a preoccupation with love and/or chivalry, in varying proportions and with a diversity of thematic emphases.

The modern connotations of the term 'romantic' might lead us to expect that love between the sexes is the primary focus of these narratives, but this is not normally the case. Such love provides the motive force for *Florys and Blauncheflour* alone among the romances in this volume. This is not to say that love and marriage do not play an important part in most romances, but usually they subserve other themes such as the hero's growth to maturity (*King Horn*, *Syr Tryamowre*), or are seen in relation to knightly prowess, honour (*The Erle of Tolous*) and loyalty (*Amis and Amiloun*).

More central to the Middle English romances than love are chivalry and the qualities associated with it: martial prowess, honour, *trouthe* and devotion to Christian ideals. The male protagonists of all the romances presented here are, or become, knights – even the youthful Florys. Horn and Tryamowre must prove themselves as warriors in order to earn their wives and their kingdoms. In *Amis and Amiloun* the love and loyalty between the two heroes are subsumed within a larger pattern of loyalties associated with the chivalric ideal. The principle underlying *The Erle of Tolous* is honour – though, interestingly, it is the heroine's even more than the hero's *trouthe* that is tested. *Florys and*

---

[1] A recent contribution is W. R. J. Barron, *English Medieval Romance* (London, 1987), pp. 53–60, which includes a useful survey of earlier discussions.

Blauncheflour and *Syr Launfal* alone lack the framework of chivalric values[2] – though there is perhaps a suggestion in the latter that knightly prowess and *trouthe* in love are interdependent.[3]

Several motifs are shared by two or more of these six romances (wicked stewards, wronged queens, 'wooing women', judicial combats), but in each they are made to serve different ends. These and related themes recur throughout the corpus of Middle English romance.

No study of romance in medieval England is complete without some consideration of the Anglo-Norman works which preceded, and in some cases provided direct sources for, the Middle English romances. Only by placing the latter within their literary-historical context can we properly appreciate the distinctive nature of their achievement.[4]

King Horn

King Horn is probably the earliest, and arguably one of the finest, of the Middle English romances. Usually dated to *c.* 1225, it is one of several English treatments of a story told at much greater length in the twelfth-century Anglo-Norman *Romance of Horn* by Thomas (hereafter *RH*).[5] Much discussion has been generated by the complexity of the interrelationships between *King Horn*, *RH* and the fourteenth-century *Horn Childe and Maiden Rimnild*,[6] but the general consensus is now that *King Horn* and *Horn Childe* are probably independently derived from *RH*.[7]

[2] On *Syr Launfal*'s fairy-tale ethos, see pp. xix–xx below.

[3] See p. xx below.

[4] See in particular Judith Weiss, *The Birth of Romance: An Anthology* (London, 1992) (hereafter *BR*), in which four Anglo-Norman romances, including versions of the Horn and Amis and Amiloun stories, are translated; Susan Crane, *Insular Romance: Politics, Faith, and Culture in Anglo-Norman and Middle English Literature* (Berkeley, Calif., 1986).

[5] *The Romance of Horn by Thomas*, ed. Mildred K. Pope, 2 vols (Vol. II rev. and completed T. B. W. Reid), Anglo-Norman Texts 9–10, 12–13 (Oxford, 1955–64). The Anglo-Norman text is translated in *BR*.

[6] See, e.g., Hans Helmut Christmann, 'Über das Verhältnis zwischen dem anglonormannischen und dem mittelenglischen "Horn"', *Zeitschrift für französische Sprache und Literatur*, 70 (1960), 166–81; Werner Arens, *Die anglonormannische und die englischen Fassungen des Hornstoffer. Ein historischgenetischer Vergleich*, Studien zur Anglistik (Frankfurt am Main, 1973).

[7] See Christmann, 'Über das Verhältnis', pp. 167–72; Arens, *Die anglonormannische und die englische Fassungen*, pp. 11–24; *Horn Childe and Maiden Rimnild*, ed. Maldwyn Mills, Middle English Texts 20 (Heidelberg, 1988), p. 44.

Detailed comparison between *King Horn* and *RH* can be found in the Commentary (pp. 267–83 below). While lacking the rich texture of the Anglo-Norman poem, with its detailed descriptions of courtly life and accomplishments, and its much larger cast of characters, the Middle English romance achieves through narrative compression a more coherent and satisfying structure, in which repetition and parallelism play an important part. Through these devices the story acquires something of the timelessness and universality of folktale.

The context of the action, while apparently reflecting in a general way the Viking raids on Britain, cannot be related to any specific historical event. The story of Horn (like those of other Anglo-Norman/Middle English heroes, including Havelok and Bevis of Hampton)[8] is based on a familiar 'exile and return' formula;[9] its overall structure is determined by Horn's need to prove himself as a man and a knight, to avenge his father's death and to regain his patrimony – to which, having attained maturity, he is now seen to be a worthy successor. The story of his courtship of (or, rather, by) Rymenhild subserves this theme: their eventual marriage at once marks Horn's achievement in regaining land and status[10] and consolidates his position as a powerful king and the founder, or perpetuator, of a dynasty. In *King Horn*, however, the 'love-interest' is more successfully integrated with the dynastic theme than in *RH*: this is achieved partly through the motif of the protective ring which is given to the hero by Rymenhild and which serves also as a means of recognition between them.[11] Magic rings are, of course, part of the stock-in-trade of folktale and romance;[12] but in *King Horn* (as also in *RH*) it is not enough simply that the hero should wear it: he must also remember it and the loyalty of which it is a token.[13] His prowess is thus seen to be dependent upon his loyalty; failure in loyalty brings about a loss of integrity which leads to failure not only as a man but as a knight. (A very similar idea, though here concerned with a larger complex of interdependent virtues, is more explicitly expressed

[8] *Havelok*, ed. G. V. Smithers (Oxford, 1987); *The Romance of Sir Beues of Hamtoun*, ed. Eugen Kölbing, EETS, ES 46, 48, 65 (London, 1885–94).
[9] See Crane, *Insular Romance*, pp. 24–5, 40–2, 87–8.
[10] See lines 1279–90.
[11] See *BR*, p. 48 n. 21.
[12] See Commentary on lines 571–4.
[13] See lines 611–16.

in the symbolism of the pentacle in *Sir Gawain and the Green Knight*.)[14] Personal emotion, too, is accorded greater importance in the Middle English than in the Anglo-Norman,[15] being emphasized as an expression of the protagonists' loyalty to one another.

King Horn employs a short, two- or three-stress line which is unusual, perhaps unique, in a poem of this length and seems to owe more to Old English verse forms than to syllabic French models, though it may perhaps bear some relation to the half-line unit of the *laisses* in which *RH* is written.[16] The stylistic device of repetition is much more marked in *King Horn* than in *RH* and also has a structural function. The first of Horn's three battles against pagans, for instance, corresponds more closely in *King Horn* to the encounter in which his father was killed than it does to the equivalent episode in the Anglo-Norman.[17] Significant phases in the action are demarked by repeated sea voyages, sometimes described in very similar terms.[18] Barron notes how the 'folk-tale pattern of repetition with variation' in *King Horn* emphasizes crucial stages in the development of the hero or of the romance's themes; while Susan Crane argues that a 'conservative faith in established social patterns is appropriately embodied in a verbal style that connotes the same conservative faith'.[19] The overall effect of the device, in conjunction with a lack of geographical specificity,[20] is to impart to the Middle English romance a haunting, almost mythic, quality.

The Text
King Horn is preserved in three manuscripts:

C Cambridge University Library, MS Gg.4.27(2) (*c.* 1300)
L Oxford, Bodleian Library, MS Laud Misc. 108 (late thirteenth century)

[14] See *Sir Gawain and the Green Knight*, ed. J. R. R. Tolkien and E. V. Gordon, 2nd edn, rev. Norman Davis (Oxford, 1967), lines 619–65.
[15] See Crane, *Insular Romance*, p. 30.
[16] I am indebted to Professor John Stevens for his help on this point.
[17] See Commentary on lines 585–644.
[18] See, e.g., lines 117–18, 1505–6.
[19] Barron, *English Medieval Romance*, p. 67; Crane, *Insular Romance*, p. 30. See further Georgianna Ziegler, 'Structural repetition in *King Horn*', *Neuphilologische Mitteilungen*, 81 (1980), 403–8.
[20] See Commentary on line 138.

H London, British Library, MS Harley 2253 (1330s)[21]

As Rosamund Allen says, 'The three manuscripts ... are ... respectively: part of a collection of narratives, secular and religious; a section added – at some stage – to a collection of *vitae*; and a literary miscellany from Herefordshire, probably not made by a professional scribe . . . The scribes seem to have associated *Horn* with Saints' Lives, but this is possibly fortuitous.'[22]

Allen demonstrates that all three texts contain many corruptions and makes a powerful case for thoroughgoing emendation of the base-text.[23] The present edition limits its aim to that of presenting a readable text from a single manuscript, with minimal emendation. The text chosen is that of MS C, where *King Horn* keeps company with a text of *Florys and Blauncheflour* and a poem on the Assumption of Our Lady.

Florys and Blauncheflour

Despite the enormous popularity of the story of Florys and Blauncheflour in the Middle Ages, the version that has come down to us in Middle English is, if not unique, in several respects untypical of medieval romance: in the youth of the protagonists, in the quasi-magical glamour of the setting, and in the focus on passionate love to the exclusion of other values and considerations, including the religious and the chivalric.[24]

First composed in western France *c.* 1160, the story was translated and adapted into a variety of European languages.[25] Two principal versions can be distinguished: (1) the 'aristocratic'

[21] In the dating of the manuscripts, I accept the conclusions in *King Horn: An Edition based on Cambridge University Library MS Gg.4.27 (2)*, ed. Rosamund Allen, Garland Medieval Texts 7 (New York and London, 1984) (hereafter *KHA*).

[22] *KHA*, pp. 15–16.

[23] *Ibid.*, pp. 1–2.

[24] The youthful protagonists and the 'all for love' theme are, however, matched in the thirteenth-century French *Aucassin and Nicolette*; and the exotic setting may be influenced by the legend of Alexander the Great (see below).

[25] See *Floris and Blauncheflur*, ed. F. C. de Vries (Groningen, 1966) (hereafter De Vries), pp. 54–5; Laura A. Hibbard, *Mediæval Romance in England: A Study of the Sources and Analogues of the Non-Cyclic Metrical Romances* (New York, 1924), pp. 185–6; *King Horn, Floriz and Blauncheflur, The Assumption of Our Lady*, re-ed. George H. McKnight, EETS, OS 14 (London, 1901; repr. 1962), pp. xxxi–xxxvii.

(or 'courtly'), an idyllic romance which emphasizes sentiment; (2) the 'popular', where the hero wins his beloved through physical prowess, here stressed at the expense of sentiment and bringing the story closer in ethos to *chanson de geste*.[26]

The Middle English romance (*c.* 1250) belongs to the first of these groups and is derived from a French original. Although at times it follows the French extremely closely, translating word for word,[27] it also adapts its original freely, omitting or condensing passages of description, reflection and dialogue, and concentrating rather on practical action.[28] This has the effect of divorcing the theme of youthful love from any sort of moral context: love conquers all and is all-important, the end justifies the means.

Much discussion of the Florys and Blauncheflour story has focused on its 'oriental' elements and possible origins.[29] Parallels to several of the narrative motifs it employs have been found in the *Arabian Nights* and other oriental sources. Barron, however, sounds a salutary note of warning here: 'The origin of a particular incident or motif is often untraceable since its occurrence in more than one culture may result from mutual reflection of common social factors rather than oral transmission or literary borrowing. So, though there are European romances with oriental settings, with incidents paralleled in the *Arabian Nights*, direct derivation has not been clearly established.'[30] The popularity in the Middle Ages of the Alexander legend and the 'Marvels of the East' it described may have contributed something to the creation of a more-or-less spurious eastern setting.[31] Again, this exotic back-

---

[26] Cf. De Vries, p. 54 n. 62.

[27] Cf. *King Horn [etc.]*, re-ed. McKnight, pp. xxxvii–xxxviii.

[28] The principal differences between the Middle English and French versions are listed in *King Horn, [etc.]*, re-ed. McKnight, p. xxxix. The emphasis on action as opposed to reflection is fairly characteristic of English, by comparison with French, romance: cf., e.g., *Ywain and Gawain [etc.]*, ed. Maldwyn Mills (London, 1992), p. xi. Geraldine Barnes, 'Cunning and ingenuity in the Middle English *Floris and Blauncheflur*', *Medium Ævum*, 53 (1984), 10–25, sees even love as being subordinated to the *engin* by which Florys achieves his goal.

[29] See De Vries, pp. 63–6; Sharon S. Geddes, 'The Middle English poem of *Floris and Blauncheflur* and the *Arabian Nights* tale of "Ni'amah and Naomi": a study in parallels', *Emporia State Research Studies*, 19 (1970), 14–24; Roberto Giacone, '*Floris and Blauncheflur*: critical issues', *Rivista di studi classici*, 27 (1979), 395–405; and cf. Hibbard, *Mediæval Romance in England*, p. 190.

[30] Barron, *English Medieval Romance*, p. 182.

[31] See Commentary on line 584.

ground to the action helps to set the protagonists' love apart from the realities of life.

Florys and Blauncheflour is written in octosyllabic couplets, with effective use of incremental repetition.[32] The plethora of natural images (especially those associating the lovers with sweetness and flowers)[33] stresses their youthful innocence. Although MSS A and C make a token gesture in the direction of Christianity at the end of the romance,[34] in general religious considerations (unusually for medieval romance) are conspicuous by their absence;[35] nothing is made, for instance, of the difference in creed between Florys and Blauncheflour, or of the thematic potential of that other 'virtuous pagan', the emir. *Florys and Blauncheflour* remains an enchanting but essentially amoral tale.

The Text

There are four manuscripts of *Florys and Blauncheflour*:

A Edinburgh, National Library of Scotland, MS 19.2.1 (the Auchinleck MS) (*c.* 1330)
C Cambridge University Library, MS Gg.4.27(2) (*c.* 1300)
S London, British Library, MS Egerton 2862 (late fourteenth/early fifteenth century)
V London, British Library, MS Cotton Vitellius D.iii (late fourteenth century)

MS A is a substantial miscellany of religious, didactic and political works interspersed with romances, including *Amis and Amiloun*, *Sir Bevis of Hampton*, *Sir Orfeo* and *Horn Childe*;[36] MS C has been described above;[37] MS S is unusual in that it contains only romances, including *Amis and Amiloun* and *Sir Bevis of Hampton*; in MS V *Florys and Blauncheflour* is sandwiched

[32] See, e.g., Commentary on lines 269–70, 457–8, 535–8.
[33] See, e.g., lines 119–20, 782–4.
[34] See Commentary on lines 1086–7.
[35] Cf., however, Edmund Reiss, 'Symbolic detail in medieval narrative: *Floris and Blancheflour*', *Papers on Language and Literature*, 7 (1971), 339–50, where a case is made for regarding certain symbolic details as adumbrating a theme of Christian charity.
[36] See the Scolar Press facsimile, *The Auchinleck Manuscript: National Library of Scotland MS. 19.2.1*, introd. Derek Pearsall and I. C. Cunningham (London, 1977).
[37] See p. xi above.

between a French item on biblical history and a Latin prose commentary on Macrobius' *Saturnalia*.

As De Vries's parallel-text edition shows, there is considerable variation among the manuscripts. MS S has been chosen as the basis of the present edition – not because it is in all respects the best text, but because it gives the fullest extant version of the Middle English romance (all manuscripts lack the beginning of the poem).

Amis and Amiloun

The story of the friendship between Amis and Amiloun was one of the most popular of the Middle Ages. The earliest known version is a Latin text of the end of the eleventh century, but the story also survives in Anglo-Norman, continental French, Italian, Spanish, Hungarian, Welsh, Dutch, German and Norse, as well as Middle English.[38] These versions may be classified into two groups: secular and hagiographic. The Middle English romance (composed toward the end of the thirteenth century) belongs to the secular group and is most closely related to the Anglo-Norman *Amis e Amilun*,[39] particularly to the text in Karlsruhe, Badische Landesbibliothek, MS Durlac 38 (= MS C).[40] Although the Middle English is not directly derived from the Anglo-Norman, with which it probably shares a lost source, the two are sufficiently closely related in narrative substance and in thematic emphasis to warrant close comparison.[41]

In the Middle English poem the protagonists' *trouthe* to each other is seen more critically than in *AA* in relation to other loyalties – to earthly overlord, to family and to God.[42] In particular, there is less certainty here on Amis's part as to whether his action in sacrificing his sons in order to help his friend is right[43] – despite the

---

[38] *A Manual of the Writings in Middle English 1050–1500*, ed. J. Burke Severs, Fasc. 1 (New Haven, Conn., 1967), p. 168; Hibbard, *Mediæval Romance in England*, p. 65.

[39] *Amis and Amiloun. Zugleich mit der altfranzösischen Quelle*, ed. Eugen Kölbing, Altenglische Bibliothek (Heilbronn, 1884) (hereafter *AA*), pp. 111–87.

[40] See Commentary on *Amis and Amiloun, passim.*

[41] See Susan Dannenbaum, 'Insular tradition in the story of Amis and Amiloun', *Neophilologus*, 67 (1983), 611–22 (esp. p. 611); see also Commentary on *Amis and Amiloun, passim.*

[42] Cf. Commentary on lines 605–9.

[43] See Commentary on lines 2257–2310.

fact that he is urged by an angel (as against the unspecified *voiz* of *AA*) to this extreme course.[44] The specifically angelic nature of the promptings the two heroes receive is one of the means by which the Middle English narrator seeks to justify the romance's exaltation of the claims of male friendship at the expense of family and other considerations; he also underpins the rather shaky moral fabric of his story by developing the character of Amiloun's 'unkende' wife and making *her* the mouthpiece for adverse criticism of the more dubious aspects of the heroes' conduct.[45]

The romance's folkloric elements have been much discussed,[46] but none more so than those relating to Amiloun's leprosy. Although leprosy was traditionally regarded in the Middle Ages as a punishment for sin,[47] we should probably regard Amiloun's affliction with the disease less as the result of wrongdoing than as a supreme test of his friendship for Amis. Both in the Middle English poem and in *AA*, the supernatural warning occurs *before* he has committed the action to which it relates, and he disregards it out of loyalty to his friend and truth to his word. Thus, Amiloun may be seen as an innocent sufferer who maintains his loyalty, the ultimate value upheld by the poem, at huge personal cost and himself becomes a touchstone for the loyalty of others – Amis, his own wife and Owein/Amoraunt.

Stylistically, *Amis and Amiloun* displays many of the faults commonly ascribed to the tail-rhyme romances – redundancies of expression, meaningless clichés and excessive repetition.[48] Sometimes, however, these very features can be turned to good account – as in the episode of Amis's sacrifice of his children (lines 2257–2304), where they seem to mirror his own uncertainties and hesitations.[49]

The Text
Texts of *Amis and Amiloun* are found in four manuscripts:

A Edinburgh, National Library of Scotland, MS 19.2.1 (the Auchinleck MS) (*c.* 1330)

44 See Commentary on line 2188.
45 See Commentary on lines 1474–1500.
46 See *Amis and Amiloun*, ed. MacEdward Leach, EETS, OS 203 (London, 1937), pp. xxxii–lxxxix; *BR*, p. xxx.
47 See Commentary on lines 1249–72.
48 See *AA*, pp. xxxvii–lxiv.
49 Cf. also Dannenbaum, 'Insular tradition', pp. 613–14.

S London, British Library, MS Egerton 2862 (late fourteenth/early fifteenth century)

D Oxford, Bodleian Library, MS Douce 326 (late fifteenth century)

H London, British Library, MS Harley 2386 (fifteenth century)

MSS A and S have been described above;[50] MS D contains only *Vita de Amys & Amylion* and a short poem beginning 'Goe lytyll byll', which is written in a later hand; MS H contains historical pieces in Latin, miscellaneous ephemera, of which many relate to Norwich, and a copy of Mandeville's Travels.

Amis and Amiloun is incomplete in all manuscripts except D, where, however, the text is (as in H) careless and unreliable. The best text is that of A, which has been used as the basis of this edition. However, it lacks the beginning and the end of the romance; these have been supplied from S. It proved impossible to use S itself as the base-text, since even where the text is extant physical damage to the manuscript has made many lines illegible: their readings are accessible only through, at best, informed guesswork.

Syr Tryamowre

The late fourteenth-century romance of *Syr Tryamowre* has received surprisingly little attention – the lack of a readily accessible edition being, no doubt, partly responsible.[51] Most studies have been concerned with the story's relations to folklore and ballad. Unlike the romances discussed so far, *Syr Tryamowre* as a whole has no known direct source or close analogues, though the principal elements of the plot (the 'calumniated queen', the faithful dog and the eventual recognition between father and son) are found elsewhere in folklore and romance.

The motif of the queen who is unjustly accused of adultery or some other iniquity and banished, with the result that father and

---

[50] See p. xiii above.

[51] The two principal editions are: *The Romance of Syr Tryamoure, from a Manuscript preserved in the University Library, Cambridge*, ed. James Orchard Halliwell, Percy Society 16 (London, 1846); *Syr Tryamowre: A Metrical Romance*, ed. Anna Johanna Erdman Schmidt (Utrecht, 1937) (hereafter *STS*).

son(s) are separated, occurs frequently in Middle English romance.[52] The combination of this motif with that of the faithful dog which guards its master's grave and kills his slayer was well known in the Middle Ages from the French story of Sebilla and the Dog of Montargis, which occurs in the Anglo-Latin *Gesta Romanorum*, compiled in England in the late thirteenth century.[53] The second part of the poem has been judged less interesting and appealing to modern tastes, a 'fair specimen of the old romances with all their vices and virtues, prolixity, improbabilities, exaggeration, with their wild graces also, their chivalrousness, their pageantry'.[54] The two parts are, however, successfully integrated through their concern with Tryamowre's maturation and his need to prove himself and to define himself in relation to his father.[55] In this theme *Syr Tryamowre* offers points of comparison with *King Horn*.

Stylistically *Syr Tryamowre* leaves much to be desired: not only does it share the usual faults of the tail-rhyme romance,[56] but the tail-rhyme stanza itself is handled with monotonous irregularity. The basic unit is a twelve-line stanza, but this breaks down at line 120, and thereafter the stanza varies in length from three to eighteen lines. This, together with the many textual obscurities,[57] suggests that the text as we have it is fairly corrupt.

The Text
Syr Tryamowre is preserved in two manuscripts:

C Cambridge University Library, MS Ff.2.38 (late fifteenth/ early sixteenth century)
P London, British Library, MS Add. 27879 (c. 1642–50)

MS C, which provides the base-text for this edition, is a sizeable collection of religious and didactic pieces, with ten

---

[52] E.g., in *Octavian* (in *Six Middle English Romances*, ed. Maldwyn Mills (London, 1973; repr. 1992), pp. 75–124), in *Emaré* (*ibid.*, pp. 46–74), and in *Valentine and Orson*, ed. Arthur Dickson, EETS, OS 204 (London, 1937). See also Jennifer Fellows, 'Mothers in Middle English romance', in *Women and Literature in Britain, c. 1100–1500*, ed. Carol M. Meale (forthcoming, Cambridge, 1993).
[53] See Hibbard, *Mediæval Romance in England*, pp. 283–5.
[54] G. W. Hales, quoted *ibid.*, p. 285.
[55] Cf. Fellows, 'Mothers in Middle English romance'.
[56] See p. xv above.
[57] See Commentary on *Syr Tryamowre*, *passim*.

romances (including *The Erle of Tolous*, *Syr Tryamowre* and *Sir Bevis of Hampton*) grouped together at the end;[58] MS P is a late compilation containing 195 texts, of which many may have been copied from printed editions.[59]

Although it is so little known now, *Syr Tryamowre* was evidently popular during the Middle Ages, and it continued to be printed until well into the sixteenth century. The relationships between the extant manuscript and printed texts suggest that a number of intermediate copies are no longer extant.[60] The text of MS P is more closely related to that of William Copland's two editions of the 1560s than it is to that of MS C.

Syr Launfal

Dating probably from the very end of the fourteenth century, *Syr Launfal* belongs to a type of narrative known as the 'Breton lay', a form whose most celebrated exponent was Marie de France, in the latter half of the twelfth century.[61] It is, indeed, derived from Marie's own lay of *Lanval*, via the fourteenth-century Middle English *Sir Landevale*;[62] though its author, Thomas Chestre,[63] has adapted the story freely.

Despite the fact that the two poems use different metrical forms,[64] there are many extremely close verbal parallels between *Syr Launfal* and *Landevale*, but by reworking certain episodes and adding others – some from sources such as the anonymous lay of *Graelent*, some apparently from his own invention[65] – Chestre

[58] See the Scolar Press facsimile, *Cambridge University Library MS Ff.2.38*, introd. Frances McSparran and P. R. Robinson (London, 1979).

[59] See Gillian Rogers, 'The Percy Folio manuscript revisited', in *Romance in Medieval England*, ed. Maldwyn Mills, Jennifer Fellows and Carol M. Meale (Cambridge, 1991), pp. 38–64.

[60] See *STS*, p. 3.

[61] See Mortimer J. Donovan, *The Breton Lay: A Guide to Varieties* (Notre Dame, Ind., and London, 1969); *Thomas Chestre: 'Sir Launfal'*, ed. A. J. Bliss, Nelson's Medieval and Renaissance Library (London and Edinburgh, 1960) (hereafter *SLB*), pp. 16–24.

[62] For convenience, references to Lanval and *Sir Landevale* are to the texts printed in *SLB*.

[63] See Commentary on line 1039.

[64] On Chestre's handling of the twelve-line tail-rhyme stanza, see *SLB*, pp. 33–6. *Landevale* is in octosyllabic couplets.

[65] See, e.g., Commentary on lines 85–216, 319–33, 505–612, etc.

has considerably modified the tone and character of the story. In particular, the supernatural aura becomes less pervasive, and the action is seen to a more marked degree through the eyes of the hero.[66]

Introducing his edition of *Syr Launfal*, A. J. Bliss describes the story as follows: 'It tells of a man who, having fallen into the depths of poverty through no fault of his own, is raised through no merit of his own to the highest point of happiness. Sought out by a fairy mistress, he is given at the same moment both inexhaustible wealth and the love of the most beautiful woman in the world. Despite his disobedience to her express wishes, the fairy mistress remains loyal to him . . . and they ride away together to live happily ever after.'[67] Many attempts have been made to define the romance's themes in terms of manhood, honour or knightly pride;[68] but essentially, despite Chestre's modifications, the ethos of the story remains closer to that of fairy-tale than to that of romance.[69] The hero is a curiously passive figure, whose good fortune is indeed unearned. He is not distinguished by any particular virtue save *largesse*, which he carries to excess; and, having been goaded into betraying his fairy mistress's trust through an assault on his male self-esteem, he is forgiven only too readily, without the need to make any amends. Indeed, Chestre's poem seems to take this betrayal less seriously than does *Landevale*, in this respect standing closer to Marie's lay.[70] As often in fairy-tale, the hero claims our sympathy because he *is* the hero and, though he may not be notably 'good' in any respect, is pitted against forces which are unquestionably 'bad' –

[66] See Dieter Mehl, *The Middle English Romances of the Thirteenth and Fourteenth Centuries* (London, 1968), pp. 44, 46; also Theo Stemmler, 'Die mittelenglischen Bearbeitungen zweier Lais der Marie de France', *Anglia*, 80 (1962), 243–63.

[67] *SLB*, p. 1.

[68] E.g., Earl R. Anderson, 'The structure of *Sir Launfal*', *Papers on Language and Literature*, 13 (1977), 115–24; E. M. Bradstock, '"Honoure" in *Sir Launfal*', *Parergon*, 24 (1979), 9–17; John C. Hirsh, 'Pride as theme in "Sir Launfal"', *Notes and Queries*, n.s. 14 (1967), 288–91; Anthony S. G. Edwards, 'Unknightly conduct in "Sir Launfal"', *Notes and Queries*, n.s. 15 (1968), 328–9.

[69] Cf. B. K. Martin, '*Sir Launfal* and the folktale', *Medium Ævum*, 35 (1966), 199–210. Dorothy Everett, 'A characterization of the English medieval romances', in her *Essays on Middle English Literature*, ed. Patricia Kean (Oxford, 1955; repr. 1967), pp. 1–22 (pp. 21–2), expresses reservations about classifying the Breton lays as romances at all.

[70] See Commentary on lines 1015–17.

in this case represented by Guinevere, who receives particularly harsh treatment at Chestre's hands.[71]

In the episode of Launfal's combat with Sir Valentyne, which does not occur in *Landevale*,[72] the hero distinguishes himself with the aid of supernatural helpers provided by his mistress, Tryamour. Although it is probably the case that a medieval audience would have seen nothing to disapprove in this,[73] nevertheless it weakens any sense of particular merit or desert on Launfal's part. But, if it does not fundamentally modify the overall themes or structure of the romance, the episode may have a more local symbolic value in indicating the interdependence of the knightly virtues of loyalty and chivalric prowess:[74] while Launfal's faith remains un-breached, he is preeminent; when he betrays his lady's trust, he risks disgrace and death.

The Text

There is only one extant manuscript of *Syr Launfal*: London, British Library, MS Cotton Caligula A.ii. The first section of this manuscript dates from the first half of the fifteenth century and contains thirty-eight items, including poems by Lydgate and ten romances. *Syr Launfal* is grouped with *Octavian* and *Libeaus Desconus*, perhaps also the work of Thomas Chestre.[75] The text of *Syr Launfal* contains a number of minor carelessnesses and some orthographical peculiarities – in, for example, the distribu-tion of *d* and *th* – but it presents no major problems.

The Erle of Tolous

Although *The Erle of Tolous* (*c.* 1400) calls itself a Breton lay (line 1214), it could hardly be more different from the other Breton lay in this volume, *Syr Launfal*. It is a highly fictionalized account of historical events concerning Bernard I, count of Barcelona and Toulouse, and the Empress Judith, wife of Louis the Pious (778–840).[76]

The motif of the unjustly accused wife is common in romance

---

71 See Commentary on lines 46–8, 1006–8.
72 See Commentary on lines 505–612.
73 See *SLB*, p. 43.
74 Cf. p. ix above.
75 See Commentary on line 1039.
76 Hibbard, *Mediæval Romance in England*, pp. 37–40.

and folktale,[77] though *The Erle of Tolous* is distinctive in containing the episode of the judicial combat.[78] What sets *The Erle of Tolous* apart is the unusual degree to which the participants in the action are characterized, especially the young Sir Antore[79] and the empress herself: 'Memorable in truth . . . is this unnamed Empress of Almayne for the vigor of her scorn against her false guardians and the treacherous Trylabas, and for the grave and beautiful dignity with which she requites the reckless gallantry of the Earl's attempt to see her. In no version, perhaps, is she a finer or purer or more vitalized character . . . '[80] The portrayal of the emperor too – as wrongheaded, blustering and domineering but ultimately honourable – both furnishes a foil to the earl and makes the exemplary loyalty of the empress the more laudable.

The pervasive theme of the romance is honour and *trouthe*: just as the honourable and trusting earl is deceived by the treacherous Trylabas, so is the empress deceived by the two knights who plot her downfall – and her own honour shines the brighter by contrast to their lack of it,[81] as she faces the prospect of death rather than break her promise of secrecy.

The often careful choice of the oaths used in the romance[82] reinforces this theme and relates the loyalty and honour between the protagonists to notions of *trouthe* as a more specifically religious virtue. The ecclesiastical ambience of much of the action[83] has the same effect, as well as contributing to our sense that the love between the earl and the empress is pure, high-minded and disinterested. (Note also that the earl is only prepared to defend the empress if he is assured of her innocence.) The use of comparatively sophisticated theological vocabulary[84] suggests that the author may well himself have been a cleric.

The Erle of Tolous makes exceptionally skilful use of the tail-rhyme stanza, especially in passages of direct speech, where its climactic potential is exploited to the full.[85]

[77] See pp. xvi–xvii above.
[78] Hibbard, *Mediæval Romance in England*, p. 37.
[79] See Commentary on lines 706–56.
[80] Hibbard, *Mediæval Romance in England*, p. 42.
[81] Cf. Commentary on line 676.
[82] See, e.g., Commentary on line 190.
[83] See Commentary on line 245.
[84] See, e.g., line 540.
[85] E.g., in lines 1135–94. Cf. also Urs Dürmüller, *Narrative Possibilities of the Tail-Rime Romance*, Schweizer Anglistische Arbeiten 83 (Berne, 1975), esp. pp. 119–42.

The Text
The Erle of Tolous is preserved in four manuscripts:

C Cambridge University Library, MS Ff.2.38 (late fifteenth/ early sixteenth century)

A Oxford, Bodleian Library, MS Ashmole 45 (early sixteenth century)

R Oxford, Bodleian Library, MS Ashmole 61 (late fifteenth century)

L Lincoln, Dean and Chapter Library, MS 91 (the Lincoln Thornton MS) (*c.* 1430–50)

MS C has been described above;[86] MS A originally contained only *The Erle of Tolous* but has had various items (including a disquisition on the virtues of parsnips) added to it; MS R (the work of the scribe John Rate) contains mostly religious pieces, but includes four romances in addition to *The Erle of Tolous*: *Sir Isumbras*, *Libeaus Desconus*, *Sir Cleges* and *Sir Orfeo*;[87] MS L (one of two manuscripts compiled by Robert Thornton in the mid-fifteenth century) contains among its sixty-four items, both religious and secular, nine romances, including a prose life of Alexander, the alliterative *Morte Arthure*, *Octavian* and *Sir Isumbras*.[88] The present edition uses as its basis the text in MS C.

Editorial procedure

Spelling follows that of the manuscripts, except that the use of *i/j* and of *u/v* has been regularized in accordance with modern practice, and the letters þ and ȝ have been resolved as *th* and as *y* or *gh* respectively. Scribal flourishes have been disregarded except where a nasal consonant (*m* or *n*) is unquestionably indicated. Punctuation, capitalization and word-division are editorial.

Emendation has been kept to a minimum and has been undertaken only where the text is obviously corrupt and the correct reading can be ascertained from manuscript evidence with

---

[86] See p. xi above.

[87] See Lynne Blanchfield, 'The romances in MS Ashmole 61: an idiosyncratic scribe', in *Romance in Medieval England*, ed. Mills, Fellows and Meale, pp. 65–87.

[88] See the Scolar Press facsimile, *The Thornton Manuscript (Lincoln Cathedral MS. 91)*, introd. D. S. Brewer and A. E. B. Owen (London, 1975).

a reasonable degree of certainty. Variant readings from other manuscripts have been cited only where they bear directly on emendations of the base-text. Lines apparently omitted from the base-text have been supplied only where they are strictly necessary to the sense, or where the omission can be clearly seen to be the result of mechanical scribal error. Words included in the text but omitted from the base-manuscript are enclosed in square brackets; letters or words which are illegible on account of some physical defect in the manuscript are enclosed in angle brackets.

Jennifer Fellows, 1993

ACKNOWLEDGEMENTS

I am grateful to the staffs of the British Library, the National Library of Scotland, the Bodleian Library and Cambridge University Library for allowing me to consult manuscripts and rare books in their possession or supplying me with reproductions.

I also wish to express my gratitude for various kinds of help to the following people: Rosamund Allen (who first fired my enthusiasm for Middle English romance), Malcolm Andrew, Lynne Blanchfield, Ardis Butterfield, Helen Cooper, Howard Davies, Eleanor Fellows (for her extraordinary forbearance and her moral support), Peter Fisher, Charmian Hearne, Frances Horgan, Andrew King, Carol Meale, Maldwyn Mills, Ad Putter, Gillian Rogers, Richard Smith, John Stevens and (last only through the exigencies of alphabetical order) Judith Weiss, to whom this edition is dedicated. The dedication also commemorates my father, Geoffrey Fellows, who died in May 1992, a few months before the book was completed.

ABBREVIATIONS

AA	*Amis and Amiloun*, ed. Kölbing
BR	Weiss, *The Birth of Romance*
De Vries	*Floris and Blauncheflur*, ed. De Vries
EETS, ES	Early English Text Society, Extra Series
EETS, OS	Early English Text Society, Original Series
Floire	*Le Conte de Floire et Blancheflor*, ed. Leclanche
French & Hale	*Middle English Metrical Romances*, ed. French and Hale
KHA	*King Horn*, ed. Allen
KHH	*King Horn*, ed. Hall
MED	*Middle English Dictionary*
RH	*The Romance of Horn*, ed. Pope
Sands	*Middle English Verse Romances*, ed. Sands
SLB	*Sir Launfal*, ed. Bliss
STS	*Syr Tryamowre*, ed. Schmidt

(Full details of books listed above will be found in the Select Bibliography.)

SELECT BIBLIOGRAPHY

General

ANTHOLOGIES

French, Walter Hoyt, and Charles Brockway Hale (eds), *Middle English Metrical Romances*, 2 vols in 1 (1930; repr. New York, 1964)

Mills, Maldwyn (ed.), *Six Middle English Romances* (London, 1973; repr. 1992)

————— *Ywain and Gawain [etc.]* (London, 1992)

Sands, Donald B. (ed.), *Middle English Verse Romances* (New York, 1966)

Schmidt, A. V. C., and Nicolas Jacobs (eds), *Medieval English Romances*, 2 vols (London, 1980)

Speed, Diane (ed.), *Medieval English Romances*, 2nd edn, 2 vols (Sydney, 1989)

Weiss, Judith, *The Birth of Romance: An Anthology* (London, 1992)

FACSIMILES

Brewer, D. S., and A. E. B. Owen (introd.), *The Thornton Manuscript (Lincoln Cathedral MS. 91)* (London, 1975)

McSparran, Frances, and P. R. Robinson (introd.), *Cambridge University Library MS Ff.2.38* (London, 1979)

Pearsall, Derek, and I. C. Cunningham (introd.), *The Auchinleck Manuscript: National Library of Scotland MS. 19.2.1* (London, 1977)

STUDIES

Barron, W. R. J., *English Medieval Romance* (London and New York, 1987)

Crane, Susan, *Insular Romance: Politics, Faith, and Culture in Anglo-Norman and Middle English Literature* (Berkeley, Calif., 1986)

Donovan, Mortimer J., *The Breton Lay: A Guide to Varieties* (Notre Dame, Ind., and London, 1969)

Everett, Dorothy, 'A characterization of the Middle English romances', in her *Essays on Middle English Literature*, ed. Patricia Kean (Oxford, 1955; repr. 1967)

Guddat-Figge, Gisela, *Catalogue of Manuscripts containing Middle English Romances*, Texte und Untersuchungen zur englischen Philologie 4 (Munich, 1976)

Hibbard, Laura A., *Mediæval Romance in England: A Study of the Sources and Analogues of the Non-Cyclic Metrical Romances* (New York, 1924)

Legge, M. D., *Anglo-Norman Literature and its Background* (Oxford, 1963)

Mehl, Dieter, *The Middle English Romances of the Thirteenth and Fourteenth Centuries* (London, 1968)

Mills, Maldwyn, Jennifer Fellows, and Carol M. Meale (eds), *Romance in Medieval England* (Cambridge, 1991)

Pearsall, Derek, 'The development of Middle English romance', *Mediaeval Studies*, 27 (1965), 91–116

Ramsey, Lee C., *Chivalric Romances: Popular Literature in Medieval England* (Bloomington, Ind., 1983)

Severs, J. Burke (ed.), *A Manual of the Writings in Middle English*, Fasc. I (New Haven, Conn., 1967)

Trounce, A. McI., 'The English tail-rhyme romances', *Medium Ævum*, 1 (1932), 87–108, 168–82; 2 (1933), 34–57, 189–98; 3 (1934), 30–50

Wittig, Susan, *Stylistic and Narrative Structures in the Middle English Romances* (Austin, Tx, and London, 1978)

King Horn

EDITIONS

Allen, Rosamund (ed.), *King Horn: An Edition based on Cambridge University Library MS Gg.4.27 (2)*, Garland Medieval Texts 7 (New York and London, 1984)

Hall, Joseph (ed.), *King Horn: A Middle-English Romance* (Oxford, 1901)

McKnight, George H. (ed.), *King Horn, Floriz and Blauncheflur, The Assumption of Our Lady*, EETS, OS 14 (London, 1901; repr. 1962)

Pope, Mildred K. (ed.), *The Romance of Horn by Thomas*, 2 vols (Vol. II rev. and completed T. B. W. Reid), Anglo-Norman Texts, 9–10, 12–13 (Oxford, 1955–64)

STUDIES

French, Walter Hoyt, *Essays on King Horn*, Cornell Studies in English 30 (Ithaca, NY, 1940)

Hill, D. M., 'An interpretation of *King Horn*', *Anglia*, 75 (1957), 157–72

Pope, Mildred K., 'The *Romance of Horn* and *King Horn*', *Medium
Ævum*, 25 (1956), 164–7
Ziegler, Georgianna, 'Structural repetition in *King Horn*', *Neu-
philologische Mitteilungen*, 81 (1980), 403–8

Florys and Blauncheflour

EDITIONS
De Vries, F. C. (ed.), *Floris and Blauncheflur* (Groningen, 1966)
Leclanche, Jean-Luc (ed.), *Le Conte de Floire et Blancheflor*, Les class-
iques français du moyen âge (Paris, 1980)
McKnight, George H. (ed.), *King Horn, Floriz and Blauncheflur, The
Assumption of Our Lady*, EETS, OS 14 (London, 1901; repr. 1962)

STUDIES
Barnes, Geraldine, 'Cunning and ingenuity in the Middle English *Floris
and Blauncheflur*', *Medium Ævum*, 53 (1984), 10–25
Giacone, Roberto, '*Floris and Blauncheflur*: critical issues', *Rivista di
studi classici*, 27 (1979), 395–405
Reiss, Edmund, 'Symbolic detail in medieval narrative: *Floris and
Blancheflour*', *Papers on Language and Literature*, 7 (1971), 339–50
Wentersdorf, Karl P., 'Iconographic elements in *Floris and Blancheflour*',
Annuale mediaevale, 20 (1981), 76–96

Amis and Amiloun

EDITIONS
Kölbing, Eugen (ed.), *Amis and Amiloun. Zugleich mit der
altfranzösischen Quelle*, Altenglische Bibliothek (Heilbronn, 1884)
Leach, MacEdward (ed.), *Amis and Amiloun*, EETS, OS 203 (London,
1937)

STUDIES
Brody, Saul Nathaniel, *The Disease of the Soul: Leprosy in Medieval
Literature* (Ithaca, NY, and London, 1974)
Dannenbaum, Susan, 'Insular tradition in the story of Amis and
Amiloun', *Neophilologus*, 67 (1983), 611–22
Hume, Kathryn, '*Amis and Amiloun* and the aesthetics of Middle English
romance', *Studies in Philology*, 70 (1973), 19–41
————'Structure and perspective: romance and hagiographic features
in the Amicus and Amelius story', *Journal of English and Germanic
Philology*, 69 (1970), 89–107

Kratins, Ojars, 'The Middle English *Amis and Amiloun*: chivalric romance or secular hagiography?', *PMLA*, 81 (1966), 347–54

Mathew, Gervase, 'Ideals of friendship', in *Patterns of Love and Courtesy: Essays in Memory of C. S. Lewis*, ed. John Lawlor (London, 1966)

Syr Tryamowre

EDITIONS

Hales, John W., and Frederick J. Furnivall (eds), *Bishop Percy's Folio Manuscript: Ballads and Romances*, Vol. II (London, 1868), pp. 78–135

Halliwell, James Orchard (ed.), *The Romance of Syr Tryamoure, from a Manuscript preserved in the University Library, Cambridge*, Percy Society 16 (London, 1846)

Schmidt, Anna Johanna Erdman (ed.), *Syr Tryamowre: A Metrical Romance* (Utrecht, 1937)

Syr Launfal

EDITION

Bliss, A. J. (ed.), *Thomas Chestre: 'Sir Launfal'*, Nelson's Medieval and Renaissance Library (London and Edinburgh, 1960)

STUDIES

Anderson, Earl R., 'The structure of *Sir Launfal*', *Papers on Language and Literature*, 13 (1977), 115–24

Bradstock, E. M., '"Honoure" in *Sir Launfal*', *Parergon*, 24 (1979), 9–17

Carlson, David, 'The Middle English *Lanval*, the corporal works of mercy, and Bibliothèque Nationale, nouv. acq. fr. 1104', *Neophilologus*, 72 (1988), 79–106

Martin, B. K., '*Sir Launfal* and the folktale', *Medium Ævum*, 35 (1966), 199–210

Mills, M., 'The composition and style of the "Southern" *Octavian*, *Sir Launfal* and *Libeaus Desconus*', *Medium Ævum*, 31 (1962), 88–109

———— 'A note on *Sir Launfal*, 733–744', *Medium Ævum*, 35 (1966), 122–4

The Erle of Tolous

EDITION

Lüdtke, Gustav (ed.), *The Erl of Tolous and the Emperes of Almayn*, Sammlung englischer Denkmäler 3 (Berlin, 1881)

STUDIES

Cabaniss, Allen, 'Judith Augusta and her time', *University of Mississippi Studies in English*, 10 (1969), 67–109

Dürmüller, Urs, *Narrative Possibilities of the Tail-Rime Romance*, Schweizer Anglistische Arbeiten 83 (Berne, 1975)

Reilly, Robert, '*The Earl of Toulouse*: a structure of honor', *Mediaeval Studies*, 37 (1975), 515–23

KING HORN

Alle beon he blithe,   *they, glad*
That to my song lythe!^[n]   *listen*
A sang ihc schal you singe   *I*
Of Mury the kinge.
5 King he was bi weste,   *in the west*
So longe so hit laste.
Godhild het his quen –   *was called*
Faire[r] ne mighte non ben.
He hadde a sone, that het Horn –
10 Fairer ne miste non beo born,   *might*
Ne no rein upon birine,   *rain upon*
Ne sunne upon bischine.
Fairer nis non thane he was: *is not*
He was bright so the glas,   *as*
15 He was whit so the flur,
Rose red was his colur.^[n]
In none kingeriche   *kingdom*
Nas non his iliche.   *equal*
Twelf feren he hadde,^[n]   *companions*
20 That alle with him ladde,   *accompanied him*
Alle riche mannes sones,
And alle hi were faire gomes,   *(young) men*
With him for to pleie.
And mest he luvede tweie: *most, two*
25 That on him het Hathulf child,   *was called*
And that other Fikenild.
Athulf was the beste,

6 i.e. for as long as his life lasted.
8 Fairer] Faire C.

And Fikenylde the werste.
Hit was upon a someres day,
30 Also ihc you telle may,   *As*
   Muri, the gode king,
   Rod on his pleing,   *sport*
   Bi the se side,   *sea*
   Ase he was woned ride.   *accustomed to*
35 He fond bi the stronde,   *shore*
   Arived on his londe,[n]
   Schipes fiftene,
   With Sarazins kene.[n]   *fierce*
   He axede what [hi] soghte
40 Other to londe broghte.   *Or*
   A payn hit ofherde,   *heathen, heard*
   And hym wel sone answarede:
   'Thi lond folk we schulle slon,   *subjects, kill*
   And alle that Crist luveth upon,
45 And theselve right anon: *straightaway*
   Ne schaltu todai henne gon.'   *You shall not, hence*
   The kyng alighte of his stede –   *dismounted from*
   For tho he havede nede –   *then*
   And his gode knightes two:
50 Al to fewe he hadde tho!
   Swerd hi gunne gripe,
   And togadere smite.   *together*
   Hy smyten under schelde
   That sume hit yfelde.   *felt*
55 The king hadde al to fewe,
   Toyenes so vele schrewe: *Against, many, evil men*
   So fele mighten ythe   *many easily*
   Bringe hem thre to dithe.   *death*
   The pains come to londe,   *heathens*
60 And neme hit in here honde.   *took*
   That folc hi gunne quelle,   *people, destroy*
   And churchen for to felle.   *raze*
   Ther ne moste libbe   *might live*
   The fremde ne the sibbe,   *Strangers nor kinsmen*

---

32 Rode out for sport.
39 hi soghte] isoȝte C.
44 And all who believe in Christ.

65 Bute hi here laghe asoke	
And to here toke.	
Of alle wymmanne,	
Wurst was Godhild thanne:	
For Murri heo weop sore,	*she wept*
70 And for Horn yute more.	*still more*
He wente ut of halle,	*She*
Fram hire maidenes alle,	
Under a roche of stone.	
Ther heo livede alone;	*rock*
75 Ther heo servede Gode,	
Ayenes the paynes forbode;	*Against, heathens', prohibition*
Ther he servede Criste,	
That no payn hit ne wiste.	*In such a way that, knew*
Evre heo bad for Horn child,	*prayed*
80 That Jesu Crist him beo myld.[n]	*merciful*
Horn was in paynes honde,	
With his feren of the londe.	*companions*
Muchel was his fairhede,	*Great, beauty*
For Jhesu Crist him makede.	
85 Payns him wolde slen,	*intended to kill him*
Other al quic flen:	*Or flay him alive*
Yef his fairnesse nere,	
The children alle aslaghe were.[n]	
Thanne spak on admirad –[n]	*heathen officer*
90 Of wordes he was bald:	*bold*
'Horn, thu art wel kene,	*brave*
And that is wel isene;	*plain to see*
Thu art gret and strong,	
Fair and evene long;	*fully grown*
95 Thu schalt waxe more,	*grow bigger*
Bi fulle seve yere	
Yef thu mote to live go,	
And thine feren also –	
Yef hit so bifalle,	*If*
100 Ye scholde slen us alle.	*would kill*
Tharvore thu most to stere,	*you must (be put) into a boat*

65–6 Unless they renounced their faith and adopted that of the heathens.
71 wente] wenten C.
87–8 Had it not been for his beauty, the youths would all have been killed.
96–7 If you live another full seven years.

Thu and thine ifere.
To schupe schulle ye funde,   *ship, hasten*
And sinke to the grunde:
105   The se you schal adrenche —   *drown*
Ne schal hit us noght ofthinche.
For if thu were alive,
With swerd other with knive,
We scholden alle deie
110   And thi fader deth abeie!'ⁿ   *pay for*
The children hi broghte to stronde,
Wringinde here honde,
Into schupes borde,
At the fuiste worde.ⁿ
115   Ofte hadde Horn beo wo,   *sorrowful*
A[c] nevre wurs than him was tho.   *But, worse, then*
The se bigan to flowe,
And Horn child to rowe.ⁿ
The se that schup so fasste drof   *drove*
120   (The children dradde therof: *were afraid*
Hi wenden, to wisse,   *thought, certainly*
Of here lif to misse),   *To lose their lives*
Al the day and al the night,
Til hit sprang dailight,
125   Til Horn sagh on the stronde   *saw*
Men gon in the londe.   *going about on land*
'Feren,' quath he, 'yonge,
Ihc telle you tithinge: *tidings*
Ihc here fogheles singe,   *birds*
130   And that gras him springe.   *And (see)*
Blithe beo we on lyve — ⁿ
Ure schup is on ryve.'   *Our, has reached land*
Of schup hi gunne funde,   *From, hasten*
And setten fout to grunde;   *foot*
135   Bi the se side,
Hi leten that schup ride.   *ride at anchor*
Thanne spak him child Horn
(In Suddene he was iborn):ⁿ
'Schup bi the se flode,

106   We shall not regret it.
116   Ac] At C.

140 Daies have thu gode!
    Bi the se brinke,   *sea's edge*
    No water the na drinke.   *Drink no water*
    Yef thu cume to Suddenne,
    Gret thu wel of myne kenne,   *my kinsmen*
145 Gret thu wel my moder,
    Godhild quen the gode;
    And seie the paene kyng,   *tell*
    Jesu Cristes withering,   *enemy*
    That ihc am hol and fer,   *well and sound*
150 On this lond arived her;
    And seie that hei schal fonde   *experience*
    The dent of myne honde.'ⁿ   *blow*
    The children yede to tune,ⁿ   *went*
    Bi dales and bi dune.   *valleys, hills*
155 Hy metten with Almair king – ⁿ
    Crist yeven him his blessing! – ⁿ
    King of Westernesse – ⁿ   *give*
    Crist yive him muchel blisse!
    He him spac to Horn child
160 Wordes that were mild:
    'Whannes beo ye, faire gumes,   *Whence, (young) men*
    That her to londe beoth icume –
    Alle throttene   *thirteen*
    Of bodie swithe kene?   *very strong*
165 Bi God that me makede,
    A swihc fair verade   *Such a fair company*
    Ne saugh ihc in none stunde,   *at no time*
    Bi westene londe!
    Seie me wat ye seche.'
170 Horn spak here speche;   *was their spokesman*
    He spak for hem alle,
    Vor so hit moste bivalle: *For, befall*
    He was the faireste,
    And of wit the beste:
175 'We beoth of Suddenne,
    Icome of gode kenne –   *of good birth*
    Of Cristene blode,
    And kynges suthe gode.   *very*
    Payns ther gunne arive,
180 And duden hem of lyve: *killed them*

Hi sloghen and to-droghe[n]
Cristene men inoghe.   *many*
So Crist me mote rede,   *As Christ may guide me*
Us he dude lede   *they*
185 Into a galeie,[n]   *boat*
With the se to pleie,
Dai hit is igon and other.   *Two days ago*
Withute sail and rother,   *rudder*
Ure schip bigan to swymme   *float*
190 To this londes brymme.   *edge*
Nu thu might us slen, and binde
Ure honde bihynde.
Bute yef hit beo thi wille,
Helpe that we ne spille!'   *perish*
195 Thanne spak the gode kyng
(Iwis, he nas no nithing):   *Certainly, villain*
'Seie me, child, what is thi name?
Ne schaltu have bute game.'
The child him answerde,
200 Sone so he hit herde,
'Horn ihc am ihote,   *called*
Icomen ut of the bote,
Fram the se side.
Kyng, wel mote the tide!'   *may good fortune be yours*
205 Thanne hym spak the gode kyng:
'Wel bruc thu thi nevening!
Horn, thu go wel schulle,
Bi dales and bi hulle.
Horn, thu lude sune,[n]   *may you sound loudly*
210 Bi dales and bi dune.
So schal thi name springe   *reputation spread*
Fram kynge to kynge,
And thi fairnesse
Abute Westernesse,
215 The strengthe of thine honde
Into evrech londe.   *every*
Horn, thu art so swete,

198 You shall have nothing but pleasure.
206 thi nevening] þin euening C; þi naming L. May you live up to your name!
(*Literally*, Well may you enjoy your name!)

Ne may ihc the forlete.'   *part with*
Hom rod Aylmar the kyng,   *Home*
220 And Horn mid him, his fund[l]yng,   *foundling*
And alle his ifere,
That were him so dere.
The kyng com into halle,
Among his knightes alle.
225 Forth he clupede Athelbrus,   *called*
That was stiward of his hus:[n]   *steward, household*
'Stiward, tak nu here
Mi fundlyng, for to lere   *teach*
Of thine mestere,   *skill*
230 Of wude and of rivere;
And tech him to harpe,
With his nayles scharpe;
Bivore me to kerve,   *Before, carve*
And of the cupe serve.[n]
235 Thu tech him of alle the liste,   *your craft*
That thu evre of wiste.   *ever, knew*
[And] his feiren thou wise   *companions, instruct*
Into othere servise.[n]
Horn thu undervonge,   *take in charge*
240 And tech him of harpe and songe.'
Ailbrus gan lere   *teach*
Horn and his yfere;
Horn in herte laghte   *apprehended*
Al that he him taghte.
245 In the curt and ute,
And elles al abute,
Luvede men Horn child.
And mest him lovede Rimenhild,   *most*
The kynges oghene do[gh]ter: *own*
250 He was mest in thoghte;
Heo lovede so Horn child   *She*
That negh heo gan wexe wild,   *nearly, go mad*
For heo ne mighte at borde   *Because, at table*
With him speke no worde,

220 fundlyng] fundyng C.
230 i.e. of hunting and hawking.
237 And] In C.
249 doghter] doster C.

255 Ne noght in the halle
    Among the knightes alle,
    Ne nowhar in non othere stede –   *place*
    Of folk heo hadde drede –
    Bi daie ne bi nighte,
260 With him speke ne mighte,
    Hire soreghe ne hire pine   *sorrow, nor, pain*
    Ne mighte nevre fine.   *never, end*
    In heorte heo hadde wo,
    And thus hire bithoghte tho: *she decided then*
265 Heo sende hire sonde   *message*
    Athelbrus to honde,
    That he come hire to,
    And also scholde Horn do –
    Al into bure,   *bower*
270 For heo gan to lure   *lower/look gloomy*
    And the sonde seide
    That sik lai that maide,[n]
    And bad him come swithe,   *quickly*
    For heo nas nothing blithe.   *very unhappy*
275 The stuard was in herte wo,
    For he nuste what to do.   *did not know*
    Wat Rymenhild hure thoghte
    Gret wunder him thughte: *Seemed to him very strange*
    Abute Horn the yonge,
280 To bure for to bringe.
    He thoghte upon his mode   *in his mind*
    Hit nas for none gode;
    He tok him another –
    Athulf, Hornes brother.[n]
285 'Athulf,' he sede, 'right anon,   *straightaway*
    Thu schalt with me to bure gon,
    To speke with Rymenhild stille,   *privately*
    And witen hure wille.   *find out what she wishes*
    In Hornes ilike,   *As Horn's substitute*
290 Thu schalt hure biswike.   *deceive*
    Sore ihc me ofdrede,   *I am greatly afraid*
    He wolde Horn misrede.'   *She, lead astray*
    Athelbrus gan Athulf lede,

258 i.e. because she was afraid of what other people might say.

	And into bure with him yede.	*went*
295	Anon upon Athulf child	
	Rymenhild gan wexe wild:	*became passionate*
	He wende that Horn hit were	*believed*
	That heo havede there.[n]	
	Heo sette him on bedde;	
300	With Athulf child he wedde.	*she displayed passion*
	On hire armes tweie	*In, two*
	Athulf heo gan leie.	*embrace*
	'Horn,' quath heo, 'wel longe	*said*
	Ihc habbe the luved stronge.	
305	Thu schalt thi trewthe plighte	
	On myn hond her righte,[n]	
	Me to spuse holde	
	And ihc the lord to wolde.'	
	Athulf sede on hire ire,	*ear*
310	So stille so hit were,	*As quietly as might be*
	'Thi tale nu thu lynne,	*cease*
	For Horn nis noght herinne![n]	
	Ne beo we noght iliche:	*equal*
	Horn is fairer and riche –	
315	Fairer bi one ribbe	*rib*
	Thane eni man that libbe![n]	*lives*
	Thegh Horn were under molde,	
	Other elleswher he wolde,	
	Other henne a thusend mile,	*from here*
320	Ihc nolde him ne the bigile!'	*nor, deceive*
	Rymenhild hire biwente,	*turned*
	And Athelbrus fule heo schente:	*foully, upbraided*
	'Hennes thu go, thu fule theof!	*wretch*
	Ne wurstu me nevremore leof.	
325	Went ut of my bur,	*Go*
	With muchel mesaventur.	
	Schame mote thu fonge,	*receive*
	And on highe rode anhonge,	*gallows, hang*

305–8 You shall plight me your troth, by giving me your hand, that you will have me as your wife and I shall possess you as my lord.
317–18 Even if Horn were (buried) under the earth, or anywhere else he wished to be.
324 You will nevermore be dear to me.
326 And ill fortune go with you.

Ne spek ihc noght with Horn —   *Unless I speak*
330 Nis he noght so unorn.   *ugly*
Hor[n] is fairer thane beo he.
With muchel schame mote thu deie!'   *may you die*
Athelbrus, in a stunde,   *immediately*
Fel anon to grunde:
335 'Lefdi, myn oghe,   *Lady, own*
Lithe me a litel throghe: *Listen, while*
Lust whi ihc wonde   *Hear, hesitated*
Bringe the Horn to honde.
For Horn is fair and riche
340 (Nis nowhar his iliche),
Aylmar, the gode kyng,
Dude him on mi lokyng.   *Placed, care*
Yef Horn were herabute,
Sore y me dute,   *I am sorely afraid*
345 With him ye wolden pleie,
Bitwex youselve tweie;
Thanne scholde, withuten othe,   *without doubt*
The kyng maken us wrothe.   *cause us distress*
Rymenhild, foryef me thi tene,   *anger*
350 Lefdi, my quene!
And Horn ihc schal the fecche,
Whamso hit recche!
Rymenhild, yef he cuthe,   *as well as she could*
Gan lynne with hire muthe;   *cease*
355 Heo makede hire wel blithe —
Wel was hire that sithe.   *time*
'Go nu,' quath heo, 'sone,
And send him after none,   *noon*
On a squieres wise,   *garb*
360 Whane the kyng arise,
To wude for to pleie —   *for the sake of sport*
Nis non that him biwreie.   *shall betray*
He schal with me bileve   *remain*
Til hit beo nir eve,   *near evening*
365 To haven of him mi wille;   *have, desire*
After ne recche [ihc] what me telle!'   *care, is said*

331 Horn] Hor C.
352 Whatever anyone says (*literally,* Whoever cares about it).
358–9 *Lines transposed in* C.
366 recche ihc] *thus* L; recchecche C; recchi H.

Aylbrus wende hire fro; *went*
Horn in halle fond he tho,
Bifore the kyng on benche,
370 Wyn for to schenche.[n] *pour*
'Horn,' quath he, 'so hende, *gracious*
To bure nu thu wende,
After mete stille, *secretly*
With Rymenhild to duelle. *remain*
375 Wordes suthe bolde, *very*
In herte thu hem holde.
Horn, beo me wel trewe –
Ne schal hit the nevre rewe.' *You will never regret it*
Horn in herte leide *kept*
380 Al that he him seide.
He yeode in wel righte *at once*
To Rymenhild the brighte; *beautiful*
On knes he him sette
And sweteliche hure grette. *greeted*
385 Of his feire sighte,
Al the bur gan lighte.
He spac faire speche –
Ne dorte him no man teche: *needed, instruct*
'Wel thu sitte and softe, *remain*
390 Rymenhild the brighte,
With thine maidenes sixe,
That the sitteth nixte. *sit beside you*
Kinges stuard ure *our*
Sende me into bure:
395 With the speke ihc scholde.
Seie me what thu woldest – *wish*
Seie, and ihc schal here,
What thi wille were.'
Rymenhild up gan stonde,
400 And tok him bi the honde;
Heo sette him on pelle, *coverlet*
Of wyn to drinke his fulle;
Heo makede him faire chere, *She looked kindly upon him*
And tok him abute the swere; *neck*
405 Ofte heo him custe, *kissed*

385–6 The whole room shone with the beauty of his appearance.

So wel so hire luste.   *desired*
'Horn,' heo sede, 'withute strif,   *assuredly*
Thu schalt have me to thi wif.
Horn, have of me rewthe,   *pity*
410 And plist me thi trewthe!'[n]   *plight*
Horn tho him bithoghte   *considered*
What he speke mighte.
'Crist,' quath he, 'the wisse,   *guide*
And yive the hevene blisse
415 Of thine husebonde,
Wher he beo in londe,   *Wherever*
Ihc am ibore to lowe[n]   *I am too low-born*
Such wimman to knowe:
Ihc am icome of thralle,   *slave*
420 And fundling bifalle.   *have become*
Ne feolle hit the of cunde
To spuse beo me bunde:
Hit nere no fair wedding
Bitwexe a thral and a king.'
425 Tho gan Rymenhild mislyke,   *was displeased*
And sore gan to sike.   *sigh*
Armes heo gan bughe;[n]   *bend*
Adun he feol i swoghe.   *she fell in a swoon*
Horn in herte was ful wo,
430 And tok hire on his armes two;
He gan hire for to kesse
Wel ofte, mid ywisse.   *certainly*
'Lemman,' he sede, 'dere,   *Beloved*
Thin herte nu thu stere!   *control*
435 Help me to knighte,   *become a knight*
Bi al thine mighte,
To my lord, the king,
That he me yive dubbing.   *dub me a knight*
Thanne is mi thralhod
440 Iwent into knighthod,   *Transformed*
And I schal wexe more   *my status will increase*
And do, lemman, thi lore.'[n]   *what you say*
Rymenhild, that swete thing,
Wakede of hire swoghning.

421–2 It would not befit one of your birth to be bound to me as my wife.

445 'Horn,' quath heo, 'vel sone   *very soon*
    That schal beon idone:
    Thu schalt beo dubbed knight
    Are come seve night.   *Within a week*
    Have her this cuppe,   *Take*
450 And this ryng theruppe,   *as well*
    To Aylbrus [the] stuard,
    And se he holde foreward.   *keeps, agreement/promise*
    Seie ihc him biseche,   *beseech*
    With loveliche speche,   *gracious*
455 That he adun falle
    Bifore the king in halle,
    And bidde the king arighte   *at once*
    Dubbe the to knighte –
    With selver and with golde,
460 Hit wurth him wel iyolde!   *He shall be well repaid*
    Crist him lene spede
    Thin erende to bede!'ⁿ
    Horn tok his leve,
    For hit was negh eve.
465 Athelbrus he soghte,
    And yaf him that he broghte;
    And tolde him, ful yare,   *quickly*
    Hu he hadde ifare;   *fared*
    And sede him his nede,   *what he needed*
470 And bihet him his mede.   *promised, reward*
    Athelbrus, also swithe,   *as soon as possible*
    Wente to halle blive: *quickly*
    'Kyng,' he sede, 'thu leste   *hear*
    A tale mid the beste.   *among*
475 Thu schalt bere crune   *wear*
    Tomoreghe in this tune:ⁿ
    Tomoreghe is thi feste –
    Ther bihoveth geste.
    Hit nere noght forloren   *would not be in vain*
480 For to knighti child Horn,
    Thine armes for to welde –   *weapons, wield*

451 the] *thus* H; & C.
461–2 Christ grant him success in presenting your errand (to the king).
478 It is fitting that there should be festivities.

God knight he schal yelde!'   *prove to be*
The king sede sone,
'That is wel idone!
485 Horn me wel iquemeth: *pleases*
God knight him bisemeth.   *he is likely to be*
He schal have mi dubbing,
And after [wurth] mi derling;[n]   *become, favourite*
And alle his feren twelf
490 He schal knighten himself:
Alle he schal hem knighte
Bifore me this nighte.'
Til the light of day sprang
Ailmar him thughte lang.
495 The day bigan to springe;   *break*
Horn com bivore the kinge,
Mid his twelf yfere –
Sume hi were luthere.   *wicked*
Horn he dubbede to knighte,
500 With swerd and spures brighte.[n]
He sette him on a stede whit –
Ther nas no knight hym ilik.
He smot him a litel wight,   *gentle blow*
And bed him beon a god knight.   *bade*
505 Athulf fel a knes thar,
Bivore the king, Aylmar:
'King,' he sede, 'so kene,   *brave*
Grante me a bene!   *favour*
Nu is knigh[t] Sire Horn,
510 That in Suddenne was iboren.   *born*
Lord he is of londe
Over us, that bi him stonde.
Thin armes he hath and scheld,
To fighte with upon the feld.
515 Let him us alle knighte,
For that is ure righte!'
Aylmar sede sone, ywis,   *indeed*
'Do nu that thi wille is.'

---

488 after wurth] afterward C; be my nowne L; by myn oþer H.
493–4 It seemed long to Aylmar until daybreak.
509 knight] kniȝ C.

Horn adun lighte,
520 And makede hem alle knightes.
Merie was the feste,
Al of faire gestes;   *festivities*
Ac Rymenhild nas noght ther,   *But*
And that hire thughte seve yer.
525 After Horn heo sente,
And he to bure wente.
Nolde he noght go one: *He would not go alone*
Athulf was his mone.   *companion*
Rymenhild on flore stod
530 (Hornes come hire thughte god),   *coming*
And sede, 'Welcome, Sire Horn,
And Athulf, knight the biforn!
Knight, nu is thi time
For to sitte bi me.
535 Do nu that thu er of spake –   *formerly*
To thi wif thu me take.
Ef thu art trewe of dedes,
Do nu ase thu sedes.
Nu thu hast wille thine,
540 Unbind me of my pine.'   *Release me from my pain*
'Rymenhild,' quath he, 'beo stille!ⁿ
Ihc wulle don al thi wille.
Also hit mot bitide,   *Whatever happens*
Mid spere I schal furst ride,   *With*
545 And mi knighthod prove,
Ar ihc the ginne to woghe.   *woo*
We beth knightes yonge,   *are*
Of o dai al isprunge,   *one, come into being*
And of ure mestere   *calling*
550 So is the manere: *custom*
With sume othere knighte
Wel for his lemman fighte,   *sweetheart*
Or he eni wif take.   *Before*
Forthi me stondeth the more rape.
555 Today, so Crist me blesse,
Ihc wulle do pruesse,   *deeds of valour*

524 And it seemed to her like seven years.
554 Therefore my haste is the greater.

For thi luve, in the felde,
Mid spere and mid schelde.
If ihc come to lyve,
560 Ihc schal the take to wyve.'ⁿ   *survive*
'Knight,' quath heo, 'trewe,
Ihc wene ihc mai the leve.   *I believe I can trust you*
Tak nu her this gold ring;
God him is the dubbing.   *The decoration on it is good*
565 Ther is upon the ringe
Igrave "Rymenhild the yonge";   *Engraved*
Ther nis no betere anonder sunne,   *under*
That eni man of telle cunne.   *can tell of*
For my luve thu hit were,   *wear*
570 And on thi finger thu him bere.
The stones beoth of suche grace   *power*
That thu ne schalt, in none place,
Of none duntes beon ofdrad,   *blows, afraid*
Ne on bataille beon amad,ⁿ   *discomfited*
575 Ef thu loke theran
And thenke upon thi lemman.
And Sire Athulf, thi brother,
He schal have another.
Horn, ihc the biseche,
580 With loveliche speche,
Crist yeve god erndinge,   *good (outcome to your) mission*
The ayen to bringe!'   *back*
The knight hire gan kesse,
And heo him to blesse.
585 Leve at hire he nam,   *He took leave of her*
And into halle cam.
The knightes yeden to table,   *went*
And Horne yede to stable;
Thar he tok his gode fole,   *horse*
590 Also blak so eny cole.   *Just as, charcoal*
The fole schok the brunie,   *chain-mail*
That al the curt gan denie;   *courtyard, resound*
The fole bigan to springe,   *prance*
And Horn murie to singe.   *merrily*
595 Horn rod in a while   *short time*
More than a myle;
He fond a schup stonde,   *riding at anchor*

With hethene honde.[n]   *heathen dogs*
He axede what hi soghte,   *asked*
600 Other to londe broghte.
An hund him gan bihelde,   *(heathen) dog saw him*
That spac wordes belde: *bold*
'This lond we wullez wynne,   *intend to*
And sle that ther is inne.'
605 Horn gan his swerd gripe,
And on his arme wype.
The Sarazins he smatte,   *struck*
That his blod hatte.   *So that, grew hot*
At evreche dunte,   *blow*
610 The heved of wente.   *head, off*
Tho gunne the hundes gone
Abute Horn alone.
He lokede on the ringe,
And thoghte on Rimenilde;
615 He slogh ther on haste   *slew*
On hundred, bi the laste.   *altogether*
Ne mighte no man telle   *count*
That folc that he gan quelle.   *kill*
Of alle that were alive
620 Ne mighte ther non thrive.   *prosper*
Horn tok the maisteres heved,
That he hadde him bireved,
And sette hit on his swerde,   *cut off*
Anoven, at than orde.[n]   *stuck*
                                                 Above, at the point
625 He verde hom into halle,   *went*
Among the knightes alle.
'Kyng,' he sede, 'wel thu sitte,   *may you remain*
And alle thine knightes mitte!   *with you*
Today, after mi dubbing,
630 So I rod on mi pleing,   *As, sport*
I fond o schup rowe,   *float*
Tho hit gan to flowe,[n]
Al with Sarazines kyn,   *kin*
And none londisse men.   *native*
635 Todai, for to pine   *hurt*
The and alle thine,
Hi gonne me assaille.
Mi swerd me nolde faille:

I smot hem alle to grunde,
640 Other yaf hem dithes wunde.   *mortal wounds*
That heved I the bringe
Of the maister kinge.
Nu is thi wile iyolde,
King, that thu me knighti woldest!'ⁿ
645 A moreghe, tho the day gan springe,   *Next morning, when*
The king him rod anhuntinge;
At hom lefte Fikenhild,
That was the wurste moder child!
H[orn] ferde into bure,
650 To sen aventure:ⁿ
He sagh Rymenild sitte,   *saw*
Also he were of witte;   *As if she were out of her mind*
Heo sat on the sunne,   *i.e. at the window*
With tieres al birunne.   *tears, streaming*
655 Horn sede, 'Lef, thin ore!   *Dear one, pardon me*
Wi wepestu so sore?'
Heo sede, 'Noght I ne wepe,
Bute ase I lay aslepe,   *Except that*
To the se my net I caste,
660 And hit nolde noght ilaste.   *hold*
A gret fiss, at the furste,   *fish, at once*
Mi net he gan to berste.
Ihc wene that ihc schal leose   *believe, lose*
The fiss that ihc wolde cheose!'ⁿ   *choose*
665 'Crist,' quath Horn, 'and Seint Steveneⁿ
Turne thine swevene!
Ne schal I the biswike,   *deceive*
Ne do that the mislike.   *distresses*
I schal me make thin owe,   *own*
670 To holden and to knowe,
For evrech othere wighte: *Despite, creature*
And tharto mi treuthe I the plighte.'
Muchel was the ruthe   *sorrow*
That was at thare truthe;   *exchange of vows*
675 For Rymenhild weop ille,   *bitterly*

643–4 Now, king, your willingness to knight me is rewarded.
649 Horn] Heo C; And horn L.
651 He] Heo C.
666 Turn your dream (to good).

And Horn let the tires stille.[n] *wept silently*
'Lemman,' quath he, 'dere,
Thu schalt more ihere:
Thi sweven schal wende, *dream, turn (to good)*
680 Other sum man schal us schende; *Or, destroy*
The fiss that brak the lyne,
Ywis, he doth us pine; *Indeed, harm*
That schal don us tene, *cause us distress*
And wurth wel sone isene.' *(that) will very soon be seen*
685 Aylmar rod bi sture,[n]
And Horn lai in bure.
Fykenhild hadde envye, *malice*
And sede thes folye:[n] *madness*
'Aylmar, ihc the warne:
690 Horn the wule berne.[n] *burn/destroy*
Ihc herde whar he sede —
And his swerd forth leide — [n]
To bringe the of lyve,
And take Rymenhild to wyve.
695 He lith in bure,
Under coverture, *sheets*
By Rymenhild, thi doghter,
And so he doth wel ofte.
And thider thu go alright, *If, at once*
700 Ther thu him finde might.
Thu do him ut of londe, *banish him*
Other he doth the schonde!' *injury*
Aylmar ayen gan turne,
Wel modi and wel murne; *angry, sorrowful*
705 He fond Horn in arme,
On Rymenhilde barme.[n] *bosom*
'Awei, ut!' he sede. 'Fule theof! *Vile scoundrel*
Ne wurstu me nevremore leof!
Wend ut of my bure,
710 With muchel missaventure! *Great misfortune go with you!*
Wel sone bute thu flitte, *unless, depart*
With swerde ihc the anhitte. *strike*
Wend ut of my londe,
Other thu schalt have schonde!' *injury*

708 You will nevermore be dear to me.

715 Horn sadelede his stede,
And his armes he gan sprede;ⁿ
His brunie he gan lace,   *chain-mail*
So he scholde, into place;
His swerd he gan fonge.   *take*
720 N'abod he noght to longe: *He did not tarry, too*
He yede forth blive   *quickly*
To Rymenhild, his wyve.ⁿ
He sede, 'Lemman, derling,
Nu havestu thi swevening: *you have your dream*
725 The fiss that thi net rente   *tore*
Fram the he me sente!   *He sent me away from you*
Rymenhild, have wel godne day.   *good*
No leng abiden I ne may;   *longer, stay*
Into uncuthe londe,   *foreign*
730 Wel more for to fonde.   *To seek yet more (adventure)*
I schal wune there   *dwell*
Fulle seve yere:
At seve yeres ende,
Yef I ne come ne sende,   *If*
735 Tak the husebonde –   *for yourself*
For me thu ne wonde.ⁿ   *hesitate*
In armes thu me fonge,   *take*
And kes me wel longe.'
He custe h[e]m wel a stunde,   *They kissed each other*
740 And Rymenhild feol to grunde.
Horn tok his leve –
Ne mighte be no leng bileve.   *longer, delay*
He tok Athulf, his fere,
Al abute the swere,   *neck*
745 And sede, 'Knight so trewe,
Kep wel mi luve newe!
Thu nevre me ne forsoke.
Rymenhild thu kep and loke.'   *guard*
His stede he gan bistride,
750 And forth he gan ride.
To the havene he ferde,
And a god schup he hurede,   *hired*
That him scholde londe

739 He custe hem] *thus* H; He custe him C; He kusten L. (Cf. line 1211.)

In westene londe.[n]
755 Athulf weop with ighe,   *eye*
And al that him isighe.   *saw*
To lond he him sette,
And fot on stirop sette.
He fond bi the weie
760 Kynges sones tweie:
That on him het Harild,   *was called*
And that other Berild.
Berild gan him preie
That he scholde him seie
765 What his name were,
And what he wolde there.
'Cutberd,' he sede, 'ihc hote,[n]   *am called*
Icomen ut of the bote,
Wel feor fram bi weste,   *far*
770 To seche mine beste.'   *profit*
Berild gan him nier ride,   *nearer*
And tok him bi the bridel:
'Wel beo thu, knight, ifounde!   *Well met, knight!*
With me thu lef a stunde.[n]   *dwell, for a time*
775 Also mote I sterve,   *As surely as I shall die*
The king thu schalt serve.
Ne sagh I nevre my lyve
So fair knight aryve!'   *(in) my life*
Cutberd [he] ladde into halle,   *they*
780 And he a kne gan falle: *on his knees*
He sette him a-knewelyng,   *kneeling*
And grette wel the gode kyng.   *greeted*
Thanne sede Berild sone,
'Sire king, of him thu hast to done.
785 Bitak him thi lond to werie,   *Entrust to, defend*
Ne scha[l] hit no man derie;   *harm*
For he is the faireste man
That evre yut on thi londe cam.'   *yet*
Thanne sede the king so dere,
790 'Welcome beo thu here!

779 he] heo C.
784 i.e. he might be of service to you.
786 schal] schat C.

Go nu, Berild, swithe, *quickly*
And make him ful blithe. *glad*
And whan thu farst to woghe, *go wooing*
Tak him thine glove.[n] *Give*
795 Iment thu havest to wyve, *(Where) you have intended*
Awai he schal the dryve;
For Cutberdes fairhede
Ne schal the nevre wel spede!' *benefit you*
Hit was at Cristesmasse,
800 Neither more ne lasse; *before nor after*
Ther cam in at none *noon*
A geaunt suthe sone,[n] *giant, very*
Iarmed, fram paynyme, *Armed, heathen lands*
And seide thes ryme: *speech*
805 'Site stille, sire kyng,
And herkne this tythyng! *news*
Her buth paens arived – *are heathens*
Wel mo thane five *more*
Her beoth on the sonde,
810 King, upon thi londe.
On of hem wile fighte *One*
Ayen thre knightes: *Against*
Yef o[w]er thre slen ure, *your, ours*
Al this lond beo youre;
815 Yef ure on overcometh your threo, *our one*
Al this lond schal ure beo.
Tomoreghe be the fightinge,
Whane the light of daye springe.'
Thanne sede the kyng, Thurston,
820 'Cutberd schal beo that on,
Berild schal beo that other, *the second*
The thridde Alrid, his brother; *third*
For hi beoth the strengeste,
And of armes the beste.
825 Bute what schal us to rede?
Ihc wene we beth alle dede!'
Cutberd sat at borde, *table*

792 *Probably*, give him good entertainment.
813 ower] *thus* H; oþer C; þyne L.
825 But what will be our (best) counsel?

And sede thes wordes:
'Sire king, hit nis no righte
830 On with th[r]e to fighte –
Ayen one hunde,   *dog*
Thre Cristen men to fonde!   *strive*
Sire, I schal alone,
Withute more ymone,   *further companion*
835 With mi swerd wel ethe   *easily*
Bringe hem thre to dethe.'
The kyng aros a-moreghe,
That hadde muchel sorghe.   *sorrow*
And Cutberd ros of bedde;
840 With armes he him schredde.   *clad*
Horn his brunie gan on caste,   *chain-mail*
And lacede hit wel faste,
And cam to the kinge
At his uprisinge.
845 'King,' he sede, 'cum to fel[de],   *field (of conflict)*
For to bihelde
Hu we fighte schulle,   *How*
And toga[de]re go wulle.'   *together*
Right at prime tide,[n]   *the hour of Prime*
850 Hi gunnen ut ride,
And funden on a grene
A geaunt suthe kene,   *fierce*
His feren him biside,
Hore deth to abide.   *Awaiting their death*
855 The ilke bataille   *same force*
Cutberd gan assaille.
He yaf dentes inoghe;   *many blows*
The knightes felle iswoghe.   *swooning*
His dent he gan withdraghe,   *withhold*
860 For hi were negh aslaghe,   *nearly destroyed*
And sede, 'Knightes, nu ye reste
One while, ef you leste.'   *wish*
He sede hi nevre nadde   *they had never had*
Of knighte dentes so harde,
865 [Bute of the King Mory,   *Except*

830 thre] *thus* L H; þe C.
845 felde] *thus* L H; fel C.
848 togadere] togare C.
865–6 *Thus* L H (*so* om.); *lines* om. C.

That was so swythe stordy:]   *very strong*
He was of Hornes kunne,   *kin*
Iborn in Suddenne.
Horn him gan to agrise,   *grow angry*
870 And his blod arise:
Bivo[r] him sagh he stonde   *Before*
That driven him of londe,   *Those who*
And that his fader slogh.   *slew*
To him his swerd he drogh.
875 He lokede on his rynge,
And thoghte on Rymenhilde.
He smot him thuregh the herte,   *through*
That sore him gan to smerte.   *smart*
The paens, that er were so sturne,   *earlier, fierce*
880 Hi gunne awei urne.   *run*
Horn and his compaynye
Gunne after hem wel swithe highe,   *Started, quickly*
And sloghen alle the hundes,
Er hi here schipes funde.   *Before, reached*
885 To dethe he hem alle broghte:
His fader deth wel dere hi boghte!   *paid for*
Of alle the kynges knightes,
Ne scapede ther no wighte;
Bute his sones tweie
890 Bifore him he sagh deie.[n]
The king bigan to grete,   *mourn*
And teres for to lete.   *let fall*
Me leide hem in bare,   *They were laid on a bier*
And burden hem ful yare.   *buried*
895 The king com into halle,
Among his knightes alle.
'Horn,' he sede, 'I seie the,[n]
Do as I schal rede the.   *advise*
Aslaghen beth mine heirs,   *Slain*
900 And thu art knight of muchel pris,   *great renown*
And of grete strengthe,
And fair o bodie lengthe: *of fine stature*
Mi rengne thu schalt welde,   *realm, rule*
And to spuse helde

871 Bivor] Biuo C.
893 Me leide] Me leiden C; Men leyden L.

905 Reynild, mi doghter,[n]
    That sitteth on the lofte.'   *above*
    'O, sire king, with wronge
    Scholte ihc hit underfonge,   *Should, accept*
    Thi doghter that ye me bede,   *offer*
910 Ower rengne for to lede.   *Your*
    Wel more ihc schal the serve,
    Sire kyng, or thu sterve.   *before you die*
    Thi sorwe schal wende   *turn/go*
    Or seve yeres ende.
915 Wanne hit is wente,
    Sire king, yef me mi rente.   *wages*
    Whanne I thi doghter yerne,   *desire*
    Ne schaltu me hire werne.'   *refuse*
    Cutberd wonede there   *dwelt*
920 Fulle seve yere,
    That to Rymenild he ne sente,
    Ne himself ne wente.
    Rymenild was in Westernesse,
    With wel muchel sorinesse.
925 A king ther gan arive,
    That wolde hire have to wyve:
    At on he was with the king   *In agreement*
    Of that ilke wedding.   *same*
    The daies were schorte,
930 That Rimenild ne dorste   *So that, dared*
    Leten, in none wise.   *Delay*
    A writ he dude devise;   *letter*
    Athulf hit dude write,
    That Horn ne luvede noght lite.   *not a little*
935 Heo sende hire sonde   *message*
    To evereche londe,
    To seche Horn, the knight,
    Ther me him finde mighte.   *Wherever he might be found*
    Horn noght therof ne herde,
940 Til o dai that he ferde   *went*
    To wude for to schete: *shoot*
    A knave he gan mete.   *lad*
    Horn sede, 'Leve fere,   *Good fellow*

929 i.e. time was running out.
943 sede] seden C.

Wat sechestu here?'   *do you seek*
945 'Knight, if beo thi wille,
I mai the sone telle:
I seche fram bi weste
Horn of Westernesse,
For a maiden, Rymenhild,
950 That for him gan wexe wild.
A king hire wile wedde,
And bringe to his bedde —
King Modi of Reynes,
On of Hornes enemis.
955 Ihc habbe walke wide,   *wandered far*
Bi the se side:
Nis he nowar ifunde —
Walawai the stunde!   *Alack the day!*
Wailaway the while!
960 Nu wurth Rymenhild bigiled.'[n]
Horn iherde with his ires,   *ears*
And spak with bidere tires: *bitter*
'Knave, wel the bitide!   *good fortune be yours!*
Horn stondeth the biside.
965 Ayen to hure thu turne,   *Go back to her*
And seie that heo ne murne,   *grieve*
For I schal beo ther bitime —   *very soon*
A Soneday bi pryme.'[n]   *the hour of Prime*
The knave was wel blithe,
970 And highede ayen blive.   *hastened back*
The se bigan to throghe   *toss*
Under hire woghe;   *wall*
The knave there gan adrinke —   *drown*
Rymenhild hit mighte ofthinke!   *regret*
975 Rymenhild undude the dure-pin
Of the hus ther heo was in,   *house*
To loke with hire ighe
If heo oght of Horn isighe.
Tho fond heo the knave adrent,   *drowned*
980 That he hadde for Horn isent,   *she*
And that scholde Horn bringe;
Hire fingres he gan wringe.[n]
Horn cam to Thurston, the kyng,
And tolde him this tithing.

985 Tho he was iknowe: *he had made himself known*
That Rimenh[ild] was his oghe;
Of his gode kenne,   *kin*
The king of Suddenne;
And hu he slogh in felde
990 That his fader quelde.   *Those who, killed*
And seide, 'King the wise,
Yeld me mi servise!   *Repay*
Rymenhild help me winne,
That thu noght ne linne;   *Without delay*
995 And I schal do to spuse
Thi doghter, wel to huse:
Heo schal to spuse have
Athulf, mi gode felaghe,[n]   *fellow*
God knight mid the beste,   *Good, among*
1000 And the treweste.'
The king sede so stille,   *quietly*
'Horn, have nu thi wille!'
He dude writes sende   *letters*
Into Yrlonde,   *Ireland*
1005 After knightes lighte.   *agile*
Irisse men to fighte   *Irish*
To Horn come inoghe,   *many*
That to schupe droghe.[n]   *took ship*
Horn dude him in the weie,   *set out*
1010 On a god galeie.[n]   *boat*
The [wynd] him gan to blowe,
In a litel throghe.   *while*
The se bigan to posse,   *drive*
Right into Westernesse.
1015 Hi strike seil and maste,   *lowered*
And ankere gunne caste.   *dropped anchor*
Or eny day was sprunge,
Other belle irunge,[n]
The word bigan to springe
1020 Of Rymenhilde weddinge.
Horn was in the watere —
Ne mighte he come no latere!   *He was just in time!*

986 Rimenhild] Rimenh C.
995–6 And I shall cause your daughter to be well married.
1011 The wynd him gan] Þe him gan C; Þe wynd bigon H; *not in* L.

He let his schup stonde,
And yede to londe.
1025 His folk he dude abide   *made*
Under wude side.   *At the edge of a wood*
Horn him yede alone,
Also he sprunge of stone.[n]   *As if*
A palmere he thar mette,
1030 And faire hine grette: *greeted him*
'Palmere, thu schalt me telle
Al of thine spelle.'   *All that you have to say*
He sede, upon his tale,
'I come fram o brudale: *bridal party*
1035 Ihc was at o wedding,
Of a maide, Rymenhild.
Ne mighte heo adrighe,   *forbear*
That heo ne weop with ighe.[n]
Heo sede that heo nolde
1040 Ben ispused with golde –   *a gold (ring)*
Heo hadde on husebonde,   *one*
Thegh he were ut of londe;
And in strong halle,
Bithinne castel walle.[n]   *Within*
1045 Ther I was atte yate,   *gate*
Nolde hi me in late.   *They would not let me in*
Modi ihote hadde   *commanded*
To bure that me hire ladde.   *she should be led*
Awai I gan glide –
1050 That deol I nolde abide.   *sorrow, endure*
The bride wepeth sore,
And that is muche deole!'
Quath Horn, 'So Crist me rede,   *As Christ is my guide*
We schulle chaungi wede!'[n]   *garments*
1055 Have her clothes myne,
And tak me thi sclavyne.[n]
Today I schal ther drinke,
That some hit schulle ofthinke!'   *regret*
His sclavyn he dude dun legge,   *lay*
1060 And tok hit on his rigge;   *back*
He tok Horn his clothes –   *gave*
That nere him noght lothe!   *unpleasant*
Horn tok burdon and scrippe,   *staff, wallet*

And wrong his lippe.	*twisted*
1065 He makede him a ful chere,	*ugly face*
And al bicolmede his swere;	*blackened*
He makede him unbicomelich,	*unattractive*
Hes he nas nevremore ilich.	
He com to the gateward,	
1070 That him answerede hard.ⁿ	*porter*
Horn bad undo softe,	*gently, unfasten (the gate)*
Mani tyme and ofte.	
Ne mighte he awynne,	*succeed*
That he come therinne.	
1075 Horn gan to the yate turne,	
And that wiket unspurne.ⁿ	*wicket, kick open*
The boye hit scholde abugge –	*rascal, pay for*
Horn threu him over the brigge,	
That his ribbes him to-brake;	
1080 And suththe com in atte gate.	*afterwards (Horn)*
He sette him wel loghe,	*seated himself, low*
In beggeres rowe.ⁿ	
He lokede him abute,	
With his colmie snute.	*blackened nose*
1085 He segh Rymenhild sitte,	
Ase heo were of witte,	*As if she had lost her mind*
Sore wepinge and yerne:	*vehemently*
Ne mighte hure no man wurne.	*stop*
He lokede in eche halke;	*corner*
1090 Ne segh he nowhar walke	
Athulf, his felawe,	
That he cuthe knowe.	*could*
Athulf was in the ture,	*tower*
Abute for to pure	*gaze*
1095 After his comynge –	*For (Horn's) arrival*
Yef schup him wolde bringe.	
He segh the se flowe,	
And Horn nowar rowe.	*nowhere*
He sede upon his songe,	
1100 'Horn, nu thu ert wel longe!	
Rymenhild thu me toke,	*entrusted*
That I scholde loke:	*guard*

1068 Such as he was at no other time.

Ihc habbe kept hure evre.
Com nu other nevre!
1105 I ne may no leng hure kepe: *longer*
For soreghe nu y wepe.'ⁿ
Rymenhild ros of benche,
Wyn for to schenche,   *pour*
After mete in sale,   *hall*
1110 Bothe wyn and ale.
[A]n horn he bar an honde,   *drinking-horn*
So laghe was in londe.ⁿ   *custom*
Knightes and squier
Alle dronken of the ber;   *beer*
1115 Bute Horn alone   *Except*
Nadde therof no mone.   *share*
Horn sat upon the grunde;
Him thughte he was ibunde.   *bound*
He sede, 'Quen so hende,   *gracious*
1120 To me ward thu wende!   *Come to me!*
Thu yef us with the furste –
The beggeres beoth ofthurste.'ⁿ   *thirsty*
Hure horn heo leide adun,
And fulde him of a brunⁿ   *brown*
1125 His bolle of a galun,   *bowl, gallon*
For heo wende he were a glotoun.   *glutton*
He seide, 'Have this cuppe,
And this thing theruppe.ⁿ   *as well*
Ne sagh ihc nevre, so ihc wene,
1130 Beggere that were so kene!'   *eager/bold*
Horn tok hit his ifere,   *gave, companion*
And sede, 'Quen so dere,
Wyn nelle ihc, muche ne lite,   *I do not wish for*
Bute of cuppe white.
1135 Thu wenest I beo a beggere,
And ihc am a fissere: *fisher*
Wel feor icome bi este,   *far, to the east*
For fissen at thi feste.   *to fish*
Mi net lith her bi honde,   *at hand*
1140 Bi a wel fair stronde;   *shore*
Hit hath ileie there   *lain*

1111 An] *thus* L H; On C.
1121 Give to us among the first.

Fulle seve yere.
Ihc am icome to loke
Ef eny fiss hit toke;
1145 Ihc am icome to fisse.[n]
Drink to me of disse: *from the bowl*
Drink to Horn of horne.[n]
Feor ihc am i-orne!'   *I have travelled far*
Rymenhild him gan bihelde;
1150 Hire heorte bigan to chelde.   *grow cold*
Ne kneu heo noght his fissing,   *recognized*
Ne Horn hymselve nothing;
Ac wunder hire gan thinke
Whi he bad to Horn drinke.
1155 Heo fulde hire horn with wyn,   *filled*
And dronk to the pilegrym.
Heo sede, 'Drink thi fulle,   *Drink your fill*
And suththe thu me telle   *afterwards*
If thu evre isighe
1160 Horn under wude lighe.'[n]   *lie*
Horn dronk of horn a stunde,   *while*
And threu the ring to grunde.   *to the bottom (of the horn)*
The quen yede to bure,
With hire maidenes foure;
1165 Tho fond heo what heo wolde,   *wished*
A ring igraven of golde,
That Horn of hure hadde.
Sore hure dradde
That Horn iste[r]ve were,   *dead*
1170 For the ring was there.
Tho sente heo a damesele
After the palmere.
'Palmere,' quath heo, 'trewe,
The ring that thu threwe –
1175 Thu seie whar thu hit nome,   *got*
And whi thu hider come.'   *hither*
He seide, 'Bi Seint Gile,[n]
Ihc habbe go mani mile,
Wel feor bi yonde weste,   *into the west*
1180 To seche my beste.   *profit*
I fond Horn child stonde

1169 isterve] isteue C; ded L H.

To schupeward in londe: *About to take ship*
He sede he wolde agesse   *strive*
To arive in Westernesse.
1185 The schip nam to the flode   *took*
With me and Horn the gode.
Horn was sik and deide,
And faire he me preide   *courteously he begged me*
Go with the ringe
1190 To Rymenhild the yonge.
Ofte he hit custe —   *kissed*
God yeve his saule reste!'[n]
Rymenhild sede, at the furste,
'Herte, nu thu berste!   *break*
1195 For Horn nastu namore,   *you do not have*
That the hath pined so sore!'   *grieved*
Heo feol on hire bedde,   *fell*
Ther heo knif hudde,   *Where, had hidden*
To sle with king lothe   *hated*
1200 And hureselve bothe,
In that ulke nighte,   *same*
If Horn come ne mighte.
To herte knif heo sette,
Ac Horn anon hire kepte.   *stopped*
1205 He wipede that blake of his swere,   *neck*
And sede, 'Quen so swete and dere,
Ihc am Horn, thin oghe.
Ne canstu me noght knowe?
Ihc am Horn of Westernesse:
1210 In armes thu me cusse!'
Hi custe hem, mid ywisse,   *certainly*
And makeden muche blisse.[n]
'Rymenhild,' he sede, 'y wende
Adun to the wudes ende: *Down*
1215 Ther beth myne knightes,
Redi to fighte,
Iarmed under clothe.   *Armed, garments*
Hi schulle make wrothe   *angry*
The king and his geste,
1220 That come to the feste:

1196 pined] pined þe C.

Today I schal hem teche,
And sore hem areche!"ⁿ   strike
Horn sprong ut of halle,
And let his sclavin falle.
1225 The quen yede to bure,
And fond Athulf in ture.
'Athulf,' heo sede, 'be blithe!
And to Horn thu go wel swithe —
He is under wude boghe,   bough
1230 And with him knightes inoghe.'ⁿ   many
Athulf bigan to springe   leap (for joy)
For the tithinge.
After Horn he arnde anon,   ran
Also that hors mighte gon.   As (fast as)
1235 He him overtok, ywis;
Hi makede suithe muchel blis.ⁿ
Horn tok his preie,   troop
And dude him in the weie.   went on his way
He com in wel sone
1240 (The yates were undone),
Iarmed ful thikke,
Fram fote to the nekke.   heavily
Alle that were therin —
Bithute his twelf ferin,   Apart from
1245 And the king, Aylmare —
He dude hem alle to kare,   made them all sorry
That at the feste were:
Here lif hi lete there.ⁿ   lost
Horn ne dude no wunderⁿ
1250 Of Fikenhildes false tunge.
Hi sworen othes holdeⁿ   true
That nevre ne scholde
Horn nevre bitraie,
Thegh he at dithe laie.   at (the point of) death
1255 Hi runge the belle,
The wedlak for to felle.ⁿ   fulfil
Horn him yede with his
To the kinges palais.
Ther was [brudale] suete,
1260 For riche men ther ete.   ate

1259 brudale] *thus* L H; brid & ale C.

Telle ne mighte tunge
That gle that ther was sunge.[n]   *song*
Horn sat on chaere,
And bad hem alle ihere.
1265 'King,' he sede, 'thu luste   *hear*
A tale mid the beste![n]   *One of the best stories*
I ne seie hit for no blame.[n]
Horn is mi name –
Thu me to knighte hove –   *elevated*
1270 And knighthod have preved.
To the king men seide
That I the bitraide.
Thu makedest me fleme,[n]   *flee*
And thi lond to reme.   *leave*
1275 Thu wendest that I wroghte
That y nevre ne thoghte,   *What, intended*
Bi Rymenhild for to ligge,   *lie*
And that I withsegge.[n]   *deny*
Ne schal ihc hit biginne
1280 Til I Suddene winne.
Thu kep hure a stunde,
The while that I funde   *strive (to come)*
Into min heritage,
And to mi baronage.   *(proper) rank*
1285 That lond I schal ofreche,   *gain*
And do mi fader wreche.   *vengeance*
I schal beo king of tune,   *in the city*
And bere kinges crune.   *wear, crown*
Thanne schal Rymenhilde
1290 Ligge bi the kinge!'   *Lie*
Horn gan to schupe draghe,   *take ship*
With his Yrisse felaghes,
Athulf with him, his brother;
Nolde he non other.
1295 That schup bigan to crude;   *rush*
The wind him bleu lude.   *loudly*
Withinne daies five,
That schup gan arive,[n]
Abute middelnighte.

1270 And (I) have proved myself as a knight.

1300 Horn him yede wel righte:	*at once*
He tok Athulf bi honde,	
And up he yede to londe.	
Hi founde under schelde	
A knight hende in felde.	*noble*
1305 The knight him aslepe lay,	
Al biside the way.	
Horn him gan to take,	*seize*
And sede, 'Knight, awake!	
Seie what thu kepest,	*you are guarding*
1310 And whi thu her slepest.	
Methinkth, bi thine crois lighte,[n]	*by your shining cross*
That thu longest to Ure Drighte.	*belong, Our Lord*
Bute thu wule me schewe,	*tell*
I schal the to-hewe!'	*cut you to pieces*
1315 The gode knight up aros;	
Of the wordes him gros.	*he was terrified*
He sede, 'Ihc have, ayenes my wille,	
Payns ful ylle!	
Ihc was Cristene a while;	*at one time*
1320 Tho icom to this ille	*island*
Sarazins blake,	*black*
That dude me forsake;	*made*
On Crist ihc wolde bileve.	
On him hi makede me reve	
1325 To kepe this passage –	*guard, road*
Fram Horn, that is of age,	
That wunieth bi este,	*dwells in the east*
Knight with the beste.	
Hi sloghe with here honde	
1330 The king of this londe,	
And with him fele hundred;	*many*
And therof is wunder	
That he ne cometh to fighte.	*i.e. Horn*
God sende him the righte!	
1335 And wind him hider drive	
To bringe hem of live!	*out of, life*
Hi sloghen Kyng Murry,	

1324 They made me reeve (guardian) against him (i.e. Horn).
1334 God grant that right be on his side!

Hornes fader, king hendy.   *noble*
Horn hi ut of londe sente;
1340 Tuelf felaghes with him wente,
Among hem Athulf the gode,
Min oghene child, my leve fode.   *dear creature*
Ef Horn child is hol and sund,   *whole and sound*
And Athulf bithute wund –   *without wound*
1345 He luveth him so dere,
And is him so stere – [n]
Mighte I seon hem tueie,   *If I might see them both*
For joie I scholde deie!'
'Knight, beo thanne blithe,
1350 Mest of alle sithe!   *Most, times*
Horn and Athulf, his fere,
Bothe hi ben here!'
To Horn he gan gon,
And grete him anon.   *greeted*
1355 Muche joie hi makede there,
The while hi togadere were.
'Childre,' he sede, 'hu habbe ye fare?   *fared*
That ihc you segh hit is ful yare!
Wille ye this lond winne,
1360 And sle that ther is inne?'
He sede, 'Leve Horn child,   *Dear*
Yut lyveth thi moder, Godhild.   *Still*
Of joie heo miste,   *She might well be joyful*
If heo the alive wiste.'   *knew you were alive*
1365 Horn sede, on his rime,   *speech*
'Iblessed beo the time
I com to Suddenne
With mine Irisse menne!
We schulle the hundes teche
1370 To speke ure speche:
Alle we hem schulle sle,
And al quic hem fle!'   *alive, flay*
Horn gan his horn to blowe.
His folk hit gan iknowe: *recognize*
1375 Hi comen ut of stere,   *boat*

1358 It is a very long time since I saw you!
1370 i.e. to dance to our tune.

Fram Hornes banere.[n]   *banner*
Hi sloghen and fughten
The night and the ughten;   *the early morning (before dawn)*
The Saracins cunde
1380 Ne lefde ther non in th'ende.[n]
Horn let wurche   *had built*
Chapeles and chirche;
He let belles ringe,
And masses let singe.
1385 He com to his moder halle,
· In a roche walle.[n]   *i.e. in a cave*
Corn he let ferie,   *had brought*
And makede feste merie.
Merie lif he wroghte;
1390 Rymenhild hit dere boghte!   *paid dearly for it*
Fikenhild was prut on herte,   *arrogant*
And that him dude smerte.   *caused him pain*
Yonge he yaf and elde,
Mid him for to helde.
1395 Ston he dude lede,   *had brought*
Ther he hopede spede.   *expected, succeed*
Strong castel he let sette,   *had built*
Mid see him biflette,   *sea, surrounded*
Ther ne mighte lighte   *alight*
1400 Bute foghel with flighte;   *Except, bird*
Bute whanne the se withdroghe,
Mighte come men ynoghe.[n]
Fikenhild gan wende
Rymenhild to schende.   *undo*
1405 To woghe he gan hure yerne;   *woo, ardently*
The kyng ne dorste him werne.[n]   *dared not, forbid*
Rymenhild was ful of mode: *anxiety*
He wep teres of blode.[n]
That night Horn gan swete,   *sweat*
1410 And hevie for to mete   *dream*
Of Rymenhild, his make,   *lover*
Into schupe was itake.

1379–80 None of the Saracen race was left there in the end.
1393–4 He gave to (i.e. bribed) young and old to side with him.
1401 i.e. at low tide.

The schup bigan to blenche;   *toss*
His leman scholde adrenche.   *drown*
1415 Rymenhild, with hire honde,
      Wolde up to londe.
      Fikenhild ayen hire pelte   *back, pulled*
      With his swerdes hilte.[nn]
      Horn him wok of slape;
1420 So a man that hadde rape,   *As, haste*
      'Athulf,' he sede, 'felaghe,
      To schupe we mote draghe!   *We must take ship*
      Fikenhild me hath idon under,   *got the better of me*
      And Rymenhild to do wunder.[n]
1425 Crist, for his wundes five,[n]
      Tonight me thuder drive!'   *thither*
      Horn gan to schupe ride,
      His feren him biside.
      Fikenhild, or the dai gan springe,
1430 Alright he ferde to the kinge   *At once*
      After Rymenhild the brighte,   *For*
      To wedden hire bi nighte.   *at night*
      He ladde hure bi the derke   *in the dark*
      Into his nywe werke.   *new building*
1435 The feste hi bigunne
      Er that ros the sunne,[n]
      Er thane Horn hit wiste.   *knew*
      Tofore the sunne upriste,
      His schup stod under ture,   *i.e. Horn's ship*
1440 At Rymenhilde bure.
      Rymenhild, litel weneth heo   *thinks*
      That Horn thanne alive beo.
      The castel thei ne knewe,   *i.e. Horn and his men*
      For he was so nywe.   *i.e. the castle*
1445 Horn fond sittinde Arnoldin,
      That was Athulfes cosin,
      That ther was in that tide   *at that time*
      Horn for t'abide.[n]   *to await*
      'Horn knight,' he sede, 'kinges sone,
1450 Wel beo thu to londe icome!

1416 i.e. she tried to reach land.
1424 And brought great distress to Rymenhild.

Today hath ywedde Fikenhild
Thi swete lemman, Rymenhild.
Ne schal I the lie —
He hath giled the twie!   *betrayed you twice*
1455 This tur he let make
Al for thine sake:
Ne mai ther come inne
No man, with none ginne.   *cunning/strategy*
Horn, nu Crist the wisse,   *guide*
1460 Of Rymenhild that thu ne misse!'
Horn cuthe al the liste   *knew, cunning*
That eni man of wiste.
Harpe he gan schewe,   *produce*
And tok felaghes fewe,
1465 Of knightes suithe snelle,   *swift*
That schrudde hem at wille.
Hi yeden bi the gravel[n]
Toward the castel.
Hi gunne murie singe,   *merrily*
1470 And makede here gleowinge.   *minstrelsy*
Rymenhild hit gan ihere,
And axede what hi were.   *asked*
Hi seden hi weren harpurs,
And sume were gigours.[n]   *fiddlers*
1475 He dude Horn in late,   *They, let*
Right at halle gate.
He sette him on the benche,
His harpe for to clenche.[n]   *pluck*
He makede Rymenhilde lay,   *song*
1480 And heo makede 'Walaway.'   *Alas*
Rymenhild feol yswoghe;   *fell swooning*
Ne was ther non that loughe.   *laughed*
Hit smot to Hornes herte,
So bitere that hit smerte.   *smarted*
1485 He lokede on the ringe,
And thoghte on Rymenhilde.[n]
He yede up to borde;
With gode suerdes orde,   *point*

1460 So that you do not lose Rymenhild.
1466 Who dressed themselves as they would.

Fikenhildes crune   *crown (of his head)*
1490 Ther ifulde adune;   *he felled*
And al his men, a rowe,   *by turn*
H[e] dude adun throwe.
Whanne hi weren aslaghe,
Fikenhild h[e] dude to-draghe.[n]
1495 Horn makede Arnoldin thare
King, after King Aylmare,
Of al Westernesse,
For his meoknesse.   *meekness*
The king and his homage   *vassals*
1500 Yeven Arnoldin trewage.[nn]   *tribute*
Horn tok Rymenhild bi the honde,
And ladde hure to the stronde;   *shore*
And ladde with him Athelbrus,
The gode stuard of his hus.
1505 The se bigan to flowe,
And Horn gan to rowe.
Hi gunne for arive
Ther King Modi was sire.   *Where, king*
Athelbrus he makede ther king,[n]
1510 For his gode teching.   *guidance*
He yaf alle the knightes ore   *favour*
For Horn knightes lore.[n]   *counsel*
Horn gan for to ride;   *sail*
The wind him bleu wel wide.   *far*
1515 He arivede in Yrlonde,
Ther he wo fonde.[n]
Ther he dude Athulf child
Wedden maide Reynild.[n]
Horn com to Suddenne,
1520 Among al his kenne.   *kin*
Rymenhild he makede his quene,
So hit mighte wel beon.   *As was fitting*
Al folk hem mighte rewe,   *pity*
That loveden hem so trewe.[n]
1525 Nu ben hi bothe dede –

1492 He] *thus* L H; Hi C.
1494 he] *thus* L; hi C; *not in* H.
1516 fond♢] fondede C.

Crist to hevene hem lede!
Her endeth the tale of Horn,
That fair was and noght unorn.   *ugly*
Make we us glade evre among,   *continually*
1530 For thus him endeth Hornes song.
Jesus, that is of hevene king,
Yeve us alle his suete blessing! **Amen.**[n]

Ex ----------------------------- **pli** ------------------------------- **cit**

FLORYS AND BLAUNCHEFLOUR[n]

Ne thurst men never in londe	*need*
After feirer children fonde.	*seek*
The Cristen woman fedde hem thoo –	*nurtured, then*
Ful wel she lovyd hem, both twoo.	
5 So longe she fedde hem in feere	*together*
That they were of elde of seven yere.[n]	*age*
The king behelde his sone dere,	
And seyde to him on this manere:	
That harme it were muche more	
10 But his sone were sette to lore,	*Unless, learning*
On the book letters to know,	
As men don, both hye and lowe.	*high*
'Feire sone,' he seide, 'thou shalt lerne:	
Lo that thou do ful yerne!'	
15 Florys answerd with wepyng,	
As he stood byfore the kyng:	
Al wepyng seide he,	
'Ne shal not Blancheflour lerne with me?	
Ne can y noght to scole goon	
20 Without Blaunchefloure,' he seide than;[n]	
'Ne can y in no scole syng ne rede	
Without Blauncheflour,' he seide.	
The king seide to his soon,	*son*
'She shal lerne, for thy love.'	
25 To scole they were put;	
Both they were good of wytte.	*intelligent*
Wonder it was of hur lore,	

13 he] she S.
14 Look that you do it in good earnest!

And of her love wel the more:[n]
The children lovyd togeder soo,
30 They myght never parte atwoo.
When they had five yere to scoole goon,
So wel they had lerned thoo,
Inowgh they couth of Latyne,   Much, knew
And wel wryte on parchemyn.
35 The kyng understod the grete amoure   love
Bytwene his son and Blanchefloure,
And thought when they were of age
That her love wolde noght swage,   abate
Nor he myght noght her love withdrawe
40 When Florys shuld wyfe after the lawe.   in accordance with
The king to the queene seide thoo,
And tolde hur of his woo –
Of his thought and of his care
How it wolde of Floreys fare.   What would become of Florys
45 'Dame,' he seide, 'y tel the my reed: what I suggest
I wyl that Blaunchefloure be do to deed.   wish, put to death
When that maide is yslawe,   slain
And brought of her lyf dawe,   life days
As sone as Florys may it underyete,   understand
50 Rathe he wylle hur foryete;   Quickly, forget
Than may he wyfe after reed.'   advisedly
The queene answerd then and seid –
And thought with hur reed   advice
Save the mayde fro the deed: death
55 'Sir,' she seide, 'we aught to fond   strive
That Florens lyf with menske in lond,   honour
And that he lese not his honour   lose
For the mayden, Blauncheflour.
Whoso myght that mayde clene,
60 That she were brought to deth, bydene,   As if, at once
Hit were muche more honour
Than slee that mayde, Blancheflour.'   slay
Unnethes the king graunt that it be soo: Grudgingly
'Dame, rede us what is to doo.'
65 'Sir, we shul oure soon, Florys,
Sende into the londe of Mountargis:
Blythe wyl my suster be,   Glad

27–8 Their learning was wonderful, and their love even more so.

That is lady of that contree;
And when she woot for whoom   *knows on whose account*
70 That we have sent him us froom,
She wyl doo al hur myght,
Both by day and by nyght,
To make hur love so undoo   *their*
As it had never ben soo.
75 And sir,' she seide, 'y rede eke   *advise, also*
That the maydens moder make hur seek: *feign sickness*
That may be that other resoun
For that ylk encheson – ⁿ   *same decision*
That she may not fro hur moder goo.'
80 Now ben these children swyth woo,   *very sorrowful*
Now they may not goo in fere –   *together*
Drewryer thinges never noon were!   *More woeful creatures*
Florys wept byfore the kyng,
And seide, 'Sir, without lesyng,   *lying*
85 For my harme out ye me sende,
Now she ne myght with me wende: *go*
Now we ne mot togeder goo,   *may*
Al my wele is turned to woo.'   *joy*
The king seide to his soon, aplyght,   *indeed*
90 'Sone, withynne this fourtenyght,
Be her moder quykke or deed,   *alive*
Sekerly,' he him seide,   *Certainly*
'That mayde shal come the too.'
'Ye, sir,' he seid, 'y pray yow it be soo!   *Yes*
95 Yif that ye me hur sende,
I rekke never wheder y wende!'
That the child graunted the kyng was fayn,   *agreed, glad*
And him betaught his chamburlayn.   *entrusted him to*
With muche honoure they theder coom,   *thither*
100 As fel to a ryche kynges soon.   *befitted*
Wel feire him receyvyd the Duke Orgas,   *courteously*
That king of that castel was,   *Who*
And his aunt, with muche honour;
But ever he thought on Blanchefloure.
105 Glad and blythe they ben him withe,
But, for no joy that he seith,   *sees*

95–6 If you send her to me, I do not care where I go!

Ne myght him glade game ne gle,
For he myght not his lyf see.   *beloved*
His aunt set him to lore,   *learning*
110 There as other children wore,   *were*
Both maydons and grom;   *girls and boys*
To lerne mony theder coom.
Inowgh he sykes, but noght he lernes: *Much, sighs*
For Blaunchefleur ever he mornes,   *grieves*
115 Yf eny man to him speke.
Love is on his hert steke;   *fastened*
Love is at his hert roote,[n]
That nothing is so soote: *sweet*
Galyngale ne lycorys[n]   *Galingale nor liquorice*
120 Is not so soote as hur love is,
Ne nothing, ne non other.
So much he thenketh on Blanchefleur,
Of oo day him thynketh thre,
For he ne may his love see.
125 Thus he abydeth, with muche woo,
Tyl the fourtenyght were goo.
When he saw she was nought ycoom,
So muche sorow he hath noom   *taken*
That he loveth mete ne drynke,
130 Ne may noon in his body synke.
The chamberleyn sent the king to wete   *know*
His sones state, al ywrete.   *condition, in writing*
The king ful sone the waxe to-brake,   *broke the seal*
For to wete what it spake.
135 He begynneth to chaunge his mood,
And wel sone he understode;
And with wreth he cleped the queene,   *wrath, called*
And tolde hur alle his teene;   *anger*
And with wrath spake and sayde,
140 'Let do bryng forth that mayde:
Fro the body the heved shal goo!'[n]   *head*
Thenne was the quene ful woo;
Than spake the quene, that good lady:
'For Goddes love, sir, mercy!

107 No sport or merriment could make him glad.
123 One day seems to him as long as three.
140 Have that maiden brought forth.

145 At the next haven that here is   *nearest harbour*
    Ther ben chapmen ryche, ywys —   *merchants, indeed*
    Marchaundes of Babyloyn ful ryche,[n]
    That wol hur bye blethelyche.   *buy, gladly*
    Than may ye, for that lovely foode,   *creature*
150 Have muche catell and goode.   *property and goods*
    And soo she may fro us be brought,
    Soo that we slee hur nought.'   *In such a way that*
    Unnethes the king graunted this,
    But, forsoth, so it is.   *indeed*
155 The king let sende after the burgeise,[n]   *burgess*
    That was hende and curtayse,   *gracious and courteous*
    And welle selle and bygge couth,
    And moony langages had in his mouth.
    Wel sone that mayde was him betaught, *entrusted to*
160 An[d] to the haven was she brought.
    Ther have they for that maide yolde   *given*
    Twenti mark of reed golde,[n]   *red*
    And a coupe good and ryche —   *cup*
    In al the world was non it lyche: *equal to*
165 Ther was never noon so wel grave —   *engraved*
    He that it made was no knave!   *fool*
    Ther was purtrayd on, y weene,   *depicted, think*
    How Paryse ledde awey the queene;   *Paris*
    And on the covercle above   *lid*
170 Purtrayde was ther both her love;[n]   *Depicted, there, their*
    And in the pomel theron   *knop*
    Stood a charbuncle stoon: *carbuncle*
    In the world was not so depe soler   *cellar*
    That it nold lyght the botelere   *cupbearer*
175 To fylle both ale and wyne;[n]
    Of sylver and gold both good and fyne.[n]
    Enneas the king, that nobel man,   *Aeneas*
    At Troye in batayle he it wan,
    And brought it into Lumbardy,
180 And gaf it his lemman, his amy.[n]   *sweetheart, beloved*
    The coupe was stoole fro King Cesar — [n]
    A theef out of his tresour hous it bar;

157 And knew well how to buy and sell.
160 And] An S.

And sethe that ilke same theef,   *afterwards, very same*
For Blaunchefloure he it yeef,   *gave*
185 For he wyst to wynne suche three,   *knew how to obtain*
Myght he hur bryng to his contree.[n]   *If he might*
Now these marchaundes saylen over the see,
With this mayde, to her contree.
So longe they han undernome   *travelled*
190 That to Babyloyn they ben coom:
To the amyral of Babyloyn   *emir*
They solde that mayde swythe soon.   *very*
Rath and soone they were at oon: *Quickly, in agreement*
The amyral hur bought anoon,
195 And gafe for hur, as she stood upryght,[n]
Sevyn sythes of gold her wyght;   *times, weight*
For he thought, without weene,   *doubt*
That faire mayde have to queene.
Among his maydons, in his bour,
200 He hur dide with muche honour.   *placed*
Now these merchaundes that may belete,   *left that maiden*
And ben glad of hur byyete.   *profit*
   Now let we of Blancheflour be,
   And speke of Florys in his contree.
205 Now is the burgays to the king coom,
With the gold and his garyson,   *payment*
And hath take the king to wolde
The selver and the coupe of golde.
They lete make, in a chirche,
210 A swithe feire grave wyrche,   *build*
And lete ley theruppon
A new, feire peynted ston,
With letters al aboute wryte,
With ful muche worshipp.   *honour*
215 Whoso couth the letters rede,
Thus they spoken and thus they seide:
'Here lyth swete Blaunchefloure,
That Florys lovyd paramoure.'[nn]   *with all his heart*
Now Florys hath undernome,   *set out*
220 And to his fader he is coome.

207 And has given into the king's keeping.
210 A] As S.

In his fader halle he is lyght;
His fader him grette anoonryght,   *greeted at once*
And his moder, the queene, also.
But unnethes myght he that doo,
225 That he ne asked where his lemman bee;
Nonskyns answere chargeth hee.
So longe he is forth noom,   *gone*
Into chamber he is coom.
The maydenys moder he asked ryght,
230 'Where is Blauncheflour, my swete wyght?'   *creature*
'Sir,' she seide, 'forsothe, ywys,   *truly, indeed*
I ne woot where she is!'   *know*
She bethought hur on that lesyng,
That was ordeyned byfore the king.[n]
235 'Thou gabbest me!' he seyde thoo.   *trick*
'Thy gabbyng doth me muche woo.   *causes me*
Tel me where my leman be!'
Al wepyng seide thenne shee,
'Sir,' shee seide, 'deed!' 'Deed?' seide he.   *dead*
240 'Sir,' she seide, 'forsothe, yee!'
'Allas! When died that swete wyght?'
'Sir, withynne this fourtenyght
The erth was leide hur above,
And deed she was for thy love.'
245 Flores, that was so feire and gent,   *gentle*
Sownyd there, verament.   *Swooned, truly*
The Cristen woman began to crye
To Jhesu Crist and Seynt Marye.
The king and the queene herde that crye;
250 Into the chamber they ronne on hye,
And the queene herde her byforn
On sowne the childe that she had born.   *In a swoon*
The kinges hert was al in care,
That sawe his son for love so fare.
255 When he awooke and speke moght,   *could*
Sore he wept and sore he syght,   *sighed*
And seide to his moder, ywys,   *indeed*

224–5 But he could scarcely do that, without asking where his sweetheart was.
226 He does not demand any sort of answer.
233–4 She called to mind that lie, which had been directed by the king.
243 above] *thus* V; aboute S.

'Lede me there that mayde is.'

Theder they him brought on hyghe;   *in haste*

260 For care and sorow he wold dyghe.   *wished to die*

As sone as he to the grave com,

Sone there behelde he then,

And the letters began to rede,

That thus spake and thus seide:

265 'Here lyth swete Blaunchefleur,

That Florys lovyd paramoure.'

Thre sithes Florys sownydde nouth;   *times, swooned, now*

Ne speke he myght not with mouth.

As sone as he awoke and speke myght,

270 Sore he wept and sore he syght.[n]

'Blaunchefleur!' he seide. 'Blaunchefleur!

So swete a thing was never in boure.   *bower*

Of Blaunchefleur is that y meene,   *For, lament*

For she was com of good kyn.

275 Lytel and muche loveden the,   *Small and great*

For thy goodnesse and thy beaute.

Yif deth were dalt aryght,   *apportioned fairly*

We shuld be deed both on oo nyght.   *one*

On oo day born we were;

280 We shul be ded both in feere.   *together*

Deeth,' he seide, 'ful of envye   *malice*

And of alle trechorye,

Refte thou hast me my lemman: *Deprived*

Forsoth,' he seide, 'thou art to blame!

285 She wolde have levyd, and thou noldest,   *would not*

And fayn wolde y dye, and thou woldest.[n]   *gladly*

After deeth clepe no more y nylle,   *call*

But slee myself now y wille.'

His knyf he braide out of his sheth: *drew*

290 Himself he wolde have doo to deth,

And to hert he had it smeten,   *struck*

Ne had his moder it underyeten.

Then the queene fel him uppon,

And the knyf fro him noom: *took*

295 She reft him of his lytel knyf,

And savyd there the childes lyf.[n]

292 If his mother had not perceived (what he meant to do).

Forth the queene ranne, al wepyng,
Tyl she com to the kyng.
Than seide the good lady,
300 'For Goddes love, sir, mercy!
Of twelf children have we noon[n]
On lyve now but this oon,   *Alive*
And better it were she were his make   *mate*
Than he were deed for hur sake!'
305 'Dame, thou seist soth,' seide he.   *truth*
'Sen it may noon other be,   *Since it may not be otherwise*
Lever me were she were his wyf   *I had rather*
Than y lost my sonnes lyf.'
Of this word the quene was fayn,   *glad*
310 And to her soon she ran agayn:
'Floryes, soon, glad make the —
Thy lef thou shalt on lyve see.   *beloved, alive*
Florys, son, through engynne   *ruse*
Of thy faders reed and myne,   *counsel*
315 This grave let we make,
Leve son, for thy sake: *Dear*
Yif thou that maide forgete woldest,
After oure reed wyf thou sholdest.'
Now every word she hath him tolde:
320 How that they that mayden solde.
'Is this soth, my moder dere?'
'Forsoth,' she seide, 'she is not here.'
The rowgh stoon adoun they leyde,[n]
And sawe that [there] was not the mayde.
325 'Now, moder, y think that y leve may;   *live*
Ne shal y rest, nyght ne day,
Nyght ne day ne no stound,   *moment*
Tyl y have my lemmon found.   *sweetheart*
Hur to seken y woll wend,
330 Thaugh it were to the worldes ende!'   *Even if*
To the king he goth to take his leve,
And his fader bade him byleve.   *begged, stay*
'Sir, y wyl let for no wynne: *desist, gain*
Me to bydden it were grete synne.'
335 Than seid the king, 'Seth it is soo —   *Since*

324 *thus* V; *om.* S.
334 To ask me (to do so) would be a great sin.

Seth thou wylt noon other doo —
Al that the nedeth we shul the fynde. *provide*
Jhesu the of care unbynde!'
'Leve fader,' he seide, 'y telle the *Dear*
340 Al that thou shalt fynde me.
Thou mast me fynde, at my devyse, *must, request*
Seven horses, al of prys; *value*
And twoo ycharged, uppon the molde, *loaded, ground*
Both with selver and wyth golde;
345 And twoo ycharged with moonay, *money*
For to spenden by the way; *on the journey*
And three with clothes ryche —
The best of al the kyngryche; *kingdom*
Seven horses and sevyn men,
350 And thre knaves, without hem; [n]
And thyn own chamburlayn,[n] *chamberlain*
That is a wel nobel swayn: *fellow*
He can us both wyssh and reede. *guide, advise*
As marchaundes we shull us lede.' *conduct ourselves*
355 His fader was an hynde king: *gracious*
The coupe of golde he dide him bryng —
That ilke self coupe of golde *very same*
That was Blauncheflour for yolde. *given*
'Have this, soon,' seide the king: *son*
360 'Herewith thou may that swete thing
Wynne, so may betyde, *it may be*
Blauncheflour, with the white syde — *side*
Blauncheflour, that faire may.' *maiden*
The king let sadel a palfray, *saddle-horse*
365 The oon half white so mylke *as*
And that other reed so sylk. *red*
I ne can telle nought
How rychely that sadel was wrought: *worked*
The arson was of gold fyn, *saddlebow*
370 Stones of vertu stode theryne,[n] *worth, were set*
Bygon aboute with orfreys. *Adorned, golden embroidery*
The queene was kynde and curtays;
Cast hur toward the kyng, *Turned towards*

338 Jesus deliver you from sorrow!
350 And three servants in addition to them.

And of hur fynger she brayde a ryng: *drew*
375 'Have now this ylke ryng:
While is it thyn, dought nothyng — *fear*
Of fire brennyng, ne water in the see; *burning*
Ne yren ne steele shal dere thee.'[n] *iron, harm*
He took his leve for to goo;
380 Ther was ful muche woo;
They made him noon other chere
Than her soon were leide in bere.
Furth he went, with al his mayn; *retinue*
With him went the chamberlayn.
385 So have they her [wey] nome
That they ben to the havyn come
There Blaunchefloure was al nyght.
Wel rychely they ben dyght. *equipped*
The lord of the ynne was welle hende: *gracious*
390 The child he sette next the ende,[n]
In al the feirest seete. *the best seat of all*
Alle they dronken and al they yete. *ate*
Ete ne drynke myght he nought;
On Blaunchefloure was al his thought.
395 The lady of that underyat *perceived*
That the childe mornyng sat, *grieving*
And seide to her lord, with styl dreme, *in a low voice*
'Sir, nym now good yeme *now take good heed*
How the child mournyng syttes:
400 Mete and drynke he foryetes — *forgets*
Lytel he eteth and lasse he drynketh; *less*
He is a marchaund, as methynketh.'
To Flores then seide she,
'Al ful of mournyng y the see.
405 Ther sate ther, this sender day, *the other day*
Blaunchefloure, that swete may.
Heder was that mayde brought,
With marchaundes that hur had bought:
Heder they brought that mayde swete;
410 They wold have solde hur for byyete. *profit*

381–2 They behaved towards him no otherwise than if their son were laid on a bier.
385 wey] hauyn S.

To Babyloyn they wyll hur bryng,
[And selle hir to kaiser other to king.   *emperor or*
Thou art ilich here of alle thinge,]
Both of semblant and of mornyng.
415 When Florys herd speke of his lemman,
Was he never so glad a man,
And in his hert bygan to lyght;   *be glad*
The coupe he let fulle anoonryght.   *fill at once*
'Dame,' he seide, 'the fessel is thyn –   *vessel*
420 Both the coupe and the wyn,
The wyn and the gold eke –   *also*
For thou of my leman speke.
On hur y thought, for hur y syght;   *sighed*
I ne wyst where I hur fynde myght.   *knew*
425 Wynde ne weder shal me assoyn   *hinder*
That y ne shal seche hur in Babyloyn.'
Now Florys resteth him al a nyght;
At morn, when it was daylyght,
He dide him into the wylde flood;[n]
430 Wynde and weder with him stood.
Sone so Florys com to londe,   *As soon as*
There he thanked Goddes sonde;   *providence*
To the londe ther his lyf ynne is;   *beloved*
Him thought he was in Paradyse.
435 Sone to Florys tydyng men tolde,
That the amyral wold fest holde:
His erls, barouns comyn sholde,   *emir*
And al that wold of him lond holde,[n]
For to herkyn his hest,   *hear his command*
440 And for to honoure his feest.
Glad was Florys of that tydyng:
He hoped to com to that gestnyng,
Yif he myght, in that halle,   *festivity*
His lemman see among hem alle.
445   Now to that citee Florys is com;
Feire he hath his ynne ynoom
At a palaise – was non it lyche;

412–13 *Lines om.* S; *supplied from* A.
413–14 You are like her in all respects, both in appearance and in your grief.
446 He has taken handsome lodgings.

The lord of that ynne was fulle ryche —
He hadde ben fer[r]e and wyde.
450 The childe he set next his syde,
In al the feirest seete;
Alle they dronken and ete.
Al that therynne were,
Al they made good chere.
455 They ete and dronke, echoon with other,   *each one*
But Florys thought al another: *quite differently*
Ete ne drynke he myght noght;
On Blauncheflour was al his thought.[n]
Than spake the burgays,
460 That was hende and curtays,
'Ow, child, methynketh welle   *Oh*
That muche thou thynkest on my catell.'   *property*
'Nay, sir, on catel thenke y nought' —
On Blauncheflour was al his thought —
465 'But y thynke, on al wyse,
For to fynde my marchaundise;
And yit it is the most woo,
When y it fynd y shal it forgoo.'   *lose*
Than spak the lord of that ynne:
470 'This sender day, ther sate hereyn   *The other day*
That faire maide, Blauncheflour.
Both in halle and in boure,
Ever she made mornyng chere,   *had a sorrowful countenance*
And bement Florys, her lyf fere;
475 Joye ne blis made she noon,
But for Florys she made her moon.'   *lament*
Florys toke a coupe of sylver clere,   *bright*
A mantyl of scarlet with menyvere:[n]   *(trimmed) with fur*
'Have this, sir, to thyn honour:
480 Thou may thonke it Blauncheflour.
He myght make myn hert glade,
That couth me tel wheder she is ladde.'   *whither*
'Child, to Babyloyn she is brought.
The amyral hur hath bought:

449 ferre] feree S.
474 And grieved for Florys, her beloved friend.
480 You may thank Blauncheflour for it.

485 He gaf for hur, as she stood upryght,	
Seven sithes of gold hur wyght;	*times, weight*
For he thenketh, without weene,	*doubt*
That feire may have to queene.	*maiden*
Among his maydons, in his toure,	
490 He hur dide with muche honoure.'	*placed*
Now Flores resteth him there al nyght,	
Tyl, on the morow, the day was lyght.	
He roos on the morownyng;	
He gaf his ost an hundryd shelyng –	*shillings*
495 To his ost and to his ostesse –	
And toke his leve, and feire dide kysse.	
And yerne his ost he besought	*eagerly, begged*
That he him help, yif he myght ought,	*in any way*
Yif he myght, with any gynne,	*by any ruse*
500 That feire may to him wynne.	
'Childe,' he seide, 'to a brygge thou shalt com,	*bridge*
The senpere fynde at hoom:ⁿ	
He woneth at the brygges ende –	*dwells*
Curtays man he is and hende.	
505 We arn bretheren, and trouthes plyght;	
He can the wyssh and rede aryght.	*guide and advise*
Thou shalt bere him a rynge	
Fro myself, to tokenynge	*as a token*
That he help the, in boure and halle,	
510 As it were myself befalle.'	
Florys taketh the ryng and nemeth leve;	
For long wold he nought beleve.	*delay*
By that it was undern hyghe,	*broad day*
The brygge com he swyth nye.	*very near*
515 The senperes name was Darys;	
Florys gret him wel feire, ywys,	*indeed*
And he him the ryng araught,	*handed*
And ful feire it him betaught.	*gave*
Throwgh the token of that ilk ryng,	
520 Florys had ful faire gestnyng –	*entertainment*
Off fyssh and flessh and tender breed,	*bread*

502 The senpere fynde at hoom:ⁿ

505 We are (as) brothers and have sworn faith to each other.
509–10 That he should help you, under all circumstances (*literally*, everywhere), as if it were myself.

Of wyn, both white and reed.
And ever Florys sate ful colde,[n]   *disconsolate*
And Dares bygan the childe beholde:
525 'Leve child, what may this be,
Thus thoughtful as y the see?
Art thou nought al in feere,   *in good health*
That thou makist thus sory chere?
Or thou lykkest noght this yn?'
530 Than Floreys answerd him,
'Yis, sir, by Goddes ore!   *grace*
So good ne had y mony day yore.
God let me abyde that daye   *live to see*
That y the quyte wel may!   *reward*
535 But y thenke, on al wyse,
Most uppon my marchaundyse;
And yit it is most woo,
When y hit fynde y shal it forgoo.'
'Childe, woldest thou telle me thy gryf,   *distress*
540 To hele the me were ful lyf.'[n]
Every word he hath him tolde:
How the mayde was fro him solde,
And how he was of Spayn a kynges son,
For grete love theder ycom,
545 To fonde, with qua[yn]tyse and with gyn,
Blauncheflour for to wynne.
'Now,' seith Dares, 'thou art affolt!'   *befooled*
And for a foole the childe he halt.
'Now y woot how it gooth –
550 Thou desirest thyn own deeth!
The amyral hath to his justinges[n]
Other half hundred of ryche kinges,   *A hundred and fifty*
And the alder rychest king   *most powerful king of all*
Durst not begynne suche a thing!   *Would not dare undertake*
555 Yif amyral myght it understond,[n]   *learn of it*
He shulde be drawe in his owne londe.[n]   *torn apart*
About Babyloyn, y wene,[n]   *believe*
Six longe myle and tene;   *ten*

532 I have had none so good for many days.
540 I would gladly find a remedy for you.
545 quayntyse] quanytyse S. To strive, with cunning and ingenuity.
548 And he considered the young man a fool.

At every myle i[n] a walle therate,
560 Seven sithes twenty yate;   *times*
And twenty toures ther ben ynne,
That every day chepyng is ynne —   *market*
Every day and nyght, throughout the yere,
The chepyng is ylyche plenere;   *equally, in full progress*
565 And thaugh al the men that ben bore
Had on hur lyf swore
To wynne that maide feire and free,
Al shul they die, so moot y the!   *as I hope to prosper*
In that bour[h], in mydward ryght,   *city, centre*
570 Stondeth a toure, y the plyght.   *assure*
An hundryd fathum it is hye — ⁿ   *fathoms*
Whosoo beholdeth hit, fer or nere,   *far or near*
An hundred fathum it is yfere.   *altogether*
It is made, without pere,   *equal*
575 Of lyme and of marbulston —
In al this world is suche noon.
Now is the morter made so wele,
Ne may it breke iren ne steele.
The pomel that above is leide,   *finial/ornamental globe*
580 It is made with muche pride,   *splendour*
That man ne thar in the tour berne   *need, burn*
Nouther tor[che] ne lantern,   *Neither*
Suche a pomel was ther bygon —   *set*
Hit shyne[th] anyght so doth the soon.ⁿ   *at night*
585 Now arn in that ilk toure
Twoo and fourty nobell boure:
Wel were that ilke man
That myght woon in that oon!   *dwell*
Ne durst him nevermore, ywys,   *He would never need*
590 Covete after more blysse!
Now arn ther serjauntes in that stage,
That serven the maydons of hyghe parage;   *noble birth*

559 in] is S.
563 throughout] þrouȝtout S.
569 bourh] *thus* A C; bour S.
578 Neither iron nor steel can breach it.
582 torche] torthee S.
584 shyneth] *thus* V; shyned S.
587 Happy would be the man.
591 Now, there are attendants on that upper floor.

But no serjeaunt may serve therynne
That bereth in his breche that gynne   *breeches, instrument*
595 To serve hem, day and nyght,
But he be as a capon dyght.
At the yate is a yateward;   *porter*
He is not a coward;[n]
He is wonder proude withalle;   *haughty, besides*
600 Every day he goth in ryche palle.   *sumptuous garments*
And the amyral hath a wonder woon,   *custom*
That he that is com of Cristendom,[n]
Every yere to have a new wyf;
Then he lovith his queene as his lyf.
605 Then shul men bryng doun of the toure
Al the maidens of grete honoure,
And bryng hem into an orchard —
The feirest of al mydlerd.[n]   *in the world*
Theryn is mony fowles song;
610 Men myght leve theryn ful long.[n]
About the orchard is a walle;
The fowlest ston is cristall.
And a well spryngeth therynne,
That is made with muche gynne.   *skill*
615 The wel is of muche prys;   *worth*
The stremes com froo Paradyse.
The gravel of the ground is precious stoones,   *bottom*
And al of vertu for the noones.[n]
Now is the well of muche aught: *renown*
620 Yif a woman com that is forlaught,   *unchaste*
And she be doo to the streeme,   *put into*
For to wesshe her honndes clene,
The water wylle yelle as it were wood,   *as if it were mad*
And bycom reed as blood.[n]
625 On what maide the water fareth soo,
Sone she shal to deth be doo.
Thoo that ben maidens clene,   *Those*
They may wessh theryn, y wene:
The water woll stonde feire and clere —   *remain*
630 To hem maketh it no daungere.[n]   *harm/resistance*
At the walles hed stondeth a tree,   *well's*

596 i.e. unless he is a eunuch.

The feirest that on erthe may be.
It is cleped the Tree of Love;   *called*
Floures and blossomes spryngen above.

635   Then they that maydons clene bene,
      Thei shul be brought under the tren,
      And whichso falleth the floure
      Shal be queene, with muche honour.
      Yif any mayden ther is

640   That the amyral telleth of more pris,
      The flour shal be to her sent,
      Through art of enchauntement.
      The amyral cheseth hem by the flour,   *chooses*
      And ever he herkeneth after Blauncheflour.[n]

645   Thre sithes Flores sownyd anoon,
      Right byfore hem, everychoon.
      When he awoke and speke myght,
      Sore he wept and sore he syght,[n]
      And seide, 'Dares, y worth now deed,   *now I would die*

650   But that y hope of the som reed!'   *Except*
      'Leve soon, w[e]l y see   *Dear son*
      That thy trust is muche on me.
      Then is the best reed that y can —
      Other reed ne can y noon —

655   Wende tomorn to the toure,
      As thou were a good gynoure.   *engineer/builder*
      Take on thy honde squyer and scantlon,   *square, measure*
      As thou were a free mason;[n]
      Behold the tour up and doun.

660   The porter is cruel and feloun; [n]   *harsh, hostile*
      Wel sone he wyl com to the,
      And aske what maner man thou be,
      And bere on the felonye,   *be hostile towards you*
      And sey thou art come to be a spye.

665   And thow shalt answere swetlych,   *gently*
      And sey to him myldelyche:
      Sey thou art a gynoure,
      To beholde that feire toure,   *survey*

637   And on whichever the flower falls.
640   By whom the emir sets greater store.
651   wel y] *thus* A; wyl ʒe S.

For to loke, and for to fonde   *attempt*
670 To make such another in thy londe.
Wel sone he wyl com the nere,   *nearer*
And wyl byd the pley at the chekere.   *chess*
When thou art at cheker brought,
Without selver [pley] thou nought.
675 Thou shalt have redy with the
Twenty marke beside thy knee.[n]
Yif thou wynne ought of his,   *anything from him*
Thow tel therof lytel prys;   *Hold it of little account*
And yf he wynne ought of thyn,
680 Loke thow leve it with hym.
So thou shalt, al with gynne,   *guile*
The porters love, forsoth, wynne,   *indeed*
That he the help on this day –
But he the help, no man may!
685 Wel yerne he wyl the bydde and pray   *eagerly, beg and pray*
Com another day to playe.   *the next day*
Thou shalt seye thou wylt soo;
Thou shalt take with the suche twoo.   *i.e. twice as much*
The thrydde day take an hundred pound,
690 And thy coupe, hool and sound.
Yeve him markes and poundes of thy male: *wallet*
Of thy tresoure tel thou no tale.   *keep no account*
Wel yerne he wyl the bydde and pray
To lay thy coupe and to play.   *wager*
695 Thou shalt answere, altherfirst,   *first of all*
Lenger to play the ne lyst.   *you are not inclined*
Ful muche he wylle for the coupe bede;   *offer/stake*
Yif he myght the better spede,[n]
Thou shalt it blethly yeve him,   *willingly*
700 Yif it be of gold fyne.   *Even though*
And he wol ful muche love the,
And to the bowe also, parde,   *by God*
That he wyl falle to thy foote,
And becom thyn, yif he moote.   *can*
705 And homage thou shalt fonge,
And the trouth of his honde.'[n]
As he seide he dide, ywys;

674 pley] *thus* A C; *om.* S.

And as he ordeyned, so it is.   *directed*
The porter is Florys man bycom,
710 For his gold and his waryson.   *reward*
Florys seide, 'Now art thou my moon,   *man*
Al my trust is the uppon.
Now my consel y wyl the shewe: *secret*
Rede me ryght, yif thou be trew.'
715 Now every word he hath him tolde:
How the mayde was fro him solde,
And how he was of Spayn a kynges soon,
For grete love theder ycoom,
To fonden, with som gynne,
720 That feire mayde for to wynne.
The porter that herde, and sore syght,   *sighed*
And seide, 'Y am betrayde aryght: *truly*
Through thy catel y am dismayde –
Therfore y am wel evyl apayde!   *ill-pleased*
725 Now y woot how it gooth,
For the shal y suffer deth.
I shal the faile nevermoo,
The while y may ryde and goo:
Thy forwardes shal y holde alle,   *agreements*
730 Whatsoever may befalle.
Wynde now hoom to thyn ynne,
While y bethenke me of sum gynne:
Bytwene this and the thrydde day,
Fonde y shal what y do may.'   *I shall try to decide*
735 Flores spake, and wept among,   *besides*
And thought the terme al to long.   *interval*
The porter thought the best reed,
And let geder floures in a meed: *gather, meadow*
He wist it was the maydons wylle.
740 To lepes he lete of floures fylle: *Two baskets*
That was the best reed, as him thought thoo,
Flores in that oon lep to doo.[n]
Twoo maydens the lepe bore:
So hevy charged never they wore,   *burdened*

716 solde] sholde S.
723 Through (coveting) your property I am undone.
739 He knew it was what the maiden wished.
742 Flores] *thus* A C; ffloures S.

745 And bade God yeve h[i]m evyl fyn — *end*
    To mony floures he dide therynne! *Too*
    To Blaunchefloures chamber they shuld tee; *come*
    They yede to another, and let that be.
    They shuld have gon to Blaunchefour,
750 And yede to swete Clarys boure,
    And cursed him so fele brought to honde;
    They yede hoom, and lete hem stonde.
    Clarys to the lepe com wolde,
    The flores to hondel and to beholde.
755 Florys wende it hadde be his swete wyght:
    Of the lepe he stert upryght; *leapt straight up*
    And the mayde, al for drede,
    Bygan to shrell and to grede. *shriek, cry out*
    When he sawgh it was not shee,
760 Into the lepe ayen stert he,
    And held him betrayde clene: *quite*
    Of his lyf tolde he not a beene.
    Ther com maydons, and to Clarys lepe
    By ten, by twelf, on an heepe; *in a crowd*
765 And they asked what hur were,
    And why she made suche a bere. *outcry*
    Clarys bythought hur, anoonryght,
    That hit was Blaunchefour the white,
    And gave the maydons answere anoon, *soon*
770 That to her chamber were goon,
    That to the lepe com she wold
    The flowres to hondel and to beholde:
    'And, or y it ere wyst, *before I knew it*
    A [botterfleye] fleygh ageynst my brest:[n]
775 I was so soore adrad than
    That y loude crye can.'
    The maydons therof hadden glee, *were amused*
    And turned hem, and lete hur be.
    As sone as the maydons were gon,

745 him] *thus* A C; hem S.
751 And cursed him who had gathered so many (flowers).
762 He thought his life was not worth a bean.
765 And they asked her what was the matter with her.
768 i.e. that it concerned Blaunchefour.
774 A botterfleye] *thus* A C; An otter S.

780 To Blauncheflour she yede anoon,
And seide boldly to Blaunchefloure,
'Felow, com and see a feire flour:
Suche a flour the shal wel lyke,   *will please you well*
Have thou it sene a lyte.'

785 'Awey, Clarys!' quod Blaunchefloure.
'To scorne me, it is none honoure.   *mock*
I here, Clarys, without gabbe,   *deceit*
That the amyral wyl me to wyf habbe;   *have*
But that day shal never be

790 That he shal ever have me —
That y shal be of love so untrewe,   *disloyal*
Ne chaunge my love for no newe —
For no love, ne for noon aye,   *fear*
Forsake Floris in his contraye:[n]

795 Now y shal swete Florys mysse,   *lose*
Ne shal noon other of me have blysse!'
Clarys stood, and beheld that rewth,   *pitiful sight*
And the trewnesse of hur trewth,   *her fidelity to her word*
And seide, 'Lady Blaunchefloure,

800 Goo we see that ilk floure.'
To the lepe they went both.
Joyful man was Florys thoo,
For he had herde al this;
Of that lepe he stert, ywys.

805 Wel sone Blaunchefloure chaunged hewe.   *colour*
Ayther of hem other knewe: *Each*
Withoute speche togeder they lepe,
And klippt and kyst wonder swete.   *embraced*
Clarys beheld al this —

810 Her countenaunce and her blysse —   *behaviour*
And seide then to Blaunchefloure,
'Felow, knowist thou aught this flour?   *at all*
She shul konne ful muche of art,
That thou woldest therof geve part!'[n]

815 Now Blaunchefloure and Florys,
Both these swete thinges, ywys,

784 i.e. if you will only come and see it.
793 i.e. under any circumstances.
796 No one else shall enjoy me.

Cryen her mercy, al wepyng, *Beg her for mercy*
That she ne wrey hem to the king. *betray*
'Ne dought no more of me in alle
820 Than it were myself byfalle.
Wete ye wel, weturly, *Know, certainly*
Heele y wyl youre drury.' *Conceal, love-making*
To a bedde they ben brought,
That is of palle and of sylke wrought, *rich cloth*
825 And there they sette hem doun,
And drowgh hemself al a-room. *drew, aside*
Ther was no man that myght radde *measure*
The joye that they twoo madde.
Florys then to speke bygan,
830 And seide, 'Lord, that madest man,
I it thonke Goddes sone[n]
That al my care I have overcom.
Now my leve I have yfounde, *beloved*
Of al my care y am unbounde.'
835 Clarys hem served al at wylle,
Both dernlyche and stylle. *secretly, quietly*
Clarys, with the white syde,
Rose up on morn tyde *in the morning*
And cleped after Blaunchefloure
840 To wende with h[ur] into the toure.
She seide, 'Y am commaund';
But her answere was slepaund. *sleepy*
The amyral had suche a woon *custom*
That every day shulde com
845 Twoo maydons of hur bour
Up to him into the toure,
With water and clooth and basyn
For to wesshe his hondes ynne.
That day they servyd him feire;
850 Another day com another peire;
But most were wonyd into the toure *accustomed (to go)*
Clarys and Blauncheflour.
Clarys com thenne aloon;
The amyral asked anoon,

819–20 Fear no more from me at all than if it concerned myself.
840 hur] him S.

855 'Where is Blaunchelour so free?   *noble*
    Why cometh she not heder with the?'   *hither*
    'Sir,' she seide, anoonryght,
    'She hath wakyd al this nyght,   *been awake*
    And ycryde and yloke,   *gazed*
860 And yredde on hur booke,
    And ybede to God her oryson   *offered, prayer*
    That he geve the his benyson,   *blessing*
    And that he holde long thy lyf.   *preserve*
    And now the mayde slepeth swyth: *soundly*
865 She slepeth so fast, that mayde swete,
    That she may not com yete.'   *yet*
    'Certes,' seide the kyng,   *Indeed*
    'Now is she a swete thing:
    Wel aught me yerne her to wyf
870 That so preyeth for my lyf.'
    Another day, Clarys erly aryst;   *arose*
    That Blaunchelour well wyst,
    And seide, 'Y com anoon',
    When Clarys her clepe bygan,
875 And fel in a slepe newe –
    Sone after it made hem to rewe!   *be sorry*
    Clarys to the pyler cam – ⁿ   *pillar*
    A basyn of gold in hond she nam –
    And cleped after Blaunchefloure
880 To wende with hur into the toure.
    The amyral asked after Blaunchelour:
    'What! Is she not com yet?
    Now she me douteth al to <lyte>!'
    Forth he cleped his chamburlayn,
885 And bade him wende with his mayn   *retinue*
    To wete why she wyl not com
    As she was wonyd to doon.   *accustomed to do*
    The chamburlayn is forth noom;   *gone*
    Into chamber he is coom,
890 And stondeth byfore hur bedde,
    And fyndeth there, nebbe to nebbe –   *face*
    Nebbe to nebbe and mouth to mouth:

869 I might well wish her to be my wife.
883 lyte] *thus* A C V; *illegible in* S. Now she shows me too little respect.

To the amyral it was sone couth.   *known*
Up into the toure he steygh,   *(the chamberlain) climbed*
895 And told his lord al that he seygh.
The amyral lete him his swerd bryng,
For wete he wolde of that tydyng.
He went to hem, there they lay;
Yit was she aslepe there ay.
900 The amyral lete the clothes doun cast   *bedclothes, pull*
A lytel bynethe hur brest;
And sone he knew anoon
That oon was woman and that other groom.[n]   *young man*
He quaked for tene, there he stood: *shook with anger*
905 Hem to sloon was in his mood.
Yit he thought, or he hem quelde,   *before, killed*
What they were they shuld him telle;   *Who*
And seth he wyl with dome hem done.
The children wakyd swyth soone,
910 And saw the swerde over hem drawe:
They ben adrad and in awghe.   *afraid, terror*
Than seide Florys to Blauncheflour,
'Of oure lyf is no socour.'   *help*
But they cryde him mercy swyth,   *earnestly*
915 For to length her lyve.   *lengthen*
Up he bade hem sytte booth,
And do on both her cloth.
Seth he dide hem bynde fast,
And in prison lete hem be cast.
920 Now hath he after his barons sent,
To wreke him after jugement.   *avenge, by process of law*
Now han the barons undernome,   *set out*
And to the amyral they ben coom.
He stood up among hem al,
925 With semblaunt wroth withalle,   *demeanour, angry, besides*
And seide, 'Lordynges, with muche honour

896–7 The emir had his sword brought to him, for he wanted to know (the truth)
of what he had been told.
905 He had it in mind to kill them.
908 And afterwards he will pass judgement on them.
913 i.e. nothing can save our lives.
917 And both of them put on their clothes.
926–7 You have heard (me) speak highly of Blauncheflour.

Ye herde speke of Blaunchflour:
That y bought hur dere, aplyght,   *indeed*
For seven sithes of golde hur wyght;
930 For y wende, without wene,   *doubt*
That feire mayde to have had to quene.
Among my maydons, in my toure,
I hur dide with muche honoure.ⁿ
Byfore her bedde myself y coom;
935 I fonde theryn a naked man.
Than were they to me so looth,   *hateful*
I thought to have sleyn hem booth,   *intended to kill*
I was so wroth and so wood.   *enraged (mad)*
Yit y withdrowgh myn hoot blood   *curbed, rage*
940 Tyl y have sende after yow, by assent   *common agreement*
To wreke me with jugement.   *avenge, by process of law*
Now yit ye woot how it is goon,   *indeed*
Wreke me soon of my foon!'   *enemies*
Than spake a kyng of that londe:
945 'We have herd al this shame and shonde;   *disgrace*
But or we hem to deth deme,   *condemn*
Lat us hem see, yif it be queeme –   *pleasing*
What they wolde speke or sygge,   *say*
Yif they wyl aught ageyn us legge.
950 Hit were nought ryght jugement
Without answere make acoupement.   *accusation*
Til this is herde of more and lasse,ⁿ
What myster is to bere wytnesse?'
After the children have they sent;
955 To brenne hem was his entent.   *burn*
Two serjeauntes hem gan bryng.   *attendants*
Toward hur [deeth], al wepyng,
Drery booth these children goo: *Sorrowful*
Ayther bemeneth otheris woo.   *Each laments*
960 Than seide Florys to Blaunchflour,
'Of oure lyf is no socour.
Yf kinde of man it thole myght,

949 If they will put forth anything in reply to us (i.e. answer our charge).
950–1 It would not be a just trial if we made an accusation without hearing what
they have to say.
953 What is the use of testifying?
957 deeth] *thus* A; *om.* S.
962–3 If it was in the nature of man to endure it, I should by rights die twice.

Twyes y shuld dye, with ryght:
Oones for myself, another for the, *Once*
965 For thy deeth thou hast for me.' *on my account*
Blauncheflour seyde thoo,
'The gylt is myn of oure woo.'
Florys drough forth that ryng *drew*
That his moder him gaff at her partyng: *their*
970 'Have this ryng, lemman myn:
Thou shalt not dye while it is thyn.'
Blaunchefloure seide thoo,
'So ne shal it never goo: *That shall never be*
That this ryng shal help me,
975 And the deed on the see.'
Florys that ryng hur raught, *handed*
And she it him agayn betaught. *handed it back*
Nouther ne wyl other deed seene: *dead*
They lete it falle hem bytwene.
980 A king com after; a ryng he fonde,
And brought it forth in his honde.
Thus the children wepyng com
To the fire and hur doom. *sentence*
Byfore the folk they were brought;
985 Drery was her bothes thought.
There was noon so stern man *hard-hearted*
That the children loked oon *upon*
That they ne wolde, al wel fawe, *only too gladly*
Her jugement have withdrawe,
990 And with grete catel hem bygge, *wealth, ransom*
Yif they durst speke or sygge: *say*
For Flores was so feire a yonglyng, *youth*
And Blaunchefloure so swete a thing.
Ther wyst no man whor hem were woo, *whether*
995 For no semblaunt that they made thoo.[n]
The admyral was so wood, *enraged*
Ne myght he nought kele his hoot blood. *cool*
He bade the children fast be bound,
And into the fire slong. *thrown*
1000 That ilk king that the ryng fond,

967 Our grief is my fault.
975 And I see you dead.

To amyral he spake and round,　　　　　　　　　　*whispered*
And wolde hem save to the lyf,
And told how for the ryng they gon stryf.　　　　　　*contend*
The amyral lete hem ageyn clepe,　　　　　　　　　*back*
1005 For he wolde here hem speke,
And asked Florys what he heete;　　　　　　　　　*was called*
And he tolde him, ful skeete.　　　　　　　　　　*readily*
'Sire,' he seide, 'yf it were thy wylle,
Thou ne getest not that maide to spylle.[n]
1010 But, good sir, quel thou me,　　　　　　　　　*kill*
And late that maide on lyve be.'　　　　　　　　　*let*
Blaunchefloure seide byne,　　　　　　　　　　*interposed*
'The gylt of oure dedes is myn.'
The admyral seide thoo,
1015 'Iwys, ye shul dye boo.'　　　　　　　　　　　*both*
His swerd he breide out of his sheeth,
The children to have don to deeth.
Blaunchefloure put forth hur swire,　　　　　　　　*neck*
And Florys dide her agayn to tyre,　　　　　　　　*pulled her back*
1020 And seide: 'I am man: I shal byfore;　　　　　　　*go first*
With wrong hast thou thy lyf loore.'　　　　　　　*Unjustly, lost*
Florys forth his swer[e] putte,　　　　　　　　　*neck*
And Blauncheflour agayn him tytte.　　　　　　　*pulled him back*
The king seide, 'Drery mot ye be
1025 This routh by this children to see!'
The king that the ryng hadde,
For routh of hem sone he radde –
And at the amyral wyl he spede –
The children fro the deth to lede.
1030 'Sir,' he seide, 'it is lytel prys　　　　　　　　*hardly creditable*
These children for to slee, ywys;
And it is wel more worship　　　　　　　　　　*honourable*
Florys counsel that ye weete:　　　　　　　　　*secret*
Who him taught that ilke gynne　　　　　　　　*instructed him in*
1035 Thy toure for to com ynne,
And who him brought thare,
And other, that ye may be ware.'　　　　　　　　*on your guard*

1022 swere] *thus* A; swerd S.
1024–5 Drery] *thus* A; dredry S. You [i.e. the emir] might well be sorrowful to see
the pitiful plight of these children!

Than seide the amyral, 'As God me save,
Florys shal his lyf have,
1040 Yif he me telle who him taught therto.'   *in that*
[Quod] Florys, 'That shal y never doo,   *Said*
[But yif hit ben foryiven also   *Unless*
That the gin me taughte therto].'[n]   *(The one) who*
Now they bydden al, ywys,   *begged*
1045 That the admyral graunted this:
To foryeve that trespas,   *offence*
Yif Florys told how it was.
Now every word he hath him tolde:
How that maide was f[ro] him solde;
1050 And how he was of Spayn a kynges sone,
For grete love theder ycom,
For to fonde, with sum gynne,
That feire maide for to wynne;[n]
And how the porter was his man bycom,
1055 For his gold and for his warysoun;   *reward*
And how he was in the florys born.   *flowers, carried*
Alle the lordinges lowgh therforn.   *laughed at that*
Now the admyral — wol him tyde! —   *may good befall him*
Florys setteth next his syde;
1060 And efte he made him stonde upryght,   *afterwards*
And dubbed him there knyght;
And bade he shulde with him be,
The furthermast of his meyne.   *highest in rank, retinue*
Florys falleth doun to his feet,
1065 And prayeth geve him his sweet.   *sweetheart*
The amyral gaf him his lemman;
Al that there were thankyd him thanne.
To a chirche he let hem bryng,
And dede let wed hem with a ryng.
1070 Both these twoo swete thinges, ywys,
Fel his feet for to kysse.
And, through consel of Blauncheflour,   *advice*
Clarys was fet doun of the toure,   *fetched, from*
And amyral wedded hur to queene.

1041 Quod] *thus* A C; Of S.
1042–3 *Thus* A; *lines om.* S.
1049 fro] *thus* A C; for S (cf. *also lines* 542, 716).

1075 There was fest swythe breeme: *splendid*
       I cannot telle al the sonde,   *courses*
       But rycher fest was never in londe.
       Was it nought longe after than
       That to Florys tydyng cam
1080 That the king, his fader, was deed.
       The baronage gaf him reed   *nobles, counselled him*
       That he shuld wende hoom
       And fonge his feire kyngdoom.   *accede to*
       At the amyral they toke leve,
1085 And he byddeth them byleve.   *begs, stay*
       Hom he went, with royal array,   *pomp*
       And was crownyd within a short day.[n]   *a few days*

AMIS AND AMILOUN

For Goddes love in Trinyte,
Al that ben hend herkenith to me,   *gracious/noble*
I pray yow, paramoure:[n]   *of your kindness*
What sumtyme fel, beyond the see,   *once befell*
5 Two barons of grete bounte   *goodness*
And men of grete honoure.
Her faders were barons hende,
Lordinges com of grete kynde,   *noble stock*
And pris men in ton and toure.
10 To here of these children two,   *hear, (noble) young men*
How they were in wele and woo,   *joy, sorrow*
Ywys, it is grete douloure.   *very moving*

In weele and woo how they gan wynd,   *fare*
And how unkouth they were of kynd,
15 The children bold of chere;   *stout-hearted*
And how they were good and hend,
And how yong thei becom frend,
In cort there they were;   *court, where*
And how they were made knyght,
20 And how they were trouth plyght,
The children both in fere;   *together*
And in what lond thei were born,
And what the childres name worn –   *were*
Herkeneth, and ye mow here!   *may*

1–96 MS A, from which the greater part of the following text is taken, is physically defective and lacks the beginning and end of the romance; lines 1–96 have been supplied from MS S.
9 And men distinguished everywhere (*literally*, in town and tower).
14 And how they were without equal (?).
20 And how they pledged loyalty to each other.

25 In Lumbardy, y understond,[n]
    Whilom bifel in that lond,   *Once, happened*
    In romance as we reede,[n]   *read*
    Two barouns hend wonyd in lond,   *dwelt*
    And had two ladyes free to fond,   *noble indeed*
30 That worthy were in wede.[n]
    Of her hend ladyes two
    Twoo knave childre gat they thoo,   *boy, begot*
    That doughty were of dede,   *brave in their actions*
    And trew weren in al thing;
35 And therfore Jhesu, hevyn king,
    Ful wel quyted her mede.   *rewarded them*

    The childrenis names, as y yow hyght,   *assure*
    In ryme y wol rekene ryght   *words, recount*
    And tel in my talkyng.   *speech*
40 Both they were getyn in oo nyght,   *begotten*
    And on oo day born aplyght,   *indeed*
    Forsoth, without lesyng.   *Truly, lying*
    That oon baron son, ywys,   *indeed*
    Was ycleped childe Amys   *called*
45 At his cristenyng.
    That other was clepyd Amylyoun,
    That was a childe of grete renoun
    And com of hyghe ofspryng.   *noble lineage*

    The children gon then thryve;   *grow up healthily*
50 Fairer were never noon on lyve,   *alive*
    Curtaise, hende and good.
    When they were of yeres fyve,   *five years old*
    Alle her kyn was of hem blyth,   *kindred*
    So mylde they were of mood.   *gentle, demeanour*
55 When they were sevyn yere olde,
    Grete joy every man of hem tolde,   *reckoned*
    To beholde that frely foode.   *(those) worthy creature(s)*
    When they were twel yere olde,
    In al the londe were noon so bolde,
60 So faire of boon and blood.

    60 So fair in body (*literally*, of bone and blood).

In that tyme, y understond,
A duk wonyd in that lond,   *duke, dwelt*
Prys in ton and toure.[n]
Frely he let [sende] his [s]onde   *message*
65 After erles, barouns, fre and bond,[n]
And ladies bryght in boure.[n]   *beautiful, bower*
A ryche fest he wolde make,   *intended to*
Al for Jhesu Cristes sake,
That is oure Savyoure.
70 Muche folk, as y yow saye,
He lete after sende that daye,   *send for*
With myrth of grete honoure.

Thoo barouns twoo that y of tolde
And her sones feire and bolde,
75 To court they com ful yare.   *quickly/eagerly*
When they were comyn, yong and olde,
Mony men gan hem byholde
Of lordynges that there were:
Of body how wel they were pyght,   *built*
80 And how feire they were of syght,   *to see*
Of hyde and hew and here.   *skin, colour, hair*
And al they seide, without lesse,   *deceit*
Fairer children than they wesse   *were*
Ne sey they never yere.   *saw, before*

85 In al the court was ther no wyght,   *no one*
Erl, baron, squyer ne knyght,
Neither lef ne loothe,
So lyche they were both of syght   *in appearance*
And of waxing, y yow plyght,   *physical stature, assure*
90 I tel yow forsoothe: *truly*
In al thing they were so lyche,   *alike/equal*
Ther was neither pore ne ryche,
Whoso beheld hem both,
Fader ne moder, that couth say   *could*
95 Ne knew the hend children tway,
But by the coloure of her cloth.   *Except, clothes*

64 sende his sonde] *thus* A (*where line acephalous*); his honde S. Generously he
had his message/invitation sent out.
87 No one at all (*literally*, Neither dear nor hateful).
95 Nor could tell the two noble youths apart.

That riche douke his fest gan hold,
With erls and with barouns bold,
As ye may listen and lithe,   *hear*
100 Fourtennight, as me was told,
With [meete and drynke meryst on mold],
To glad tho bernes blithe.
Ther was mirthe and melodye
And al maner of menstracie,   *kinds, minstrelsy*
105 Her craftes for to kithe.
Opon the fiftenday, ful yare,   *early(?)*
Thai token her leve for to fare,   *depart*
And thonked him mani a sithe.   *time*

Than the lordinges schuld forth wende,   *When*
110 That riche douke, comly of kende,[n]   *of noble nature*
Cleped to him that tide   *Called*
Tho tvay barouns, that were so hende,   *two*
And prayd hem, also his frende,   *as*
In court thai schuld abide,   *remain*
115 And lete her tvay sones fre   *two, noble*
In his servise with him to be,
Semly to fare bi his side;   *In fitting manner*
And he wald dubbe hem knightes to,
And susten hem for evermo   *provide for*
120 As lordinges proude in pride.[n]   *lordly in splendour*

The riche barouns answerd ogain,
And her levedis gan to sain   *ladies*
To that douke ful yare   *at once*
That thai were bothe glad and fain   *happy*
125 That her levely children tvain   *their, lovable, two*
In servise with him ware.   *should be*
Thai yave her childer her blisceing,   *gave, their blessing*
And bisought Jhesu, heven king,   *prayed*
He schuld scheld hem fro care;   *shield, sorrow*

101 meete . . . mold] *thus* S; erls & wiþ barouns bold A. With food and drink
the most pleasing on earth.
102 To entertain those men merrily.
105 To show their (i.e. the minstrels') skills.
106 *The phrase* ful yare *is perhaps no more than a meaningless tag here.*
117 i.e. to be part of his retinue.

130 And oft thai thonked the douke that day,
     And token her leve and went oway;
     To her owen cuntres thai gun fare.   *countries, go*

     Thus war tho hende childer, ywis,
     Child Amiloun and child Amis,[n]
135 In court frely to fede,   *nobly, to be raised*
     To ride anhunting under riis.
     Over al the lond than were thai priis   *renowned*
     And worthliest in wede.[n]
     So wele tho children loved hem tho,
140 Nas never children loved hem so,
     Noither in word no in dede.   *Neither, nor*
     Bitvix hem tvai, of blod and bon,[n]
     Trewer love nas never non,
     In gest as so we rede.[n]   *story*

145 On a day the childer war and wight[n]   *prudent, brave*
     Trewethes togider thai gun plight,
     While thai might live and stond,
     That, bothe bi day and bi night,
     In wele and wo, in wrong and right,   *joy*
150 That thai schuld frely fond   *unstintingly strive*
     To hold togider at everi nede,   *To be loyal to each other*
     In word, in werk, in wille, in dede,
     Where that thai were in lond;   *Wherever*
     Fro that day forward nevermo
155 Failen other, for wele no wo –   *each other*
     Therto thai held up her hond.[nn]

     Thus, in gest as ye may here,   *story*
     Tho hende childer in cuntre were,
     With that douke for to abide.
160 The douke was blithe and glad of chere;
     Thai were him bothe leve and dere,   *beloved*
     Semly to fare bi his side.

136 *Literally*, under branch (i.e. in the woods).
139–40 Those young men loved each other so well then that there were never
young men who loved each other so much.
146 Gave their word to each other.
162 Cf. line 117.

Tho thai were fiften winter old,   *When*
He dubbed bothe tho bernes bold   *(young) men*
165 To knightes in that tide,[n]   *at that time*
And fond hem al that hem was nede –
Hors and wepen and worthly wede –   *fine clothes*
As princes prout in pride.[n]   *lordly in splendour*

That riche douke, he loved hem so,
170 Al that thai wald he fond hem tho,
Bothe stedes white and broun,   *horses*
That, in what stede thai gan go,   *place*
Alle the lond spac of hem tho,   *spoke*
Bothe in tour and toun;
175 Into what stede that thai went,   *whatever place*
To justes other to turnament,   *jousts*
Sir Amis and Sir Amiloun,
For douhtiest in everi dede,   *bravest*
With scheld and spere to ride on stede,
180 Thai gat hem gret renoun.[n]

That riche douke hadde of hem pris,   *esteemed them highly*
For that thai were so war and wiis   *prudent, wise*
And holden of gret bounte.   *considered, goodness*
Sir Amiloun and Sir Amis,
185 He sett hem bothe in gret office,
In his court for to be:
Sir Amis, as ye may here,
He made his chef botelere,[n]   *cupbearer*
[For he was hend and fre];
190 And Sir Amiloun of hem alle
He made chef steward in halle,[n]
To dight al his meine.   *direct, household*

Into her servise when thai were brought,   *posts*
To geten hem los tham spared nought;   *praise*
195 Wel hendeliche thai bigan.   *nobly*
With riche and pover so wele thai wrought,

166 And provided them with all that they needed.
170 All that they wished he provided for them then.
189 For . . . fre] *thus* S H; In his court for to be A; *om.* D.
196 They behaved so well towards both rich and poor.

Al that hem seighe, with word and thought   *saw*
Hem loved mani a man.[n]
For thai were so blithe of chere,   *cheerful in demeanour*
200 Over al the lond, fer and nere,
The los of love thai wan;   *praise*
And the riche douke, withouten les,   *deceit*
Of alle the men that olive wes   *were alive*
Mest he loved hem than.   *Most*

205 Than hadde the douke, ich understond,
A chef steward of alle his lond,
A douhti knight at crie,   *at his service*
That euer he proved, with nithe and ond,
For to have brought hem bothe to schond,   *disgrace*
210 With gile and trecherie.
For thai were so gode and hende,
And for the douke was so wele her frende,
He hadde therof gret envie.
To the douke, with wordes grame,   *angry*
215 Ever he proved to don hem schame,   *harm*
With wel gret felonie.[n]   *wickedness*

So, within tho yeres to,   *those, two*
A messanger ther com tho   *then*
To Sir Amiloun hende on hond;[n]
220 And seyd hou deth hadde fet him fro   *taken from him*
His fader and his moder also,
Thurch the grace of Godes sond.   *Through, providence*
Than was that knight a careful man;   *sorrowful*
To that douke he went him than
225 And dede him to understond   *informed him*
His fader and his moder hende
War ded, and he most hom wende   *home*
For to resaive his lond.   *receive*

That riche douke comly of kende   *of noble nature*
230 Answerd oyain with wordes hende,
And seyd, 'So God me spede,

208 Who continually strove, with malice and indignation.
231 As (I wish that) God may cause me to prosper.

Sir Amiloun, now thou schalt wende,   *depart*
Me nas never so wo for frende
That of mi court out yede.
235 Ac yif ever it bifalle so   *But if, happen*
That thou art in wer and wo   *danger*
And of min help hast nede,
Saveliche com, or send thi sond,   *Confidently, message*
And with al mi powere of mi lond   *(military?) power*
240 Y schal wreke the of that dede.'   *avenge*

Than was Sir Amiloun ferli wo   *terribly*
For to wende Sir Amis fro;
On him was al his thought.
To a goldsmitthe he gan go,
245 And lete make gold coupes to: *had made*
For thre hundred pounde he hem bought;
That bothe were of o wight,   *the same weight*
And bothe of o michel, yplight,   *size, assuredly*
Ful richeliche thai were wrought;
250 And bothe thai weren as liche, ywis,   *indeed*
As was Sir Amiloun and Sir Amis:
Ther no failed right nought.[n]

When that Sir Amiloun was al yare,   *ready*
He tok his leve for to fare,   *depart*
255 To wende in his jorne.   *journey*
Sir Amis was so ful of care,
For sorwe and wo and sikeing sare   *sighing, sore*
Almest swoned that fre.   *swooned, noble (man)*
To the douke he went with dreri mode,   *heavy heart*
260 And praid him fair, ther he stode,   *courteously*
And seyd, 'Sir, par charite,   *of your goodness*
Yif me leve to wende the fro: *Give*
Bot yif y may with mi brother go,   *Unless*
Mine hert it breketh of thre!'   *in three*

265 That riche douke comly of kende
Answerd oyain with wordes hende,

233–4 I was never so sorry at a friend's departure from my court.
252 i.e. that was so in every respect.

And seyd, withouten delay,
'Sir Amis, mi gode frende,
Wold ye bothe now fro me wende?
270 Certes,' he seyd, 'nay!   *Certainly*
Were ye bothe went me fro,   *gone*
Than schuld me waken al mi wo;
Mi joie were went oway.
Thi brother schal into his cuntre;   *shall (go)*
275 Wende with him in his jurne,
And com oyain this day.'ⁿ   *come back today*

When thai were redi for to ride,
Tho bold bernes for to abide
Busked hem redy boun.   *Made themselves ready*
280 Hende, herkneth, is nought to hide: *it cannot be denied*
So douhti knightes in that tide
That ferd out of that toun.ⁿ
Al that day as thai rade   *rode*
Ever morning bothe thai made,
285 Sir Amis and Amiloun.
And when thai schuld wende otvain,   *part from each other*
Wel fair togider opon a plain
Of hors thai light adoun.   *dismounted*

When thai were bothe afot light,   *on foot*
290 Sir Amiloun, that hendi knight,
Was rightwise man of rede,   *i.e. Gave good advice*
And seyd to Sir Amis ful right,   *indeed*
'Brother, as we er trewthe plight,
Bothe with word and dede,
295 Fro this day forward nevermo
To faily other, for wele no wo,
To help him at his nede –   *Each to help other*
Brother, be now trewe to me,
And y schal ben as trewe to the,
300 Also God me spede!

272 All my sorrow would awaken.
278 Those men redoubtable to encounter (in battle).
284 They both grieved continually.
293 Brother, as we have sworn loyalty to each other.

'Ac, brother, ich warn the biforn,   *But*
For his love that bar the croun of thorn
To save al mankende,
Be nought oyain thi lord forsworn;
305 And yif thou dost, thou art forlorn,   *lost*
Evermore, withouten ende.
Bot ever do trewthe and no tresoun,
And thenk on me, Sir Amiloun,
Now we asondri schal wende.   *apart*
310 And, brother, yete y the forbede
The fals steward felawerede –
Certes he wil the schende!'[n]   *intends to destroy you*

As thai stode so, tho bretheren bold,
Sir Ami[loun] drough forth tvai coupes of gold,
315 Ware liche in al thing,
And bad Sir Amis that he schold   *offered*
Chese whether he have wold,   *Choose which*
Withouten more duelling.   *delay*
And seyd to him, 'Mi leve brother,   *dear*
320 Kepe thou that on and y that other,
For Godes love, heven king!
Lete never this coupe fro the,
Bot loke heron and thenk on me:
It tokneth our parting.'   *is a token of*

325 Gret sorwe thai made at her parting,
And kisten hem with eighen wepeing,   *each other, eyes*
Tho knightes hende and fre.
Aither bitaught other heven king,   *Each, commended*
And on her stedes thai gun spring,
330 And went in her jurne.
Sir Amiloun went hom to his lond
And sesed it al into his hond,[n]
That his elders hadde be,

304 Do not transgress against your loyalty to your lord.
307 But always behave loyally and without treachery.
310–11 And, brother, I furthermore warn you against the treacherous steward's
friendship.
314 Amiloun] *thus* S D H; Amis A.
315 Which were alike in every respect.
333 Which had belonged to his forebears.

And spoused a levedy bright in bour,   *married*
335 And brought hir hom with gret honour
And miche solempnete.   *much ceremony*

Lete we Sir Amiloun stille be
With his wiif in his cuntre –
God leve hem wele to fare! –
340 And of Sir Amis telle we:
When he com him to court oye   *came back to the court*
Ful blithe of him thai ware.
For that he was so hende and gode,
Men blisced him, bothe bon and blod,   *blessed*
345 That ever him gat and bare,[n]
Save the steward of that lond –   *Except*
Ever he proved, with nithe and ond,
To bring him into care.   *distress*

Than on a day bifel it so   *happened*
350 With the steward he met tho;
Ful fair he gret that fre: *greeted, that noble (man)*
'Sir Amis,' he seyd, 'the is ful wo,
For that thi brother is went the fro,   *Because*
And, certes, so is me.
355 Ac of his wendeing have thou no care: *But, departure*
Yif thou wilt leve opon mi lare
And lete thi morning be,
And thou wil be to me kende,   *well disposed*
Y schal the be a better frende
360 Than ever yete was he.

'Sir Amis,' he seyd, 'do bi mi red,   *advice*
And swere ous bothe brotherhed,   *let us both swear*
And plight we our trewthes to.
Be trewe to me in word and dede,
365 And y schal, so God me spede,
Be trewe to the also.
Sir Amis answerd, 'Mi treuthe y plight

339 God grant that they may prosper!
347 Cf. line 208.
352 You are very sorrowful.
356–7 If you will trust to what I have to say and leave off your grieving.
365 schal] *thus* S D H; schal to þe A.

To Sir Amiloun, the gentil knight:
Thei he be went me fro,   *Although*
370 Whiles that y may gon and speke
Y no schal never mi treuthe breke,
Noither for wele no wo!

'For, bi the treuthe that God me sende,[n]
Ichave him founde so gode and kende
375 Seththen that y first him knewe.   *Since*
For ones y plight him treuthe, that hende,   *Because I once*
Whereso he in warld wende,
Y schal be to him trewe.
And yif y were now forsworn
380 And breke mi treuthe, y were forlorn —   *lost*
Wel sore it schuld me rewe!   *I should bitterly regret it*
Gete me frendes whare y may,
Y no schal never, bi night no day,
Chaunge him for no newe.'[n]

385 The steward than was egre of mode;   *angry/furious*
Almest for wretthe he wex ner wode,   *anger, became, mad*
And seyde, withouten delay,
And swore bi him that dyed on rode,   *the cross*
'Thou traitour, unkinde blod,
390 Thou schalt abigge this nay!   *pay for, refusal*
Y warn the wele,' he seyd than,
'That y schal be thi strong foman   *bitter enemy*
Ever after this day.'
Sir Amis answerd tho,
395 'Sir, therof yive y nought a slo,[n]   *sloe*
Do al that thou may.'[n]

Al thus the wrake gan biginne,   *hostility*
And with wretthe thai went atvinne,   *anger, they parted*
Tho bold bernes to.   *two*

370 i.e. for as long as I live.
372 Under any circumstances (*literally*, Neither for joy nor sorrow).
382 Wherever I may be able to find friends.
389 You treacherous, unnatural creature.
395–6 Sir, I do not care in the least about that, whatever you may do.

400 The steward nold never blinne: *cease*
    To schende that douhti knight of kinne   *destroy*
    Ever he proved tho.   *Continually, strove, then*
    Thus in court togider thai were,
    With wretthe and with loureand chere,   *sullen demeanour*
405 Wele half a yere and mo.
    And afterward, opon a while,
    The steward, with tresoun and gile,   *treachery*
    Wrought him ful michel wo.

    So in a time, as we tel in gest,   *story*
410 The riche douke lete make a fest
    Semly in somers tide.   *Splendid, summertime*
    Ther was mani a gentil gest,
    With mete and drink ful onest   *fitting*
    To servi bi ich a side.   *on every side*
415 Miche semly folk was samned thare –   *gathered*
    Erls, barouns, lasse and mare,   *lesser and greater*
    And levedis proude in pride.   *ladies*
    More joie no might be non
    Than ther was in that worthly won,   *splendid dwelling*
420 With blisse in borwe to bide.[n]

    That riche douke that y of told,
    He hadde a douhter fair and bold,
    Curteise, hende and fre.
    When sche was fiften winter old,
425 In al that lond nas ther non yhold   *considered*
    So semly on to se,   *So fair to look upon*
    For sche was gentil and avenaunt.   *graceful*
    Hir name was cleped Belisaunt,
    As ye may lithe at me.   *hear from me*
430 With levedis and maidens bright in bour
    Kept sche was with honour   *Attended to*
    And gret solempnite.   *ceremony/splendour*

    That fest lasted fourtennight,
    Of barouns and of birddes bright[n]   *ladies*

401 The phrase *of kinne* perhaps signifies 'of noble birth'.
408 Caused him very great distress.

435 And lordinges mani and fale.   *very many*
    Ther was mani a gentil knight,
    And mani a serjaunt wise and wight   *servant, nimble*
    To serve tho hende in halle.   *those noble (guests)*
    Than was the boteler, Sir Amis,   *cupbearer*
440 Over al yholden flour and priis,
    Trewely to telle in tale;   *To tell the truth*
    And douhtiest in everi dede,
    And worthliest in ich a wede,[n]
    And semliest in sale.[n]   *handsomest, hall*

445 Than the lordinges schulden al gon   *When, depart*
    And wende out of that worthli won,   *noble dwelling*
    In boke as so we rede,
    That mirie maide gan aske anon   *sweet, soon*
    Of hir maidens, everichon,   *each one*
450 And seyd, 'So God you spede',
    Who was hold the doughtiest knight,   *considered*
    And semlyest in ich a sight,   *most worthy, every regard*
    And worthliest in wede;
    And who was the fairest man
455 That was yholden in lond than,
    And doughtiest of dede.

    Her maidens gan answere ogain
    And seyd, 'Madame, we schul the sain
    That sothe, bi Seyn Savour:[n]   *truth*
460 Of erls, barouns, knight and swain,[n]   *young men*
    The fairest man and mest of main   *strongest*
    And man of mest honour,   *most*
    It is Sir Amis, the kinges boteler.
    In al this warld nis his per,   *is not, equal*
465 Noither in toun no tour;
    He is douhtiest in dede,
    And worthliest in everi wede,
    And chosen for priis and flour.

    Belisaunt, that birdde bright,   *lady*

440 Considered the best (*literally*, the flower) and most outstanding of them all.

470 When thai hadde thus seyd, yplight,   *assuredly*
    As ye may listen and lithe,   *hear*
    On Sir Amis, that gentil knight,
    Ywis, hir love was al alight,   *Indeed, set*
    That no man might it kithe.[n]
475 Wher that sche seighe him ride or go,   *Whether, saw, walk*
    Hir thought hir hert brac atvo   *broke in two*
    That hye no spac nought with that blithe.   *she, gentle one*
    For hye no might, night no day,
    Speke with him, that fair may,   *maiden*
480 Sche wepe wel mani a sithe.   *wept, time*

    Thus that miri maiden ying   *sweet, young*
    Lay in care and love morning   *sorrow*
    Bothe bi night and day.
    As y you tel in my talking,
485 For sorwe sche spac with him nothing,   *(that) she*
    Sike in bed sche lay.   *Sick*
    Hir moder com to hir tho   *mother, then*
    And gan to frain hir of hir wo,   *ask*
    Help hir yif hye may.   *(To) help, if*
490 And sche answerd, withouten wrong,[n]
    Hir pines were so hard and strong   *pains*
    Sche wald be loken in clay.

    That riche douk, in o morning,   *one morning*
    And with him mani a gret lording,
495 As prince prout in pride,
    Thai dight hem, withouten dueling,   *accoutred, delay*
    For to wende on dere-hunting,
    And busked hem for to ride.   *made themselves ready*
    When the lordinges, everichon,
500 Were went out of that worthli won —
    In hert is nought to hide —
    Sir Amis, withouten les,   *doubt*
    For a malady that on him wes   *Because of an illness*
    At hom he gan to abide.[n]

474 (But in such a way) that no one knew of it.
478 might] *thus* S D H; miȝt wiþ him A.
492 She would be dead and buried (*literally*, She would be enclosed in earth).
495 Cf. line 168.
501 i.e. it cannot be kept a secret.

505 When tho lordinges were out ywent
    With her men hende and bowes bent
    To hunte on holtes hare,[n]   *woods, grey*
    Than Sir Amis, verrament,   *truly*
    He bileft at hom in present   *remained, at that time*
510 To kepe al that ther ware.   *oversee*
    That hendi knight bithought him tho
    Into the gardin he wold go,
    For to solas him thare.   *enjoy himself*
    Under a bough as he gan bide,   *linger*
515 To here the foules song that tide   *time*
    Him thought a blisseful fare.[n]

    Now, hende, herkneth and ye may here
    Hou that the doukes douhter dere   *How*
    Sike in hir bed lay.
520 Hir moder com with diolful chere,   *sorrowful countenance*
    And al the levedis that ther were,
    For to solas that may.   *comfort*
    'Arise up,' sche seyd, 'douhter min,
    And go play the in the gardin   *amuse yourself*
525 This semly somers day.   *lovely*
    Ther may thou here the foules song,
    With joie and miche blis among;   *much delight besides*
    Thi care schal wende oway.'   *Your sorrow will disappear*

    Up hir ros that swete wight;   *creature*
530 Into the gardine sche went ful right,   *at once*
    With maidens hende and fre.
    The somers day was fair and bright;
    The sonne him schon thurch lem of light,
    That semly was on to se.   *to behold*
535 Sche herd the foules gret and smale,
    The swete note of the nightingale
    Ful mirily sing on tre;   *sweetly*
    Ac hir hert was so hard ibrought –   *was in such distress*
    On love longing was al hir thought –
540 No might hir gamen no gle.

    506 With their attendants to hand and bows at the ready.
    516 Seemed to him a delightful thing to do.
    533 The sun shone brightly (*literally*, with gleam of light).
    540 No merriment could give her pleasure.

And so that mirie may with pride   *sweet maiden, gay attire (?)*
Went into the orchard that tide,
To slake hir of hir care.   *rid herself*
Than seyghe sche Sir Amis biside;   *saw, nearby*
545 Under a bough he gan abide,
To here tho mirthes mare.   *then, more sweet singing*
Than was sche bothe glad and blithe;
Hir joie couthe sche no man kithe,[n]   *express*
When that sche seighe him thare;
550 And thought sche wold for no man wond   *desist*
That sche no wold to him fond,   *go*
And tel him of hir fare.   *situation*

Than was that may so blithe o mode,   *glad in her mind*
When sche seighe were he stode,
555 To him sche went, that swete;
And thought, for alle this warldes gode,
Bot yif hye spac, that frely fode,
That time no wold sche lete.
And as tite as that gentil knight   *as soon as*
560 Seighe that bird in bour so bright   *Saw*
Com with him for to mete,
Oyaines hir he gan wende;   *To meet her*
With worde bothe fre and hende
Ful fair he gan hir grete.   *courteously, greet*

565 That mirie maiden, sone anon,   *immediately*
Bad hir maidens fram hir gon   *Commanded*
And withdrawe hem oway.
And when thai were togider alon,
To Sir Amis sche made hir mon,   *lament*
570 And seyd opon hir play,
'Sir knight, on the mine hert is brought:
The to love is al mi thought,
Bothe bi night and day;
That, bot thou wolt mi leman be,   *unless, beloved*
575 Ywis, min hert breketh a thre —   *Certainly, in three*
No lenger libben y no may.   *live*

556–8 And thought, that noble creature, that she would not refrain from speaking at that time for anything in the world.
572 I can think of nothing else but loving you.

'Thou art,' sche seyd, 'a gentil knight,
And icham a bird in bour bright,   *I am*
Of wel heighe kin ycorn.   *noble lineage indeed*
580 And bothe, bi day and bi night,
Mine hert so hard is on the light,   *firmly, set*
Mi joie is al forlorn.   *lost*
Plight me thi trewthe thou schalt be trewe,
And chaunge me for no newe
585 That in this world is born,
And y plight the mi treuthe also;
Til God and deth dele ous ato,   *part us asunder*
Y schal never be forsworn.'ⁿ   *break my promise*

That hende knight stille he stode,
590 And al for thought chaunged his mode,
And seyd with hert fre,
'Madame, for him that dyed on rode,   *the cross*
Astow art comen of gentil blode
And air of this lond schal be,   *heir*
595 Bithenke the of thi michel honour.   *Be mindful of, rank*
Kinges sones and emperour
Nar non to gode to the;   *Would not be too good for you*
Certes, than were it michel unright
Thi love to lain opon a knight   *set*
600 That nath noither lond no fe.ⁿ

'And yif we schuld that game biginne,
And ani wight of al thi kinne
Might it undergo,   *find out about it*
Al our joie and worldes winne   *earthly pleasure*
605 We schuld lese, and for that sinne   *lose*
Wretthi God therto.   *Anger, as well*
And y dede mi lord this deshonour,   *If, dishonour*
Than were ich an ivel traitour —   *evil*
Ywis, it may nought be so!'ⁿ

584–5 i.e. and change me for no other friend in the world.
590 i.e. he became thoughtful; *mode* might denote his mood/feelings or his manner.
593 Since you are of gentle birth.
598 Certainly, then, it would be a great wrong.

610 Leve madame, do bi mi rede,   *Dear, advice*
    And thenk what wil com of this dede —
    Certes, nothing bot wo.'   *except sorrow*

    That mirie maiden of gret renoun
    Answerd, 'Sir knight, thou nast no croun.   *tonsure*
615 For God that bought the dere,   *By, redeemed, dearly*
    Whether artow prest other persoun,
    Other thou art monk other canoun,
    That prechest me thus here?
    Thou no schust have ben no knight,   *You should not*
620 To gon among maidens bright —
    Thou schust have ben a frere!   *friar*
    He that lerd the thus to preche,   *taught*
    The devel of helle ichim biteche,   *consign*
    Mi brother thei he were!   *Even if he were my brother*

625 'Ac,' sche seyd, 'bi him that ous wrought,   *But, created us*
    Al thi precheing helpeth nought,   *does no good*
    No stond thou never so long.[n]
    Bot yif thou wilt graunt me mi thought,   *Unless*
    Mi love schal be ful dere abought
630 With pines hard and strong.   *pains*
    Mi kerchef and mi clothes anon[n]   *kerchief*
    Y schal to-rende doun ichon   *tear down, each one*
    And say with michel wrong   *great*
    With strengthe thou hast me to-drawe;   *raped*
635 Ytake thou schalt be thurch londes lawe
    And dempt heighe to hong.'   *condemned, high*

    Than stode that hendy knight ful stille,
    And in his hert him liked ille;   *he was ill-pleased*
    No word no spac he tho.
640 He thought, 'Bot y graunt hir wille,
    With hir speche sche wil me spille,

616–18 Are you a priest or parson — otherwise you are a monk or canon — who preach to me here in this way?
627 However long you go on (*literally*, stand/remain).
629 You will pay dearly for my (unrequited) love.
635 You will be seized in accordance with the law of the land.
640–1 Unless I grant what she wishes, she will destroy me by what she will say.

Er than y passe hir fro.[n]   *Before*
And yif y do mi lord this wrong,
With wilde hors and with strong
645 Y schal be drawe also.'[n]   *torn apart*
Loth him was that dede to don,   *Reluctant*
And wele lother his liif forgon —
Was him never so wo.   *He was never so sorrowful*

And than he thought, withouten lesing,   *deceit*
650 Better were to graunt hir asking
Than his liif for to spille.   *lose*
Than seyd he to that maiden ying,
'For Godes love, heven king,
Understond to mi skille: *Give heed, argument*
655 Astow art maiden gode and trewe,
Bithenk hou oft rape wil rewe[n]   *haste, be regretted*
And turn to grame wel grille.   *bitter anguish*
And abide we al this sevennight,   *If we wait, week*
As icham trewe, gentil knight,
660 Y schal graunt the thi wille.'

Than answerd that bird bright,
And swore, 'Bi Jhesu, ful of might,
Thou scapest nought so oway!
Thi treuthe anon thou schalt me plight,   *at once*
665 Astow art trewe, gentil knight,
Thou schalt hold that day.'   *keep that appointment*
He graunted hir hir wil tho,[n]   *her wish*
And plight hem trewthes bothe to,
And seththen kist tho tvai.   *afterwards, those two*
670 Into hir chaumber sche went ogain;   *went back*
Than was sche so glad and fain,   *happy*
Hir joie sche couthe no man sai.   *could, express*

Sir Amis than, withouten duelling,   *delay*
For to kepe his lordes coming,   *attend to, homecoming*
675 Into halle he went anon.
When thai were comen fram dere-hunting,

---

647 And much more so to lose his life.
668 And they both pledged their loyalty to each other.

And with him mani an heighe lording,   *i.e. the duke, noble*
Into that worthly won,   *noble dwelling*
After his douhter he asked swithe;   *soon*
680 Men seyd that sche was glad and blithe —
Hir care was al agon.   *departed*
To eten in halle thai brought that may;   *dine, maiden*
Ful blithe and glad thai were that day,
And thonked God, ichon.

685 When the lordinges, withouten les,
Hendelich were brought on des[n]   *Graciously, dais*
With levedis bright and swete,
As princes that were proude in pres,   *crowd*
Ful richeliche served he wes,   *splendidly*
690 With menske and mirthe to mete.   *dignity, becoming*
When that maiden that y of told
Among the birdes that were bold   *merry*
Ther sche sat in her sete,
On Sir Amis, that gentil knight,
695 An hundred time sche cast hir sight;
For nothing wald sche lete.   *would, desist*

On Sir Amis, that knight hendy,
Evermore sche cast hir eyghe;
For nothing wold sche spare.   *refrain*
700 The steward, ful of felonie,   *wickedness*
Wel fast he gan hem aspie,   *closely, observe*
Til he wist of her fare.
And bi her sight he perceived tho   *looks*
That gret love was bitvix hem to,   *between, two*
705 And was agreved ful sare;[n]
And thought he schuld, in a while,
Bothe with tresoun and with gile,
Bring hem into care.   *distress*

Thus, ywis, that miri may
710 Ete in halle with gamen and play
Wele four days other five;
That ever when sche Sir Amis say,

702 Until he realized what was going on between them.

Al hir care was went oway —
Wele was hir olive.   *indeed (literally, alive)*
715 Wher that he sat or stode,   *Wherever*
Sche biheld opon that frely fode;   *noble creature*
No stint sche for no strive.
And the steward, for wretthe sake,   *out of malice*
Brought hem bothe in ten and wrake —   *distress, trouble*
720 Wel ivel mot he thrive!ⁿⁿ

That riche douke, opon a day,
On dere-hunting went him to play,
And with him wel mani a man.
And Belisaunt, that miri may,
725 To chaumber ther Sir Amis layⁿ   *where*
Sche went, as sche wele kan.
And the steward, withouten les,
In a chaumber bisiden he wes,   *next door*
And seighe the maiden than,
730 Into chaumber hou sche gan glide:
For to aspie hem bothe that tide,   *spy on*
After swithe he ran.ⁿ   *quickly*

When that may com into that won,   *maiden, apartment*
Sche fond Sir Amis ther alon.
735 'Hail!' sche seyd, that levedi bright.
'Sir Amis,' sche sayd anon,
'This day a sevennight it is gon
That trewthe we ous plight:
Therfore icham comen to the
740 To wite, astow art hende and fre   *find out*
And holden a gentil knight,
Whether wiltow me forsake,   *you will*
Or thou wilt trewely to me take   *stand by me*
And hold as thou bihight.'   *keep your promise*

745 'Madame,' seyd the knight ogain,   *replied the knight*
'Y wold the spouse now ful fain   *marry, very gladly*

717 She did not refrain because of (fear of) any opposition.
720 May ill fortune be his!
737–8 Today it is a week since we pledged loyalty to each other.

And hold the to mi wive.   *as my wife*
Ac yif thi fader herd it sain   *But if, said*
That ich hadde his douhter forlain,   *lain with*
750 Of lond he wald me drive.   *Out of*
Ac yif ich were king of this lond,
And hadde more gode in min hond   *wealth, possession*
Than other kinges five,   *i.e. Than five kings together*
Wel fain y wald spouse the than;
755 Ac, certes, icham a pover man —   *poor*
Wel wo is me olive!'

'Sir knight,' seyd that maiden kinde,   *gentle*
For love of Seyn Tomas of Ynde,[n]
Whi seystow ever nay?   *Why do you always say no?*
760 No be thou never so pover of kinde,
Riches anough y may the finde,   *plenty*
Bothe bi night and day.'[n]
That hende knight bithought him than,
And in his armes he hir nam,   *took*
765 And kist that miri may.
And so thai plaid, in word and dede,   *disported themselves*
That he wan hir maidenhede   *took her virginity*
Er that he went oway.[n]   *Before*

And ever that steward gan abide   *remain*
770 Alon under that chaumber side   *right beside that room*
Hem for to here.   *hear*
In at an hole, was nought to wide,   *not very wide*
He seighe hem bothe in that tide:
Hou thai seten yfere.   *sat/stayed, together*
775 And when he seyghe hem bothe with sight,
Sir Amis and that bird bright,
The doukes douhter dere,
Ful wroth he was and egre of mode,   *angry, resentful*
And went oway as he were wode,   *mad*
780 Her conseil to unskere.   *To betray their secret*

When the douke com into that won,[n]
The steward oyain him gan gon,   *to meet him*

756 I am wretched indeed (cf. line 714).
760 However poor you are by birth.

Her conseyl for to unwrain: *reveal*
'Mi lord the douke,' he seyd anon,
785   'Of thine harm, bi Seyn Jon,
Ichil the warn ful fain!
In thi court thou hast a thef,   *rascal*
That hath don min hert gref –   *caused, grief*
Schame it is to sain.   *Disgraceful, tell*
790   For certes he is a traitour strong,
When he, with tresoun and with wrong,
Thi douhter hath forlain.'   *lain with*

The riche douke gan sore agrame: *became very angry*
'Who hath,' he seyd, 'don me that schame?[n]   *disgrace*
795   Tel me, y the pray!'
'Sir,' seyd the steward, 'bi Seyn Jame,[n]
Ful wele y can the tel his name;
Thou do him hong this day.   *Have him hanged*
It is thi boteler, Sir Amis –
800   Ever he hath ben traitour, ywis –
He hath forlain that may.
Y seighe it meself, forsothe,   *truly*
And wil aprove biforn hem bothe,   *prove*
That thai can nought say nay.'

805   Than was the douke egre of mode;
He ran to halle as he were wode –
For nothing he nold abide.   *wait*
With a fauchoun scharp and gode   *sword*
He smot to Sir Amis, ther he stode,
810   And failed of him biside.
Into a chaumber Sir Amis ran tho,
And schet the dore bitven hem to,   *shut, between, two*
For drede his heved to hide.   *fear, head*
The douke strok after swiche a dent   *struck, such a blow*
815   That thourch the dore that fauchon went,   *through*
So egre he was that tide.

Al that ever about him stode   *Every one of those that*
Bisought the douke to slake his mode,   *Begged, calm down*

785–6 I will gladly warn you, by St John, of what harms you.
804   So that they cannot deny it.
810   And missed him, so that the blow fell beside him.

Bothe erl, baroun and swain.[n]
820 And he swore bi him that dyed on rode
He nold, for al this worldes gode,
Bot that traitour were slain:
'Ich have him don gret honour
And he hath, as a vile traitour,
825 Mi douhter forlain.
Y nold, for al this worldes won,
Bot y might the traitour slon
With min hondes tvain!'   *two*

'Sir,' seyd Sir Amis anon,
830 'Lete thi wretthe first overgon –   *anger, pass off*
Y pray the, par charite!   *of your mercy*
And yif thou may prove, bi Sein Jon,
That ichave swiche a dede don,
Do me to hong on tre.   *Have me hanged on the gallows*
835 Ac yif ani, with gret wrong,
Hath lowe on ous that lesing strong –
What bern that he be,   *Whoever he is*
He leighth on ous, withouten fail – [n]   *is lying, doubt*
Ichil aprove it in bataile
840 To make ous quite and fre.'

'Ya?' seyd the douke. 'Wiltow so?'   *Yes?*
Darstow into bataile go,   *Do you dare*
Al quite and skere you make?'
'Ya, certes, sir,' he seyd tho.
845 And here mi glove y yive therto,[n]
He leighe on ous with wrake.'   *vengefully*
The steward stirt to him than,   *leapt*
And seyd, 'Traitour, fals man,
Ataint thou schalt be take!   *You will be found guilty*
850 Y seighe it meself this ich day,   *this very day*
Where that sche in thi chaumber lay –
Your noither it may forsake.'

821–2 He wished for nothing . . . but that the traitor should be killed.
826–7 I would not wish, for the whole world, anything but that I might kill the
traitor.
836 Has told that terrible lie about us.
840 To make us clear and free (from blame).
843 To make yourselves completely clear and free of guilt.
852 Neither of you can deny it.

Thus the steward ever gan say,
And ever Sir Amis seyd, 'Nay,
855 Ywis, it nas nought so!'
Than dede the douke com forth that may,   *made, maiden*
And the steward withstode alway   *resisted*
And vouwed the dede tho.   *swore to*
The maiden wepe, hir hondes wrong,   *wept, wrung*
860 And ever swore hir moder among,   *her mother swore besides*
'Certain, it was nought so!'
Than seyd the douke, withouten fail,
'It schal be proved in batail,
And sen bitven hem to.'

865 Than was atvix hem take the fight,   *between, arranged*
And sett the day a fourtennight,
That mani man schuld it sen.
The steward was michel of might;   *very powerful*
In al the court was ther no wight   *nobody*
870 Sir Amis borwe durst ben;[n]
Bot, for the steward was so strong,   *because*
Borwes anowe he fond among –   *plenty, there*
Tventi al bidene.   *altogether*
Than seyd thai alle with resoun   *by rights*
875 Sir Amis schuld ben in prisoun,
For he no schuld nowhar flen.   *So that, flee*

Than answerd that maiden bright,
And swore, 'Bi Jhesu ful of might,
That were michel wrong!   *would be*
880 Taketh mi bodi for that knight,[n]
Til that his day com of fight,
And put me in prisoun strong.
Yif that the knight wil flen oway,
And dar nought holden up his day
885 Bataile of him to fong,
Do me than londes lawe:

864 And made apparent (in combat) between the two of them.
866 And the day appointed a fortnight thence.
870 Who dared stand surety for Sir Amis.
881 Until the day of his battle comes.
884–5 And dare not keep his appointment to do battle with him.

For his love to be to-drawe   *torn apart*
And heighe on galwes hong.'ⁿ

Hir moder seyd, with wordes bold,
890 That with gode wil als sche wold   *willingly she too*
Ben his borwe also,
His day of bataile up to hold,
That he, as gode knight, schold
Fight oyain his fo.   *against, enemy*
895 Thus tho levedis fair and bright   *those ladies*
Boden for that gentil knight,
To lain her bodis to.ⁿ
Than seyd the lordinges, everichon,
That other borwes wold thai non,   *required*
900 Bot graunt it schuld be so.   *agreed*

When thai had don as y you say,
And borwes founde withouten delay,
And graunted al that ther ware,
Sir Amis sorwed night and day –   *grieved*
905 Al his joie was went oway,
And comen was al his care.
For that the steward was so strong,   *Because*
And hadde the right and he the wrong
Of that he opon him bare,
910 Of his liif yaf he nought;ⁿ   *For, cared*
Bot of the maiden so michel he thought,
Might no man morn mare.   *lament*

For he thought that he most nede,   *needs must*
Ar that he to bataile yede,   *Before, went*
915 Swere an oth biforn
That, also God schuld him spede,
As he was giltles of that dede   *innocent*
That ther was on him born.   *Of which he was accused*

891–2 Also stand surety for him that he would keep the appointed day of battle.
896–7 Offered themselves as pledges for that noble knight.
903 And all who were there had agreed to it.
908–9 And had right on his side while he (Amis) was in the wrong concerning the accusation that he (the steward) made against him.
916 That, as he hoped that God would grant him success.

And than thought he, withouten wrong,
920 He hadde lever to ben anhong   *rather, hanged*
Than to be forsworn.   *perjured*
Ac oft he besought Jhesu tho   *prayed*
He schuld save hem, bothe to,
That thai ner nought forlorn.

925 So it bifel, opon a day,
He mett the levedi and that may   *i.e. the duchess*
Under an orchard side.
'Sir Amis,' the levedy gan say,
'Whi mornestow so, withouten play?
930 Tel me that sothe this tide.   *truth*
No drede the nought,' sche seyd than,   *Do not be afraid*
'For to fight with thi foman,   *enemy*
Whether thou wilt go or ride.
So richeliche y schal the schrede,   *equip*
935 Tharf the never have of him drede
Thi bataile to abide.'   *undergo*

'Madame,' seyd that gentil knight,
'For Jhesus love, ful of might,
Be nought wroth for this dede:
940 Ich have that wrong and he the right –
Therfore icham aferd to fight,   *afraid*
Also God me spede!
For y mot swere, withouten faile,   *must*
Also God me spede in bataile,
945 His speche is falshede.
And yif y swere, icham forsworn;   *perjured*
Than, liif and soule, icham forlorn –   *body and soul*
Certes, y can no rede!'   *I do not know what to do*

Than seyd that levedi in a while,
950 'No mai ther go no nother gile,

924 So that they would not be lost (i.e. perish).
929 Why do you grieve so, without (seeking any) diversion?
933 Whether you fight on foot or on horseback.
935 You need have of him no fear at all.
939 wroth] wrorþ A.
944–5 (That), as (I hope that) God will give me success in battle, what he says is untrue.

To bring that traitour doun?'
'Yis, dame,' he seyd, 'bi Seyn Gile!'[n]
Her woneth hennes mani a mile   *many miles hence*
Mi brother, Sir Amiloun;
955 And yif y dorst to him gon,   *dared*
Y dorst wele swere, bi Seyn Jon,[n]
So trewe is that baroun,
His owhen liif to lese to mede,
He wold help me at this nede,   *in this necessity*
960 To fight with that feloun.'   *villain*

'Sir Amis,' the levedi gan to say,
'Take leve tomorwe at day,   *daybreak*
And wende in thi jurne.   *go on your journey*
Y schal say thou schalt in thi way   *are going on your way*
965 Hom into thine owhen cuntray,
Thi fader, thi moder to se.
And when thou comes to thi brother right,   *indeed*
Pray him, as he is hendi knight
And of gret bounte,   *goodness*
970 That he the batail for ous fong   *undertake*
Oyain the steward, that with wrong   *Against*
Wil stroie ous, alle thre.'[n]   *destroy*

Amorwe Sir Amis made him yare,   *Next morning, ready*
And toke his leve for to fare,   *depart*
975 And went in his jurnay.
For nothing nold he spare: *desist*
He priked the stede that him bare   *spurred, carried*
Bothe night and day.
So long he priked withouten abod,   *resting*
980 The stede that he on rode,
In a fer cuntray,   *distant*
Was overcomen and fel doun ded.[n]   *overcome (by exhaustion)*
Tho couthe he no better red —
His song was 'Waileway!'   *Alas!*

950–1 Is there no other stratagem by which we can destroy that traitor?
958 Even if he was repaid with the loss of his own life.
983 Then he could think of nothing better to do.

985 And when it was bifallen so,
    Nedes afot he most go;   *Of necessity, on foot*
    Ful careful was that knight.   *sorrowful*
    He stiked up his lappes tho;
    In his way he gan to go,
990 To hold that he bihight.   *keep his promise*
    And al that day so long he ran,
    Into a wilde forest he cam
    Bitven the day and the night.   *i.e. at dusk*
    So strong slepe yede him on,
995 To win al this warldes won
    No ferther he no might.   *He could go no further*

    The knight, that was so hende and fre,
    Wel fayr he layd him under a tre
    And fel in slepe that tide.
1000 Al that night stille lay he,
    Til amorwe men might yse
    The day bi ich a side.
    Than was his brother, Sir Amiloun,
    Holden a lord of gret renoun
1005 Over al that cuntre wide;
    And woned fro thennes that he lay
    Bot half a jorne of a day,
    Noither to go no ride.

    As Sir Amiloun, that hendi knight,
1010 In his slepe he lay that night,
    In sweven he mett anon   *dream, dreamed*
    That he seighe Sir Amis bi sight,
    His brother that was trewethe plight,
    Bilapped among his fon: *Surrounded by his enemies*
1015 Thurch a bere wilde and wode,   *By, bear, fierce, raging*
    And other bestes that bi him stode,[n]
    Bisett he was to slon;   *He was harried to death*
    And he alon among hem stode,

988 He fastened up the skirts of his surcoat then.
994 He was so overcome by sleep.
1001-2 i.e. until it was daylight the following morning.
1007 No more than half a day's journey.
1008 i.e. whether on foot or on horseback.

As a man that couthe no gode –   *i.e. was in despair*
1020 Wel wo was him bigon!   *He was indeed oppressed by sorrow*

When Sir Amiloun was awake,
Gret sorwe he gan for him make,
And told his wiif ful yare   *at once*
Hou him thought he seighe bestes blake
025 About his brother, with wrake   *violence*
To sle with sorwe and care.   *kill (him)*
'Certes,' he seyd, 'with sum wrong,   *through some injustice*
He is in peril gret and strong;
Of blis he is ful bare.'   *He is quite bereft of joy*
030 And than seyd he, 'Forsothe, ywis,
Y no schal never have joie no blis
Til y wite hou he fare.'

As swithe he stirt up in that tide;   *Thereupon, leapt*
Ther nold he no leng abide,   *no longer stay*
035 Bot dight him forth anon.   *set out at once*
And al his meine, bi ich a side,   *retinue, on every side*
Busked hem redi to ride,   *Made themselves ready*
With her lord for to gon.   *their*
And he bad al that ther wes,
040 For Godes love, held hem stille in pes –
He bad hem so, ichon;
And swore bi him that schop mankende   *created*
Ther schuld no man with him wende,
Bot himself alon.

45 Ful richeliche he gan him schrede,   *equip*
And lepe as tite opon his stede –   *at once*
For nothing he nold abide.
Al his folk he gan forbede,
That non so hardi were of dede   *forbid*
50 After him noither go no ride.   *bold*
So al that night he rode til day,
Til he com ther Sir Amis lay,

1032 Until I know what has become of him.
1040 For the love of God, to remain quietly where they were.
1041 ichon] ich chon A.

Up in that forest wide.
Than seighe he a weri knight forgon   *exhausted*
1055 Under a tre slepeand alon;   *sleeping*
To him he went that tide.

He cleped to him anonright,   *immediately*
'Arise up, felawe! It is light,
And time for to go!'
1060 Sir Amis biheld up with his sight,   *i.e. looked up*
And knewe anon that gentil knight,   *at once recognized*
And he knewe him also.
That hendi knight, Sir Amiloun,
Of his stede light adoun,   *dismounted*
1065 And kist hem bothe to.   *And the two kissed each other*
'Brother,' he seyd, 'whi listow here,   *are you lying*
With thus mornand chere?   *such a sorrowful countenance*
Who hath wrought the this wo?'   *caused*

'Brother,' seyd Sir Amis tho,
1070 'Ywis, me nas never so wo
Seththen that y was born!   *Since*
For seththen that thou was went me fro,   *you left me*
With joie and michel blis also
Y served mi lord biforn;   *in the presence of my lord*
1075 Ac the steward, ful of envie,   *malice*
With gile and with trecherie,
He hath me wrought swiche sorn,   *distress*
Bot thou help me at this nede,   *Unless*
Certes, y can no nother rede:
1080 Mi liif it is forlorn.'

'Brother,' seyd Sir Amiloun,
'Whi hath the steward, that feloun,   *villain*
Ydon the al this schame?'   *Done/Brought, disgrace*
'Certes,' he seyd, 'with gret tresoun
1085 He wald me driven al adoun,
And hath me brought in blame.'   *disgrace/injury*
Than told Sir Amis al that cas: *case*

1079 Certainly, I do not know what else to do.
1085 He wishes to destroy me utterly.

Hou he and that maiden was
Bothe togider ysame,   *together in company*
1090 And hou the steward gan hem wrain,   *betray*
And hou the douke wald him have slain,
With wretthe and michel grame.

And also he seyd, yplight,   *assuredly*
Hou he had boden on him fight,   *challenged him to fight*
1095 Batail of him to fong;   *with, undertake*
And hou in court was ther no wight,
To save tho tvai levedis bright,   *(In order) to*
Durst ben his borwe among;   *Dared, at that time (?)*
And hou he most, withouten faile,
1100 Swere ar he went to bataile:
'It war a lesing ful strong;
And forsworn man schal never spede;   *perjured, prosper*
Certes, therfore, y can no rede –
"Allas" may be mi song!'

1105 When that Sir Amis had al told –
Hou that the fals steward wold
Bring him doun with mode –   *anger*
Sir Amiloun, with wordes bold,
Swore bi him that Judas sold   *i.e. who was sold by Judas*
1110 And died opon the rode,
'Of his hope he schal now faile;
And y schal for the take bataile.   *on your behalf*
Thei that he wer wode,   *Even if, mad*
Yif y may mete him aright,[n]
1115 With mi brond, that is so bright,   *sword*
Y schal sen his hert blode.

'Ac, brother,' he seyd, 'have al mi wede,   *clothes*
And in thi robe y schal me schrede,   *attire*
Right as theself it ware.   *Just as though I were you*
1120 And y schal swere, so God me spede,
As icham giltles of that dede
That he opon the bare.'[n]   *Of which he has accused you*

1101 It would be a very grievous falsehood.
1111 He shall be disappointed now of his hope.

Anon tho hendi knightes to
Alle her wede chaunged tho.
1125 And when thai were al yare,   *ready*
Than seyd Sir Amiloun, 'Bi Seyn Gile,
Thus man schal the schrewe bigile
That wald the forfare!

'Brother,' he seyd, 'wende hom now right   *at once*
1130 To mi levedi, that is so bright,
And do as y schal the sain;
And, as thou art a gentil knight,
Thou ly bi hir in bed ich night
Til that y com ogain;   *come back*
1135 And sai thou hast sent thi stede, ywis,
To thi brother, Sir Amis.
Than wil thai be ful fain;   *i.e. Amiloun's household*
Thai wil wene that ich it be;   *think*
Ther is non that schal knowe the,   *recognize*
1140 So liche we be, bothe tvain.'   *alike*

And when he hadde thus sayd, yplight,
Sir Amiloun, that gentil knight,
Went in his jurnay.
And Sir Amis went hom anonright
1145 To his brother levedi so bright,
Withouten more delay,
And seyd hou he hadde sent his stede
To his brother, to riche mede,   *as a fine gift*
Bi a knight of that cuntray.
1150 And al thai wende of Sir Amis   *believed as regards Sir Amis*
It had ben her lord, ywis,
So liche were tho tvay.

When that Sir Amis hadde, ful yare,
Told him al of his care,
1155 Ful wele he wend tho,
Litel and michel, lasse and mare,
Al that ever in court ware,
Thai thought it hadde ben so.[n]

1127–8 Thus the blackguard who wants to destroy you will be deceived.

And when it was comen to the night,
1160 Sir Amis and that levedi bright
To bed thai gan go.
And when thai were togider ylayd,
Sir Amis his swerd out braid,   *drew*
And layd bitvix hem tvo.[n]   *laid it between them*

1165 The levedi loked opon him tho
Wrothlich, with her eighen tvo;   *Angrily, eyes*
Sche wend hir lord were wode.
'Sir,' sche seyd, 'whi farstow so?   *i.e. what are you doing*
Thus were thou nought won to do.
1170 Who hath changed thi mode?'   *your feelings*
'Dame,' he seyd, 'sikerly,   *certainly*
Ich have swiche a malady,
That mengeth al mi blod;
And al min bones be so sare,   *sore*
1175 Y nold nought touche thi bodi bare,   *I would not wish to*
For al this warldes gode.'[n]

Thus, ywis, that hendy knight
Was holden in that fourtennight   *regarded*
As lord and prince in pride.   *splendour*
1180 Ac he foryat him never a night –
Bitvix him and that levedi bright
His swerd he layd biside.
The levedi thought in hir resoun   *mind*
It hadde ben hir lord, Sir Amiloun,
1185 That hadde ben sike that tide.
Therfore sche held hir stille tho,
And wold speke wordes no mo,   *held her peace*
Bot thought his wille to abide.   *more*

Now, hende, herkneth, and y schal say   *listen*
1190 Hou that Sir Amiloun went his way –
For nothing wold he spare.
He priked his stede night and day,   *spurred*

1169 It was never your habit to do so.
1172-3 I have such an illness that it afflicts all my blood.
1180 But he never forgot on any night.
1188 But decided to submit to his wish.

As a gentil knight, stout and gay.   *stalwart, finely clad*
To court he com ful yare   *soon*
1195 That selve day, withouten fail,   *The very day*
That was ysett of batail;   *appointed for*
And Sir Amis was nought thare.
Than were tho levedis taken bi hond,
Her juggement to understond,   *trial, undergo*
1200 With sorwe and sikeing sare.   *bitter sighing*

The steward hoved opon a stede,   *waited*
With scheld and spere bataile to bede;   *offer*
Gret bost he gan to blawe.
Bifor the douke anon he yede,
1205 And seyd, 'Sir, so God the spede,
Herken to mi sawe!   *Listen to what I have to say*
This traitour is out of lond ywent;
Yif he were here in present,
He schuld ben hong and drawe.
1210 Therefore ich aske jugement   *I ask that the verdict be*
That his borwes be to-brent,   *burned*
As it is londes lawe.'

That riche douke, with wretthe and wrake,
He bad men schuld tho levedis take
1215 And lede hem forth biside.
A strong fer ther was don make,   *fire, was made there*
And a tonne for her sake,ⁿ   *barrel, their*
To bren hem in that tide.   *burn*
Than thai loked into the feld,
1220 And seighe a knight with spere and scheld
Com prikeand ther with pride.   *riding*
Than seyd thai everichon, ywis,
'Yonder cometh prikeand Sir Amis!'
And bad thai schuld abide.   *wait*

1225 Sir Amiloun gan stint at no ston;
He priked among hem everichon;
To that douke he gan wende.

1203 i.e. he began to behave very boastfully/to swagger.
1225 Sir Amiloun did not stop (*literally*, stopped at no stone).

'Mi lord the douke,' he seyd anon,
'For schame! Lete tho levedis gon,
1230 That er bothe gode and hende.   *are*
   For icham comen hider today   *hither*
   For to saven hem, yive y may,   *if*
   And bring hem out of bende.   *captivity*
   For, certes, it were michel unright   *a great wrong*
1235 To make roste of levedis bright — ⁿ   *a roast*
   Ywis, ye eren unkende!'   *you are callous*

   Than ware tho levedis glad and blithe;
   Her joie couthe thai no man kithe;
   Her care was al oway.   *had all departed*
1240 And seththen, as ye may list and lithe,   *listen and hear*
   Into the chaumber thai went aswithe,   *at once*
   Withouten more delay.
   And richeliche thai schred that knight,   *equipped*
   With helme and plate and brini bright —
1245 His tire it was ful gay.   *He was very finely clad*
   And when he was opon his stede,
   That God him schuld save and spede   *give success*
   Mani man bad that day.   *prayed*

   As he com prikand out of toun,
1250 Com a voice fram heven adoun,   *down*
   That no man herd bot he,   *except*
   Say, 'Thou knight, Sir Amiloun,
   God that suffred passioun
   Sent the bode bi me: *a warning*
1255 Yif thou this bataile underfong,   *undertake*
   Thou schalt have an eventour strong
   Within this yeres thre;
   And or this thre yere ben al gon,   *the next three years*
   Fouler mesel nas never non   *before*
1260 In the world than thou schal be.

   'Ac, for thou art so hende and fre,
   Jhesu sent the bode bi me

1244 With helmet and breastplate and bright chain-mail.
1256 i.e. something grave will happen to you.
1259 There was never a more hideous leper.

To warn the anon.
So foule a wreche thou schalt be,
1265 With sorwe and care and poverte,
Nas never non wers bigon   *worse afflicted*
Over al this world, fer and hende.   *near*
Tho that be thine best frende   *Those*
Schal be thi most fon;   *greatest enemies*
1270 And thi wiif and alle thi kinne
Schul fle the stede thatow art inne   *place where you are*
And forsake the, ichon.'[n]   *abandon*

That knight gan hove stille so ston,   *paused, as still as*
And herd tho wordes, everichon,
1275 That were so gret and grille.   *terrible*
He nist what him was best to don –   *did not know*
To flen other to fighting gon.   *flee or*
In hert him liked ille!   *he was ill-pleased*
He thought, 'Yif y beknowe mi name,[n]   *make known*
1280 Than schal mi brother go to schame –   *be disgraced*
With sorwe thai schul him spille.   *Piteously, destroy*
Certes,' he seyd, 'for drede of care,
To hold mi treuthe schal y nought spare –
Lete God don alle his wille!'

1285 Al the folk ther was, ywis,   *who were there*
Thai wend it had ben Sir Amis
That bataile schuld bede.   *Who was going to offer battle*
He and the steward of pris   *renown*
Were brought bifor the justise   *judicial assembly*
1290 To swere for that dede.[n]
The steward swore the pople among   *before the people*
As wis as he seyd no wrong,   *surely*
God help him at his nede.
And Sir Amiloun swore and gan to say
1295 As wis as he never kist that may,
Our Levedi schuld him spede.

When thai hadde sworn as y you told,
To biker tho bernes were ful bold,   *fight, warriors*

1283 I shall not fail, through fear of any affliction, to keep my word.
1290 To take their oaths in that matter.

     And busked hem for to ride.   *made themselves ready*
1300 Al that ther was, yong and old,
     Bisought God, yif that he wold,
     Help Sir Amis that tide.
     On stedes that were stithe and strong   *hardy*
     Thai riden togider, with schaftes long,   *spears*
1305 Til thai to-schiverd bi ich a side.   *shattered*
     And than drough thai swerdes gode   *drew*
     And hewe togider as thai were wode —   *struck at each other*
     For nothing thai nold abide.   *desist*

     Tho gomes, that were egre of fight,   *men, fierce in battle*
1310 With fauchouns felle thai gun to fight,   *swords, cruel*
     And ferd as thai were wode.   *behaved as if*
     So hard thai hewe on helmes bright,   *struck*
     With strong strokes of michel might,
     That fer biforn out stode.   *i.e. sparks flew out*
1315 So hard thai hewe on helme and side,   *struck*
     Thurch dent of grimly woundes wide,
     That thai sprad al of blod.
     Fram morwe to none, withouten faile,   *morning*
     Bitvixen hem last the bataile,   *lasted*
1320 So egre thai were of mode.   *fierce*

     Sir Amiloun, as fer of flint,   *like fire from flint*
     With wretthe anon to him he wint,   *went*
     And smot a stroke with main.   *struck a blow, strength*
     Ac he failed of his dint —   *i.e. he missed his aim*
1325 The stede in the heved he hint   *head, struck*
     And smot out al his brain.[n]
     The stede fel ded doun to grounde;
     Tho was the steward that stounde   *at that time*
     Ful ferd he schuld be slain.   *Much afraid*
1330 Sir Amiloun light adoun of his stede;
     To the steward afot he yede,   *on foot*
     And halp him up ogain.   *helped*

     'Arise up, steward!' he seyd anon.
     'To fight thou schalt afot gon,

1316–17 That, through the blows of terrible and deep wounds, they were all covered in blood.

1335 For thou hast lorn thi stede.   *lost*
     For it were gret vilani, bi Seyn Jon,
     A liggeand man for to slon,   *fallen (literally, lying)*
     That were yfallen in nede.'
     The knight was ful fre to fond,   *noble indeed*
1340 And tok the steward bi the hond,
     And seyd, 'So God me spede,
     Thow thou schalt afot go,
     Y schal fight afot also,   *Although*
     And elles were gret falshed!'ⁿ   *unfairness*

1345 The steward and that douhti man,
     Anon togider thai fight gan
     With brondes bright and bare.   *swords*
     So hard togider thai fight than
     Til al her armour o blod ran —   *streamed with blood*
1350 For nothing nold thai spare.
     The steward smot to him that stounde
     On his schulder a gret wounde
     With his grimly gare,   *terrible spear*
     That thurch that wounde, as ye may here,   *by means of*
1355 He was knowen with reweli chere   *in a wretched state*
     When he was fallen in care.ⁿ

     Than was Sir Amiloun wroth and wode,
     Whan al his armour ran o blode,
     That ere was white so swan.   *formerly*
1360 With a fauchoun scharp and gode
     He s[mo]t to him with egre mode,
     Also a douhti man,   *Like*
     That even fro the schulder blade   *right from*
     Into the brest the brond gan wade —   *cleave/go*
1365 Thurchout his hert it ran.
     The steward fel adoun ded;
     Sir Amiloun strok of his hed,   *struck off*
     And God he thonked it than.   *thanked (for) it*

     Alle the lordinges that ther ware,
1370 Litel and michel, lasse and mare,

     1361 smot] somt A.

Ful glad thai were that tide.
The heved opon a spere thai bare;[n]   *carried*
To toun thai dight hem ful yare –   *set out*
For nothing thai nold abide.
375 Thai com oyaines him out of toun   *to meet*
With a fair processioun,
Semliche bi ich a side.   *Splendid in every way*
Anon thai ladde him to the tour   *led*
With joie and ful michel honour,
380 As prince proude in pride.

Into the palais when thai were gon,
Al that was in that worthli won
Wende Sir Amis it ware.
'Sir Amis,' seyd the douke anon,
385 'Bifor this lordinges, everichon,
Y graunt the ful yare.   *I grant you most readily*
For Belisent, that miri may,
Thou hast bought hir ful dere today,
With grimli woundes sare:
390 Therfore y graunt the now here
Mi lond and mi douhter dere,
To hald for evermare.'

Ful blithe was that hendi knight,
And thonked him with al his might;
395 Glad he was and fain.
In alle the court was ther no wight
That wist wat his name it hight,   *knew what his name was*
To save tho levedis tvain.   *Apart from*
Leches swithe thai han yfounde,   *Physicians*
400 That gun to tasty his wounde   *probe*
And made him hole again.   *whole/well*
Than were thai al glad and blithe,
And thonked God a thousand sithe   *times*
That the steward was slain.[n]

405 On a day Sir Amiloun dight him yare,
And seyd that he wold fare
Hom into his cuntray,
To telle his frendes, lasse and mare,

And other lordinges that there ware
1410 Hou he had sped that day.   *fared*
The douke graunted him that tide,
And bede him knightes and miche pride,   *offered, splendour*
And he answerd, 'Nay':
Ther schuld no man with him gon;
1415 Bot as swithe him dight anon,
And went forth in his way.

In his way he went alone –
Most ther no man with him gon,   *Might*
Noither knight no swain.
1420 That douhti knight of blod and bon,
No stint he never at no ston
Til he com hom ogain.
And Sir Amis, as y you say,
Waited his coming everi day   *Awaited*
1425 Up in the forest plain.[n]
And so thai mett togider same,   *together in company*
And he teld him, with joie and game,
Hou he hadde the steward slain;

And hou he schuld spousy to mede   *marry as a reward*
1430 That ich maide, worthli in wede,   *same*
That was so comly corn.   *beautiful indeed*
Sir Amiloun light of his stede,
And gan to chaungy her wede,   *(they) began*
As thai hadde don biforn.
1435 'Brother,' he seyd, 'wende hom ogain.'
And taught him hou he schuld sain,   *what he should say*
When he com ther thai worn.
Than was Sir Amis glad and blithe,
And thanked him a thousand sithe
1440 The time that he was born.[n]

And when thai schuld wende ato,
Sir Amis oft thonked him tho
His cost and his gode dede.   *trouble*
'Brother,' he seyd, 'yif it bi[falle] so   *happen*

1420 That knight stalwart of body.
1444 bifalle] bitide A. (Cf. line 235.)

1445 That the bitide care other wo   *befall you*
    And of min help hast nede,
    Savelich com, other sende thi sond,   *confidently, or, message*
    And y schal never lenger withstond,   *refuse*
    Also God me spede!
1450 Be it in periil never so strong,   *However great the danger*
    Y schal the help in right and wrong,
    Mi liif to lese to mede.'

    Asonder than thai gun wende.[n]   *Their separate ways*
    Sir Amiloun, that knight so hende,
1455 Went hom in that tide
    To his levedi, that was unkende,
    And was ful welcome to his frende,
    As prince proude in pride.
    And when it was comen to the night,
1460 Sir Amiloun and that levedi bright
    In bedde were layd biside: *beside (each other)*
    In his armes he gan hir kis,
    And made hir joie and michel blis –   *gave*
    For nothing he nold abide.

1465 The levedi, as tite, asked him tho   *at once*
    Whi that he hadde farn so   *behaved*
    Al that fourtennight –
    Laid his swerd bitven hem to,
    That sche no durst nought, for wele no wo,
1470 Touche his bodi aright.
    Sir Amiloun bithought him than
    His brother was a trewe man,
    That hadde so done, aplight.   *assuredly*
    'Dame,' he seyd, 'ichil the sain,   *I will tell you*
1475 And telle the that sothe ful fain;   *the truth, gladly*
    Ac wray me to no wight.'   *But betray*

    The levedi, as tite, him frain gan,   *ask*
    For his love that this warld wan,   *redeemed/saved*
    Telle hir whi it ware.   *why it was*
1480 Than, as tite, that hendy man

1452 Even if I lose my life by way of reward.

Al the sothe he teld hir than –   *told*
To court hou he gan fare;
And hou he slough the steward strong,
That, with tresoun and with wrong,
1485 Wold have his brother forfare;   *destroyed*
And hou his brother, that hendy knight,
Lay with hir in bed ich night
While that he was thare.

The levedi was ful wroth, yplight,
1490 And oft missayd hir lord that night   *abused*
With speche bitvix hem to,
And seyd, 'With wrong and michel unright
Thou slough ther a gentil knight –
Ywis, it was ivel ydo!'   *evilly done*
1495 'Dame,' he seyd, 'bi heven king,
Y no dede it for non other thing   *did*
Bot to save mi brother fro wo.
And ich hope yif ich hadde nede,   *hope/expect*
His owhen liif to lesse to mede,
1500 He wald help me also.'ⁿ

Al thus in gest as we sain,
Sir Amis was ful glad and fain;
To court he gan to wende.
And when he com to court oyain,
1505 With erl, baroun, knight and swain
Honourd he was, that hende.
That riche douke tok him bi hond,
And sesed him in alle his lond,ⁿ   *put him in possession of*
To held withouten ende.   *in perpetuity*
1510 And seththen, with joie, opon a day
He spoused Belisent, that may,
That was so trewe and kende.ⁿ

Miche was that semly folk in sale,   *Great (in number), hall*
That was samned at that bridale,   *assembled*
1515 When he hadde spoused that flour,   *flower*
Of erls, barouns, mani and fale,
And other lordinges, gret and smale,
And levedis bright in bour.

A real fest thai gan to hold,   royal/splendid
1520 Of erls and of barouns bold,
With joie and michel honour.
Over al that lond, est and west,
Than was Sir Amis helden the best,
And chosen for priis in tour.   distinguished, merit

1525 So, within tho yeres to,   two
A wel fair grace fel hem tho,   favourable chance, befell
As God Almighti wold:
The riche douke dyed hem fro,
And his levedi dede also,
1530 And graven in grete so cold.   (they were) buried in earth
Than was Sir Amis, hende and fre,
Douke and lord of gret pouste   power
Over al that lond yhold.
Tvai childer he biyat bi his wive —   begot
1535 The fairest that might bere live,   might live
In gest as it is told.[n]

Than was that knight of gret renoun,
And lord of mani a tour and toun,
And douke of gret pouste.
1540 And his brother, Sir Amiloun,
With sorwe and care was driven adoun,   oppressed
That ere was hende and fre.   before
Also that angel hadde him told,   Just as
Fouler messel thar nas non hold   More hideous, leper
1545 In world than was he.
In gest to rede it is gret rewthe   very piteous
What sorwe he hadde for his treuthe,   (in return) for
Within tho yeres thre.

And, er tho thre yere com to th'ende,
1550 He no wist whider he might wende,   did not know whither
So wo was him bigon;   He was so oppressed by sorrow
For al that were his best frende,
And nameliche al his riche kende,   especially, kindred
Bicom his most fon;   greatest enemies
1555 And his wiif, forsothe to say,   truly
Wrought him wers, bothe night and day,   Treated

Than thai dede, everichon.
When him was fallen that hard cas,   befallen, harsh plight
A frendeleser man than he was   more friendless
1560 Men nist nowhar non.   did not know

So wicked and schrewed was his wiif,   depraved
Sche brac his hert withouten kniif,
With wordes hard and kene;   sharp
And seyd to him, 'Thou wreche chaitif!   vile scoundrel
1565 With wrong the steward les his liif,   lost
And that is on the sene.
Therfore, bi Seyn Denis of Fraunce,[n]   On that account
The is bitid this hard chaunce –
Dathet who the bimene!'[n]
1570 Wel ofttimes his honden he wrong,   Very often
As man that thenketh his liif to long,
That liveth in treye and tene.   affliction and distress

Allas, allas! That gentil knight,
That whilom was so wise and wight,   once, strong
1575 That than was wrought so wo,   brought into such sorrow
That fram his levedi, fair and bright,
Out of his owhen chaumber anight   own, at night
He was yhote to go.   commanded
And in his owhen halle, o day,   one day
1580 Fram the heighe bord oway   high table
He was ycharged also,   ordered
To eten at the tables ende;[n]
Wald ther no man sit him hende –   near
Wel careful was he tho!   sorrowful

1585 Bi than that half-yere was ago   By the time that
That he hadde eten in halle so,
With gode mete and with drink,
His levedi wa[x] ful wroth and wo,   grew
And thought he lived to long tho,   too long

1566 i.e. the injustice of that is apparent from the punishment you have received.
1568 This harsh lot has befallen you.
1569 Cursed be he who laments for you!
1588 wax] *thus* S D; war A.

1590 Withouten ani lesing.   *deceit (i.e. I do not lie)*
   'In this lond springeth this word:
   Y fede a mesel at mi bord.   *leper, table*
   He is so foule a thing,
   It is gret spite to al mi kende;   *disgrace, kindred*
1595 He schal no more sitt me so hende,   *near*
   Bi Jhesus, heven king!'

   On a day sche gan him calle,
   And seyd, 'Sir, it is so bifalle –
   Forsothe, y telle it te –
1600 That thou etest so long in halle,   *to you*
   It is gret spite to ous alle:
   Mi kende is wroth with me.'[n]   *insult*
   The knight gan wepe, and seyd ful stille,   *quietly*
   'Do me where it is thi wille,   *Put*
1605 Ther noman may me se.   *Where*
   Of no more ichil the praye
   Bot of a meles mete ich day,
   For Seynt Charite!'[n]

   That levedi, for hir lordes sake,
1610 Anon sche dede men timber take –   *had men fetch timber*
   For nothing wold sche wond –   *desist*
   And half a mile fram the gate
   A litel loge sche lete make,   *lodge, had made*
   Biside the way to stond.[n]
1615 And when the loge was al wrought,   *built*
   Of his gode no wold he noght
   Bot his gold coupe an hond.
   When he was in his loge alon,
   To God of heven he made his mon,
1620 And thonked him of al his sond.[n]   *For, providence*

   Into that loge when he was dight,   *settled*
   In al the court was ther no wight
   That wold serve him thare,

1591 i.e. this rumour is rife.
1606–7 I will ask no more of you than food sufficient for a meal each day.
1616–17 He would (take) nothing of his wealth except his gold cup in his hand.

To save a gentil child, yplight: *Apart from, youth*
1625 Child Owaines his name it hight;   *was called*
For him he wepe ful sare.
That child was trewe and of his kende: *kindred*
His soster sone he was, ful hende.[n]   *sister's*
He sayd to hem ful yare,   *readily*
1630 Ywis, he no schuld never wond   *cease*
To serven him, fro fot to hond,   *hand and foot*
While he olives ware.   *was alive*

That child, that was so fair and bold,
Owaines was his name ytold;   *called*
1635 Wel fair he was of blode.   *by nature*
When he was of tvelve yere old,
Amoraunt than was he cald,[n]   *called*
Wel curteys, hende and gode.
Bi his lord ich night he lay,
1640 And feched her livere ever[i] day,[n]   *allowance of food*
To her lives fode.   *essential*
When ich man made gle and song,[n]
Ever for his lord among   *For his lord continually*
He made dreri mode.   *i.e. He showed his sorrow*

1645 Thus Amoraunt, as y you say,
Com to court ich day —
No stint he for no strive.   *opposition*
Al that ther was gan him pray
To com fro that lazer oway:
1650 Than schuld he the and thrive.   *prosper and thrive*
And he answerd, with milde mode,   *gently*
And swore bi him that dyed on rode
And tholed woundes five,[n]   *suffered*
For al this worldes gode to take,
1655 His lord nold he never forsake
Whiles he ware olive.

Bi than the twelmoneth was al gon,
Amorant went into that won   *i.e. Amiloun's castle*
For his lordes liveray.   *allowance of food*

1640 everi] euer A.

1660 The levedi was ful wroth anon,
     And comaunde hir men, everichon,
     To drive that child oway;[n]
     And swore bi him that Judas sold,
     Thei his lord for hunger and cold   *Even if*
1665 Dyed ther he lay,
     He schuld have noither mete no drink,
     No socour of non other thing,
     For hir, after that day.

     That child wrong his honden tvain,
1670 And weping went hom ogain,
     With sorwe and sikeing sare.   *sighing*
     That gode man gan him frain,   *ask*
     And bad him that he schuld him sain   *begged*
     And telle him whi it ware.
1675 And he answerd and seyd tho,
     'Ywis, no wonder thei me be wo –
     Mine hert it breketh for care.
     Thi wiif hath [sw]orn, with gret mode,   *anger*
     That sche no schal never don ous gode.
1680 Allas! Hou schal we fare?'

     'A, God help!' seyd that gentil knight.
     'Whilom y was man of might,   *Once*
     To dele mete and cloth;   *distribute (as alms)*
     And now icham so foule a wight
1685 That al that seth on me bi sight,
     Mi liif is hem ful loth.
     Sone,' he seyd, 'lete thi wepeing,   *leave off*
     For this is now a strong tiding,   *distressing news*
     That may we se, forsoth.
1690 For, certes, y can non other red:
     Ous bihoveth to bid our brede,
     Now y wot hou it goth.'

1667–8 Nor any other sort of assistance, if she could help it, after that day.
1676 Indeed, it is no wonder if I am sorrowful.
1678 sworn] wrorn A.
1686 My existence is very hateful to them.
1690–2 For, certainly, I do not know what else to do: we shall have to beg for our food, now I know how matters stand.

Amorwe, as tite as it was light,   *Next morning, as soon*
The child and that gentil knight
1695 Dight hem for to gon.   *Made themselves ready*
And in her way thai went ful right   *at once*
To begge her brede, as thai hadde tight,   *decided*
For mete no hadde thai none.
So long thai went up and doun,
1700 Til thai com to a chepeing toun,   *market town*
Five mile out of that won;
And, sore wepeand, fro dore to dore,
[Thai] bad her mete for Godes love –
Ful ivel couthe thai theron!

1705 So in that time, ich understond,
Gret plente was in that lond,
Bothe of mete and drink;
That folk was ful fre to fond,
And brought hem anough to hond   *plenty*
1710 Of al kines thing.   *Of all kinds of things*
For the gode man was so messais tho,   *Because, afflicted*
And for the child was so fair also,
Hem loved old and ying,   *young*
And brought hem anough of al gode.
1715 Than was the child blithe of mode,
And lete be his wepeing.

Than wex the gode man fete so sare   *became, sore*
That he no might no forther fare,   *could walk no further*
For al this worldes gode.
1720 To the tounes ende that child him bare,
And a loge he bilt him thare
As folk to chepeing yode.   *Where, market*
And al that folk of that cuntray
Com to chepeing everi day,
1725 Thai gat hem lives fode;
And Amoraunt oft to toun gan go,
And begged hem mete and drink also,
When hem most nede at stode.   *When they were most in need*

1701 i.e. five miles from Amiloun's castle.
1703 Thai bad] & bad A; To begge S D.
1704 That came very hard to them.
1708 The (local) people proved most generous.

Thus in gest rede we:	*story*
1730 Thai duelled there yeres thre,	
That child and he also,	
And lived, in care and poverte,	
Bi the folk of that cuntre,	*Through (the generosity of)*
As thai com to and fro;	
1735 So that, in the ferth yere,	*Until, fourth*
Corn bigan to wex dere,	*become expensive*
That hunger bigan to go,	*spread*
That ther was noither eld no ying	
That wald yif hem mete no drink –	
1740 Wel careful were thai tho!	

Amorant oft to toun gan gon,	
Ac mete no drink no gat he non,	
Noither at man no wive.	*From neither man nor woman*
When thai were togider alon,	
1745 Reweliche thai gan maken her mon –	*Pitifully*
Wo was hem olive!	
And his levedi, forsothe to say,	
Woned ther in that cuntray,	
Nought thennes miles five,	*thence*
1750 And lived in joie, bothe night and day,	
Whiles he in sorwe and care lay –	
Wel ivel mot sche thrive![n]	

On a day, as thai sete alon,	
That hendi knight gan m[a]ken his mon,	
1755 And seyd to the child that tide:	
'Sone,' he seyd, 'thou most gon	
To mi levedi swithe anon,	*immediately*
That woneth here biside:	*nearby*
Bid her, for him that died on rode,	*Beg*
1760 Sende me so michel of al mi gode –	
An asse on to ride;	
And out of lond we wil fare,	
To begge our mete with sorwe and care –	
No lenger we nil abide.'	*stay (here)*

1746 Cf. line 756.
1752 May ill fortune be hers!
1754 maken] meken A.
1760 Send me thus much of all my property.

1765 Amoraunt to court is went,
Bifor that levedi fair and gent;
Wel hendeliche seyd hir anon: *courteously, he said to her*
'Madame,' he seyd, 'verrament,
As mensanger mi lord me sent,
1770 For himself may nought gon,
And praieste, with milde mode,
Sende him so michel of al his gode
As an asse to riden opon;
And out of lond we schulen yfere –   *(go) together*
1775 No schal we never com eft here,   *again*
Thei hunger ous schuld slon.'

The levedi seyd sche wald ful fain
Sende him gode asses tvain,
With thi he wald oway go   *Provided that*
1780 So fer that he never eft com ogain.   *far*
'Nay, certes, dame!' the child gan sain.
'Thou sest ous never eft mo.'   *will see*
Than was the levedi glad and blithe,
And comaund him an asse as swithe,
1785 And seyd with wretthe tho,
'Now ye schul out of lond fare –
God leve you never to com here mare,
And graunt that it be so!'

That child no lenger nold abide;
1790 His asse as tite he gan bistride,   *at once*
And went him hom ogain;
And told his lord in that tide
Hou his levedi, proude in pride,
Schameliche gan to sain.   *Shamefully*
1795 Opon the asse he sett that knight so hende,
And out of the cite thai gun wende –
Therof thai were ful fain.
Thurch mani a cuntre, up an doun,
Thai begged her mete fram toun to toun,
1800 Bothe in winde and rain.

1776 Even if hunger kills us.
1787 God forbid that you ever come here again.

Over al that lond, thurch Godes wille,
That hunger wex so gret and g[r]ille,   *terrible*
As wide as thai gun go,   *However far they went*
Almest for hunger thai gan to spille;   *perish*
1805 Of brede thai no hadde nought half her fille —
Ful careful were thai tho!
Than seyd the knight, opon a day,
'Ous bihoveth selle our asse oway,   *We shall have to*
For we no have gode no mo,
1810 Save mi riche coupe of gold;   *Except*
Ac, certes, that schal never be sold,
Thei hunger schuld me slo.'ⁿ

Than Amoraunt and Sir Amiloun,
With sorwe and care and reweful roun,   *pitiful speech*
1815 Erliche in a mor[n]ing,
Thai went hem til a chepeing toun.
And when the knight was light adoun,
Withouten ani duelling,   *delay*
Amoraunt went to toun tho;
1820 His asse he ladde with him also,
And sold it for five schilling.
And while that derth was so strong,   *famine*
Therwith thai bought hem mete among,
When thai might gete nothing.

1825 And when her asse was ysold
For five schilling, as y you told,
Thai duelled ther dayes thre.
Amoraunt wex strong and bold;
Of fiftene winter was he old,
1830 Curtays, hende and fre.
For his lord he hadde grete care,
And at his rigge he dight him yare,
And bare him out of that cite.
And half a yere, and sumdel mare,   *somewhat*

1802 grille] gille A.
1815 morning] moring A.
1823–4 The sense is apparently that they were always (*among*) able to buy food
with the five shillings when they were unable to get alms.
1832 And he put him (*literally*, made him ready) on his back.

1835 About his mete he him bare —   *i.e. In search of food*
      Yblisced mot he be!

      Thus Amoraunt, withouten wrong,
      Bar his lord about so long,
      As y you tel may,
1840 That winter com, so hard and strong,
      Oft 'Allas!' it was his song,   *(That) often*
      So depe was that cuntray.   *muddy*
      The way was so depe and slider,   *slippery*
      Ofttimes bothe togider
1845 Thai fel doun in the clay.   *mud*
      Ful trewe he was and kinde of blod,   *noble by nature*
      And served his lord with mild mode —
      Wald he nought wende oway.

      Thus Amoraunt, as y you say,
1850 Served his lord, bothe night and day,
      And at his rigge him bare.   *on his back*
      Oft his song was 'Waileway!';
      So depe was that cuntray,
      His bones wex ful sare.
1855 Al her catel than was spent,   *property*
      Save tvelf pans, verrament;   *pence*
      Therwith thai went ful yare,
      And bought hem a gode croude-wain;   *push-cart*
      His lord he gan therin to lain —
1860 He no might him bere na mare.

      Than Amoraunt crud Sir Amiloun   *pushed*
      Thurch mani a cuntre, up and doun,
      As ye may understond.[n]
      So he com to a cite toun,
1865 Ther Sir Amis, the bold baroun,
      Was douke and lord in lond.
      Than seyd the knight, in that tide,
      'To the doukes court, here biside,
      To bring me thider thou fond.   *try*
1870 He is a man of milde mode;

      1836 Blessings upon him!

We schul gete ous ther sum gode,
Thurch grace of Godes sond.   *providence*

'Ac, leve sone,' he seyd than,   *dear son*
'For his love that this world wan,
1875 Astow art hende and fre,
Thou [m]e aknowe to no man –
Whider y schal, no whenes y cam,
No what mi name it be.'
He answerd and seyd, 'Nay!'[n]
1880 To court he went in his way,
As ye may listen at me,
And, bifor al other pover men,   *in front of*
He crud his wain into the fen –   *pushed, cart, mire*
Gret diol it was to se!'[n]   *sorrow/pity*

1885 So it bifel, that selve day,   *same*
With tong as y you tel may,
It was midwinter tide;
That riche douke, with gamen and play,
Fram chirche com the right way,   *direct*
1890 As lord and prince with pride.
When he com to the castel gate,
The pover men that stode therate
Withdrough hem ther beside.   *Drew aside*
With knightes and with serjaunce fale,   *attendants, many*
1895 He went into that semly sale,   *fine hall*
With joie and blis to abide.   *remain*

In kinges court, as it is lawe,   *custom*
Trumpes in halle to mete gan blawe;   *Trumpets*
To benche went tho bold.   *those bold (men)*
1900 When thai were semly set on rowe,[n]   *appropriately seated*
Served thai were opon a throwe,   *in a little while*
As men miriest on mold.   *earth*
That riche douke, withouten les,
As a prince served he wes,
1905 With riche coupes of gold;

1876–7 Thou me aknowe] Þou be aknowe A; Loke þu wray me D. Do not tell anyone who I am, where I am going or where I came from.

And he that brought him to that state
Stode bischet withouten the gate,   *shut out, outside*
Wel sore ofhungred and cold.   *grievously hungry*

Out at the gate com a knight
1910 And a serjaunt wise and wight,   *strong*
To plain hem, bothe yfere;   *amuse themselves, together*
And, thurch the grace of God Almight,
On Sir Amiloun he cast a sight —
Hou laith he was of chere;   *hideous, appearance*
1915 And seththen biheld on Amoraunt —
Hou gentil he was and of fair semblaunt —   *demeanour*
In gest as ye may here.
Than seyd thai bothe, bi Seyn Jon,
In al the court was ther non
1920 Of fairehed half his pere.   *beauty, equal*

The gode man gan to him go,
And hendeliche he asked him tho,
As ye may understond,
Fram wat lond that he com fro,
1925 And whi that he stode ther tho,
And whom he served in lond.
'Sir,' he seyd, 'so God me save,
Icham here mi lordes knave,   *servant*
That lith in Godes bond.
1930 And thou art gentil knight of blode,   *If*
Bere our erand of sum gode,[n]
Thurch grace of Godes sond.'

The gode man asked him anon
Yif he wald fro that lazer gon,
1935 And trewelich to him take;
And he seyd he schuld, bi Seyn Jon,
Serve that riche douke in that won,
And riche man he wald him make.
And he answerd, with mild mode,
1940 And swore bi him that dyed on rode
Whiles he might walk and wake,   *be awake*

1929 i.e. who lies bound by the affliction that God has sent.
1935 i.e. transfer his loyalty to him (the *gode man*).
1941 i.e. for as long as he lived.

For to winne al this warldes gode,
His hende lord, that bi him stode,
Schuld he never forsake.

1945 The gode man wende he hadde ben rage,   *mad*
Or he hadde ben a fole sage,[n]   *wise fool*
That hadde his witt forlorn;   *lost*
Other he thought that his lord with the foule visage   *Else*
Hadde ben a man of heighe parage   *noble birth*
1950 And of heighe kinde ycorn.   *noble lineage indeed*
Therfore he nold no more sain,
Bot went him into the halle ogain,
The riche douke biforn.
'Mi lord,' he seyd, 'listen to me:
1955 The best bourd, bi mi leute,   *joke, loyalty*
Thou herdest seththen thou were born.'

The riche douke badde him anon
To telle biforn hem, everichon,
Withouten more duelling.
1960 'Now, sir,' he seyd, 'bi Seyn Jon,
Ich was out atte gate ygon   *I had gone out to the gate*
Right now, on mi playing: *Just now, sport*
Pover men y seighe mani thare,
Litel and michel, lasse and mare,
1965 Bothe old and ying;
And a lazer ther y fond –
Herdestow never, in no lond,   *You never heard*
Telle of so foule a thing!

'The lazer lith up in a wain,   *is lying in a cart*
1970 And is so pover of might and main   *i.e. so feeble*
O fot no may he gon.   *One foot (in distance)*
And over him stode a naked swain –   *scantily clad/unarmed*
A gentiler child, forsothe to sain   *to tell the truth*
In world no wot y non!   *I know of none in the world*
1975 He is the fairest gome   *(young) man*
That ever Crist yaf Cristendome
Or layd liif opon.

1976–7 That Christ ever gave to Christendom or bestowed life upon.

And on the most fole he is   *the very greatest fool*
That ever thou herdest speke, ywis,   *speak (of)*
1980 In this worldes won.'

Than seyd the riche douke ogain:
'What foly,' he seyd, 'can he sain?   *foolishness*
Is he madde of mode?'   *distracted in his mind*
'Sir,' he seyd, 'y bad him fain
1985 Forsake the lazer in the wain,
That he so over stode,
And in thi servise he schuld be;
Y bihete him bothe lond and fe,   *promised, property*
Anough of warldes gode;   *Plenty*
1990 And he answerd and seyd tho
He nold never gon him fro —
Therfore ich hold him wode.'   *think he is mad*

Than seyd the douke, 'Thei his lord be lorn,   *brought low*
Paraventour the gode man hath biforn   *Perhaps*
1995 Holpen him at his nede;   *Helped*
Other the child is of his blod yborn,   *Or, related to him*
Other he hath him othes sworn
His liif with him to lede.
Whether he be fremd or of his blod,   *stranger*
2000 The child,' he seyd, 'is trewe and gode.
Also God me spede,
Yif ichim speke er he wende,
For that he is so trewe and kende,   *Because*
Y schal quite him his mede.'   *reward him*

2005 That douke as tite, as y you told,
Cleped to him a squier bold,   *Called, squire*
And hendelich gan him sain:
'Take,' he sayd, 'mi coupe of g[ol]d,
As ful of wine astow might hold   *as you*
2010 In thine hondes tvain,
And bere it to the castel yate.

1978 on] on of A; *om.* D.
1999 Whether or not they are related.
2002 If I speak with him before he departs.
2008 gold] glod A.

A lazer thou schalt finde therate,
Liggeand in a wain: *Lying*
Bid him, for the love of Seyn Martin,[n]   *Beg*
2015 He and his page drink this win,
And bring me the coupe ogain.'[n]

The squier tho the coupe hent,   *took*
And to the castel gat he went,
And ful of win he it bare.
2020 To the lazer he seyd, verrament,
'This coupe ful of win mi lord the sent:
Drink it, yive thou dare.'   *if, need*
The lazer tok forth his coupe of gold:
Bothe were yoten in o mold,   *cast, one mould*
2025 Right as that selve it ware.
Therin he pourd that win so riche;
Than were thai bothe ful yliche,   *alike/equal*
And noither lesse no mare.

The squier biheld the coupes tho,
2030 First his, and his lordes also,   *First Amiloun's*
Whiles he stode hem biforn;
Ac he no couthe nevermo   *in no way*
Chese the better of hem to,
So liche bothe thai worn.
2035 Into halle he ran ogain;
'Certes, sir,' he gan to sain,
'Mani gode dede thou hast lorn!
And so thou hast lorn this dede now:
He is a richer man than thou,
2040 Bi the time that God was born!'   *(I swear) by*

The riche douke answerd, 'Nay!
That worth never, bi night no day —   *would never happen*
It were oyaines the lawe.'[n]
'Yis, sir!' he gan to say.
2045 'He is a traitour, bi mi fay,   *faith*

2025 i.e. so that it looked as though the two cups were one and the same.
2033 Decide (*literally*, Choose) which was the better of the two.
2037 i.e. your charity has often been wasted/misdirected.

And were wele worth to drawe!ⁿ   *And well deserves*
For when y brought him the win,
He drough forth a gold coupe fin,   *fine*
Right as it ware thin awe.   *Exactly like your own*
2050 In this world, bi Seyn Jon,
So wise a man is ther non
Asundri schuld hem knawe.'   *Who could tell them apart*

'Now, certes,' seyd Sir Amis tho,
'In al this world were coupes no mo   *more*
2055 So liche in al thing,
Save min and mi brothers also,   *Except*
That was sett bitvix ous to,
Token of our parting.
And yif it be so, with tresoun
2060 Mine hende brother, Sir Amiloun,
Is slain, withouten lesing,
And yif he have stollen his coupe oway,   *i.e. the leper*
Y schal him sle meself this day,   *kill*
Bi Jhesu, heven king!'

2065 Fram the bord he resed than,   *rushed*
And hent his swerd as a wode man,   *seized, madman*
And drough it out with wrake.   *drew, rage*
And to the castel gat he ran —
In al the court was ther no man
2070 That him might atake.   *catch*
To the lazer he stirt in the wain,   *leapt*
And hent him in his honden tvain,
And sleynt him in the lake,   *slung, water*
And layd on as he were wode;   *set upon (him)*
2075 And al that ever about him stode
Gret diol gan make.   *lamentation*

'Traitour,' sayd the douke, 'so bold!
Where haddestow this coupe of gold,   *Where did you get*
And hou com thou therto?   *And how did you acquire it?*
2080 For, bi him that Judas sold,

2057 The line seems to refer loosely to the pledge made (*sett*) by Amis and
Amiloun at their parting and symbolized by the two cups.

Amiloun, mi brother, it hadde in wold,   *(his) possession*
When that he went me fro.'
'Ya, certes, sir,' he gan to say,
'It was his in his cuntray,
2085 And now it is fallen so;
Bot, certes, now that icham here,
The coupe is mine – y bought it dere,
With right y com therto.'

Than was the douke ful egre of mod –
2090 Was no man that about him stode
That durst legge on him hond.   *dared, lay*
He spurned him with his fot,   *kicked*
And laid on as he wer wode
With his naked brond;   *drawn sword*
2095 And bi the fet the lazer he drough,   *dragged*
And drad on him in the slough –   *trampled, mire*
For nothing wald he wond;   *desist*
And seyd, 'Thef, thou schalt be slawe,
Bot thou wilt be the sothe aknawe,
2100 Where thou the coupe fond!'"

Child Amoraunt stode the pople among,
And seye his lord, with wough and wrong,   *saw, evil*
Hou reweliche he was dight.   *pitifully, treated*
He was bothe hardi and strong;
2105 The douke in his armes he fong,   *seized*
And held him stille upright.   *i.e. made him stand still*
'Sir,' he seyd, 'thou art unhende,   *discourteous*
And of thi werkes unkende,   *in your deeds*
To sle that gentil knight!
2110 Wel sore may him rewe that stounde
That ever for the toke he wounde,
To save thi liif in fight.'"

When Sir Amis herd him so sain,
He stirt to the knight ogain,

2085 And now it has turned out like this.
2088 I acquired it rightfully.
2099–2100 Unless you will acknowledge the truth as to where you got the cup.
2110–11 Well may he regret the time that he was ever wounded for your sake.

2115 Withouten more delay,
 And biclept him in his armes tvain,   *embraced*
 And oft 'Allas!' he gan sain –
 His song was 'Waileway!'
 He loked opon his scholder bare,
2120 And seighe his grimly wounde thare,[n]   *dreadful*
 As Amoraunt gan him say.   *As Amoraunt had told him*
 He fel aswon to the grounde,   *in a swoon*
 And oft he seyd 'Allas!' that stounde,
 That ever he bode that day.

2125 'Allas!' he seyd. 'Mi joie is lorn!
 Unkender blod nas never born –   *creature*
 Y not wat y may do.   *do not know*
 For he saved mi liif biforn,
 Ichave him yolden with wo and sorn,   *repaid, pain*
2130 And wrought him michel wo.
 O, brother,' he seyd, 'par charite,   *of your goodness*
 This rewely dede foryif thou me,
 That ichave smiten the so!'   *struck you*
 And he foryave it him also swithe,
2135 And kist him wel mani a sithe,
 Wepeand with eighen tvo.

 Than was Sir Amis glad and fain;
 For joie he wepe with his ain,   *eyes*
 And hent his brother than,
2140 And tok him in his armes tvain,
 Right til he com into the halle oyain –
 No bar him no nother man.
 The levedi tho in the halle stode,
 And wend hir lord hadde ben wode;
2145 Oyaines him hye ran.   *To meet*
 'Sir,' sche seyd, 'wat is thi thought?
 Whi hastow him into halle ybrought,
 For him that this world wan?'

2124 that] þat þat A. That ever he should live to see that day.
2130 And caused him great distress.
2132 Forgive me for this dreadful deed.
2146 What are you thinking of?

'O, dame,' he seyd, 'bi Seyn Jon,
2150 Me nas never so wobigon,   *oppressed by sorrow*
Yif thou it wost understond;   *would know*
For be[t]ter knight in world is non,
Bot almost now ichave him slon,   *(just) now*
And schamely driven to schond.   *shamefully, humiliated*
2155 For it is mi brother, Sir Amiloun,
With sorwe and care is dreven adoun,
That er was fre to fond.'
The levedi fel aswon to grounde,   *in a swoon*
And wepe and seyd 'Allas!' that stounde,
2160 Wel sore wrengand hir hond.

As foule a lazer as he was,
The levedi kist him in that plas –
For nothing wold sche spare;
And ofttime sche seyd 'Allas!'
2165 That him was fallen so hard a cas,   *befallen, plight*
To live in sorwe and care.[n]
Into hir chaumber sche gan him lede,
And kest of al his pover wede,   *threw, clothes*
And bathed his bodi al bare;
2170 And to a bedde swithe him brought,   *quickly*
With clothes riche and wele ywrought.   *fashioned*
Ful blithe of him thai ware![n]   *i.e. of his coming*

And thus, in gest as we say,
Tvelmoneth in her chaumber he lay.[n]
2175 Ful trewe thai ware and kinde –
No wold thai nick him with no nay:
Whatsoever he asked, night or day,
It nas never bihinde: *slow in coming*
Of everich mete and everi drink
2180 Thai had hemselve, withouten lesing;   *themselves*
Thai were him bothe ful minde.

2152 better] berter A.
2156–7 Who is oppressed by sorrow and care, and who formerly was noble indeed.
2161 Though he was such a hideous leper.
2176 Nor would they refuse him anything.
2181 They were both very mindful of (his comfort).

And bi than the tvelmo[n]th was ago,   *when, passed*
A ful fair grace fel hem tho,   *(divine) dispensation*
In gest as we finde.   *story*

2185 So it bifel opon a night,
      As Sir Amis, that gentil knight,
      In slepe thought as he lay: *dreamed*
      An angel com fram heven bright,[n]
      And stode biforn his bed ful right,   *right by his bed*
2190 And to him thus gan say:
      Yif he wald rise on Cristes morn,[n]   *If, Christmas morning*
      Swiche time as Jhesu Crist was born,
      And slen his children tvay,
      And alien his [broth]er with the blode,   *anoint*
2195 Thurch Godes grace, that is so gode,
      His wo schuld wende oway.[n]

      Thus him thought al tho thre night:
      An angel out of heven bright
      Warned him evermore,   *Told*
2200 Yif he wald do as he him hight,   *commanded*
      His brother schuld ben as fair a knight
      As ever he was biforn.[n]
      Ful blithe was Sir Amis tho,
      Ac for his childer him was ful wo,
2205 For fairer ner non born.   *were not*
      Wel loth him was his childer to slo,   *reluctant*
      And wele lother his brother forgo,   *lose*
      That is so kinde ycorn.[n]   *noble indeed*

      Sir Amiloun met that night also   *dreamed*
2210 That an angel warned him tho
      And seyd to him ful yare,
      Yif his brother wald his childer slo,
      The hert blod of hem to   *two*
      Might bring him out of care.
2215 Amorwe Sir Amis was ful hende,   *Next morning*

2182 tvelmonth] tvelmoth A.
2194 brother] *thus* S D; childer A.
2197 He dreamed thus all the next three nights.

And to his brother he gan wende,
And asked him of his fare.   *how he was*
And he him answerd oyain, ful stille,   *quietly*
'Brother, ich abide her Godes wille,   *submit to*
220 For y may do na mare.'

Also thai sete togider thare,   *As, sat*
And speke of aventours, as it ware,[n]
Tho knightes hende and fre,
Than seyd Sir Amiloun ful yare,
25 'Brother, y nil nought spare
To tel the in privite: *secret*
Methought tonight in mi sweven
That an angel com fram heven;
Forsothe, he told me
30 That thurch the blod of [th]in children to
Y might aschape out of mi wo,   *escape*
Al hayl and hole to be.'   *healthy, whole*

Than thought the douk, withouten lesing,   *duke*
For to slen his childer so ying
35 It were a dedli sinne.
And than thought he, bi heven king,
His brother out of sorwe bring,
For that nold he nought blinne.[n]
So it bifel on Cristes night,   *Christmas Eve*
40 Swiche time as Jhesu ful of might
Was born to save mankinne,
To chirche to wende al that ther wes
Thai dighten hem, withouten les,
With joie and worldes winne.   *worldly pleasure*

45 Than thai were redi for to fare,   *When*
The douke bad al that ther ware
To chirche thai schuld wende —
Litel and michel, lasse and mare —

2227 It seemed to me last night in my dream.
2230 thin] *thus* S D; min A.
2234–5 That to kill his young children would be a mortal sin.
2237–8 That he would stop at nothing to deliver his brother from sorrow.
2242–3 All who were there made themselves ready to go to church.

That non bi[le]ft in chaumber thare,   *So that, remained*
2250 As thai wald ben his frende;
And seyd he wald himselve that night
Kepe his brother, that gentil knight,   *Tend to*
That was so god and hende.
Than was ther non that durst say nay;   *dared*
2255 To chirche thai went in her way;
At hom bileft tho hende.   *remained those noble (men)*

The douke wel fast gan aspie   *closely observed*
The kays of the noricerie,   *keys, nursery*
Er than thai schuld gon;
2260 And priveliche he cast his eighe,   *surreptitiously, watched*
And aparceived ful witterlye   *noticed, surely/carefully*
Where that thai hadde hem don.   *put*
And when thai were to chirche went,
Than Sir Amis, verrament,
2265 Was bileft alon,   *left*
He tok a candel fair and bright,
And to the kays he went ful right,   *at once*
And tok hem oway, ichon.ⁿ

Alon himself, withouten mo,   *more (i.e. anyone else)*
2270 Into the chaumber he gan to go,
Ther that his childer were;   *Where*
And biheld hem, bothe to,
Hou fair thai lay togider tho,
And slepe, bothe yfere.   *together*
2275 Than seyd himselve, 'Bi Seyn Jon,   *he said to himself*
It were gret rewethe you to slon,   *pity*
That God hath bought so dere!'
His kniif he had drawen that tide;
For sorwe he sleyntt oway biside,   *drew back*
2280 And wepe with reweful chere.   *sorrowful heart*

Than he hadde wopen ther he stode,   *When, wept*
Anon he turned oyain his mode,   *changed his mind*

2249 bileft] biselft A.
2250 This line should be understood with *bad* (2246): he begged them, as they
wished to be his friends . . .
2259 i.e. before the rest of his household set out for church.
2277 Whom God has redeemed so dearly.

And sayd, withouten delay,
'Mi brother was so kinde and gode:
285 With grimly wounde he schad his blod,   *shed*
For mi love, opon a day.   *For love of me*
Whi schuld y, than, mi childer spare
To bring mi brother out of care?
O, certes,' he seyd, 'nay!
290 To help mi brother now at this nede,
God graunt me therto wele to spede,
And Mari, that best may!'

No lenger stint he no stode,   *stopped, hesitated*
Bot hent his kniif with dreri mode,   *heavy heart*
295 And tok his children tho.[n]
For he nold nought spille her blode,
Over a bacine fair and gode,   *basin*
Her throtes he schar atvo.   *slit, in two*
And when he hadde hem bothe slain,
300 He laid hem in her bed ogain –
No wonder thei him wer wo! –
And hilde hem that no wight schuld se,   *covered, so that*
As no man hadde at hem be;
Out of chaumber he gan go.

305 And when he was out of chaumber gon,
The dore he steked stille anon,   *fastened quietly*
As fast as it was biforn.   *securely*
The kays he hidde under a ston,
And thought thai schuld wene, ichon,   *everyone would think*
10 That thai hadde ben forlorn.[n]   *lost*
To his brother he went him than,
And seyd to that careful man,   *sorrowful*
'Swiche time as God was born,
Ich have the brought mi childer blod:
15 Ich hope it schal do the gode,   *hope/expect*
As the angel seyd biforn.'

2288 i.e. when I can deliver my brother from sorrow.
2290–2 God and Mary, that best maiden, grant me success in helping my brother in this need.
2296 Because he did not wish to spill their blood.
2303 i.e. as if no one had touched them.
2313 At the time of God's birth.

'Brother!' Sir Amiloun gan to say.
'Hastow slayn thine children tvay?
Allas, whi destow so?'   *did you do*
2320   He wepe and seyd, 'Waileway!
Ich had lever til Domesday   *rather, the Day of Judgement*
Have lived in care and wo!'
Than seyd Sir Amis, 'Be now stille!   *silent*
Jhesu, when it is his wille,
2325   May sende me childer mo.
For me of blis thou art al bare:
Ywis, mi liif wil y nought spare
To help the now therfro.'[n]

He tok that blode, that was so bright,
2330   And alied that gentil knight,   *anointed*
That er was hende in hale;   *noble in hall*
And seththen in a bed him dight,   *laid*
And wreighe him wel warm, aplight,   *wrapped, assuredly*
With clothes riche and fale.[n]   *many*
2335   'Brother,' he seyd, 'ly now stille,
And falle on slepe, thurch Godes wille,
As the angel told in tale;   *speech*
And ich hope wele, withouten lesing,
Jhesu, that is heven king,
2340   Schal bote the of thi bale.'   *cure you, affliction*

Sir Amis lete him ly alon,
And into his chapel he went anon,
In gest as ye may here;
And for his childer, that he hadde slon,
2345   To God of heven he made his mon,
And preyd, with rewely chere,
Schuld save him fram schame that day,   *(That God) should*
And Mari his moder, that best may,
That was him leve and dere.   *beloved*
2350   And Jhesu Crist, in that stede,   *place*
Ful wele he herd that knightes bede,   *prayer*
And graunt him his praiere.   *granted*

2326 On my account you are bereft of joy.
2327–8 Indeed, I would give my own life to help you now out of that plight.

Amorwe, as tite as it was day,
The levedi com hom, al with play,   *revelry*
355 With knightes ten and five.
Thai sought the kays ther thai lay;   *had lain*
Thai founde hem nought, thai were oway —   *gone*
Wel wo was hem olive!
The douk bad al that ther wes
360 Thai schuld hold hem stille in pes,
And stint of her strive;
And seyd he hadde the keys nome;   *taken*
Schuld no man in the chaumber come,
Bot himself and his wive.[n]

365 Anon he tok his levedi than,
And seyd to hir, 'Leve leman,   *Dear sweetheart*
Be blithe and glad of mode![n]
For, bi him that this warld wan,
Bothe mi childer ich have slan,
370 That were so hende and gode.
For methought, in mi sweven,
That an angel com fram heven
And seyd me thurch her blode   *(that) by means of*
Mi brother schuld passe out of his wo —
375 Therfore y slough hem, bothe to,
To hele that frely fode.'   *heal, noble creature*

Than was the levedi ferly wo,   *wondrously*
And seighe hir lord was also;   *saw*
Sche comfort him ful yare:[n]   *readily*
380 'O, lef liif,' sche seyd tho,   *dear creature*
'God may sende ous childer mo —
Of hem have thou no care!
Yif it ware at min hert rote,
For to bring thi brother bote,
385 My lyf y wold not spare.

2360–1 That they should remain quiet and calm and stop their agitation.
2363–4 No one was to come into the (children's) chamber except for himself and his wife.
2382 Do not be sorrowful about them.
2383–5 If the cure for your brother lay at the bottom of my heart, I would not spare my own life (in order to help him).
2385–2496 These lines are missing from MS A and are supplied from S.

Shal no man oure children see;
Tomorow shal they beryed bee,   *buried*
As they faire ded ware."[n]   *As if they had died naturally*

Thus the lady faire and bryght
2390 Comfort hur lord with al hur myght,
As ye mow understonde.   *may*
And seth they went both ful ryght   *afterwards, straight*
To Sir Amylion, that gentil knyght,
That ere was free to fonde.
2395 Whan Sir Amylion waked thoo,
Al his fowlehed was agoo,   *hideousness, gone*
Through grace of Goddes sonde.
Than was he as feire a man
As ever he was yet or than,
2400 Seth he was born in londe.[n]   *Since*

Than were they al blith;
Her joy couth no man kyth;[n]
They thonked God that day.
As ye mow listen and lyth,   *hear*
2405 Into a chamber they went swyth,   *quickly*
There the children lay: *Where*
Without wemme and wound,   *blemish*
Hool and sond the children found,   *Whole and sound*
And layen togeder and play.[n]
2410 For joye thay wept, there they stood,
And thanked God, with myld mood,
Hir care was al agoo.   *Their*

When Sir Amylion was hool and fere,   *healthy*
And wax was strong of powere   *had grown*
2415 Both to goo and ryde,
Child Oweys was a bold squyer;[n]
Blithe and glad he was of chere
To serve his lord beside.
Than saide the knyght, upon a day,
2420 He wolde hoom to his contray,
To speke with his wyf that tyde;
And for she halp him so at nede,

2399 As he had ever been before that time.
2422 And because she helped him in such a way when he was in need.

Wel he thought to quyte hur mede —   *repay her*
No lenger wold he abyde.

425 Sir Amys sent ful hastely
    After mony knyght hardy,
    That doughty were of dede:
    Wel fyve hundred kene and try,   *brave, proven*
    And other barons by and by,   *in (due) succession*
430 On palfray and on steede.   *saddle-horse*
    He preked both nyght and day,   *rode*
    Til he com to his contray,
    There he was lord in lede.   *Where, among the people*
    Than had a knyght of that contre
35 Spoused his lady bryght of ble,
    In romaunce as we rede.

    But thus in romaunce, as y yow say,   *thus (it is told)*
    They com hoom that silf day   *on the very day*
    That the bridal was hold.   *marriage was celebrated*
40 To the yates they preked, without delay,
    And ther began a soory play   *wretched game*
    Among the barouns bold!
    A messengere to the hal com,
    And seide her lorde was com hom,   *husband*
45 As man meriest on molde.
    Than wox the lady blew and wan;   *blue, pale*
    Ther was mony a sory man,
    Both yong and olde.

    Sir Amys and Sir Amylion,
0   And with hem mony a stout baron,
    With knyghtes and squyers fale,   *many*
    With helmes and with haberyon,   *coats of mail*
    With swerd bryght and broun,   *burnished*
    They went into the hale.
5   Al that they there araught   *reache*
    Grete strokes there they caught,   *blows, received*
    Both grete and smale.
    Glad and blyth were they that day,

2435 Married his beautiful (*literally*, beautiful of colour/complexion) wife.
2458–60 Whoever was able to escape and flee from the wedding feast was glad
and happy that day.

Whoso myght skape away
2460 [And fle fro that bredale.ⁿ

When they had, with wrake,   *violently*
Drove oute both broun and blake]ⁿ
Out of that worthy woon,   *noble dwelling*
Sir Amylyon, for his lady sake,
2465 A grete logge he let make,
Both of lym and stoon.   *lime*
Theryn was the lady ladde,   *led*
And with bred and water was she fedⁿ
Tyl her lyve dayes were goon.   *Until her life was over*
2470 Thus was the lady brought to dede   *death*
(Who therof rought he was a queede!),
As ye have herd, echoon.

Then Sir Amylion sent his sond   *message*
To erles and barouns, fre and bond,
2475 Both feire and hende.
When they com, he sesed in hond
Child Oweys in al his lond,ⁿ
That was trew and kynde.
And when he had do thus, ywys,
2480 With his brother, Sir Amys,
Ayen then gan he wende.   *Back home*
In muche joy, without stryf,
Togeder ladde they her lyf,
Tel God after hem dide sende.

2485 Anoon the hend barons tway,
They let reyse a feire abbay,   *build*
And feffet it ryght wel thoo —   *endowed*
In Lumbardy, in that contray — ⁿ
To senge for hem tyl Domesday,   *sing*
2490 And for her eldres also.   *forebears*
Both on oo day were they dede,   *one/the same*

2460–2 And . . . blake] *thus* D; *om.* S.
2471 Whoever cared about that was a scoundrel!
2476–7 When they came, he installed the young Oweys in possession of all his land.
2491 i.e. they died on the same day as each other.

And in oo grave were they leide,
The knyghtes both twoo.
And for her trewth and her godhed,   *godliness(?)*
2495 The blisse of hevyn they have to mede,   *in reward*
That lasteth evermoo.   Amen.

SYR TRYAMOWRE

Heven blys, that all schall wynne,
Schylde us fro dedly synne   *Shield*
And graunte us the blys of hevyn!
Yf ye wyll a stounde blynne,   *be quiet a while*
5 Of a story y wyll begynne,
That gracyus ys to nevyn: *pleasing, narrate*
Of a kyng and of a quene,
What bale and blys was them bytwene,   *sorrow and joy*
Y schall yow telle full evyn.   *in full*
10 A gode ensaumpull ye may lere,   *lesson, learn*
Yf ye wyll thys story here,
And herkyn to my stevyn.[n]   *listen, voice*

He was the kynge of Arragon,
A nobull man and of grete renown:
15 Syr Ardus was hys name.
He had a quene that hyght Margaret,   *was called*
Trewe as stele, y yow behett,   *steel, assure*
That falsely was broght in blame.   *accused*
The kyngys steward Marrok hyght:
20 False and fekyll was that wyght,   *disloyal, man*
That lady for to fame.   *defame*
He lovyd well that lady gente;   *gentle*
For scho wolde not to hym assente,   *Because, yield*
He dud hur mekyll schame![n]   *great injury*

25 The kyng lovyd well the quene,
For scho was semely on to sene,   *beautiful to behold*
And trewe as stele on tree.[n]

Oftetyme togedur can they meene,
For no chylde come them betwene:
30 Sore syghed bothe sche and hee.
Therfore the kyng, as y undurstonde,
Hath made a vowe to go into the Holy Londe,
To fyght and not to flee,
That God Almyghty schulde helpe them so   *So that, might*
35 A chylde to gete betwene them two,   *beget*
That ther heyre myght bee.[n]   *heir*

When the kyng hys vowe had maked,
And at the pope the cros taked,[n]   *from*
To bedd then were they broght.
40 That nyght on hys lady mylde,
As God wolde, he gate a chylde,
But they of hyt wyste noght.   *knew nothing*
Sone on the morne, when hyt was day,   *Early, morning*
The kyng wolde forthe on hys way
45 To the londe there God [us] boght.   *redeemed us*
Than began the quene to morne,   *lament*
For he wolde no lenger soyorne;   *stay*
[H]evy sche was in thoght.   *She was heavy-hearted*

The kyng bad ordeygne hys armoryes —
50 Knyghtys, squyers and palfrays —   *saddle-horses*
All redy for to goo.
He toke hys leve at the quene,
At erlys and barons, all bedene,   *together*
And at Syr Marrok alsoo.
55 He comawndyd Marrok, on hys lyfe,
That he schulde kepe wele the quene, hys wyfe,   *look after*
Bothe in wele and in woo.
Betwene the quene and the kyng
Was grete sorowe and mornynge   *lamentation*
60 When they schulde parte in twoo.

28–9 They would often lament together, because no child was born to them.
41 In accordance with God's will, he begot a child.
45 us] was C.
48 Hevy] Prevy C.
49 The king ordered his forces should be set in order.
57 At all times (*literally*, Both in joy and in sorrow).

Now ys the kyng passyd the see:
To hys enemyes gon ys he,
And warryth there a whyle.   *fights*
But that Syr Marrok, hys steward,
65 Was faste abowtewarde
To do hys lady gyle.
He wowyd the quene bothe day and nyght;   *wooed*
To lye hur by he had hyt hyght —   *sworn*
He dredyd no peryle.   *feared no danger*
70 Feyre he spake to hur, aplyght: *Persuasively, assuredly*
Yf he hur thoght turne myght
Wyth wordys, hyt was hys wylle.

The quene was stedfaste of wylle;   *firm in determination*
Sche herde hys wordys and stode styll
75 Tyll he all had sayde.
Sche seyde, 'Traytur, what ys thy thoght?
All that thou spekyst, hyt ys for noght.   *in vain*
Owt upon the, thefe!' sche seyde.   *villain*
'My lorde, when he went to the see,
80 For specyall tryste he toke me to the,[n]   *trust, committed*
To have undur holde.   *protection*
And now thou woldyst wondur fayne   *only too gladly*
Be the furste to do me trayne!   *beguile me*
How darste thou be so bolde?'

85 He seyde, 'Ye be my lady gente,
For now ys my lorde wente
Agayne hys fone to fyght;   *Against, enemies*
And, but the more wondyr bee,
Ye schall nevyrmore hym see.
90 Therfore y rede yow ryght: *give you good advice*
Now ys he gone, my lady free,   *he is, noble*
In hys stede ye schall take me —   *place*
Am y not a knyght?

65–6 Was firmly resolved to practise deceit upon his lady.
71–2 It was his intention to persuade her to disloyalty by his words, if he could.
76 Traitor, what are you thinking of?
78 the] þe the C. seyde] seyde in þᵗ brayde C. *Owt upon the* is an untranslatable expression of rebuke.
88 And it is more than likely (*literally*, Unless the greater wonder be).

And we schall do so prevely   *act, secretly*
95 That, whethyr he leve or dye,   *live*
Ther schall wete no wyght.'   *Nobody shall know of it*

Then was the quene wondur wrothe,   *exceedingly angry*
And swere mony a grete othe,   *swore*
As sche was woman trewe: *loyal*
100 'Yf ye be so hardy   *bold/insolent*
To wayte me wyth velanye,   *seek to ensnare, wickedness*
Fowle hyt schall the rewe!   *You will bitterly regret it*
Y trowe y schall never ete bredd   *trust*
Tyll thou be broght to the dedd.[n]   *death*
105 Soche balys then schall y the brewe,   *pains, concoct*
Y may evyr aftur thys
That thou woldyst tyse me to do amys.[n]   *entice, wrong*
No game schulde the glewe!'   *sport, make you merry*

Marrok seyde, 'Madam, mercy!
110 Y seyde hyt for no velanye,   *evil intent*
But for a fondynge — [n]   *testing*
For y wolde wytt yowre wylle,
Whethur that hyt were gode or ylle,
And for no nothyr thynge.   *no other purpose*
115 And now, madame, y may see
That ye ar trewe as stele on tree[n]
Unto my lorde the kynge.
And that ys me wondur lefe;   *extremely pleasing to me*
Wherefore taketh hyt to no grefe,   *So do not take it amiss*
120 Or wyckyd askynge.'

So excusyd he hym tho,
The lady wende hyt had byn soo   *thought it was*
As Syr Marrokk sayde.
He goth forthe and holdyth hys pese;   *keeps silence*
125 More he thenkyth then he says —   *than*
He was full evyll payde!   *very ill-pleased*

99 i.e. she swore by her own loyalty.
111–12 But to test you, because I wished to know your inclination.
120 Or (regard it) as wicked solicitation.

Of the quene let we bee –
And, thorow the grace of the Trynyte,   *through*
Grete wyth chylde sche was –
130 And of Kyng Ardus speke we:
Farre in hethennes ys he,   *heathen lands*
To werre in Goddys grace.[n]

There he had grete chyvalry;   *honour as a knight*
He slewe hys enemyes wyth grete envy.   *ferocity*
135 Grete worde of hym aroos:
In hethennes and yn Spayne,
In Gaskyn and in Almayne,   *Gascony, Germany*
Wyt they of hys loos.   *His reputation was known*

When he had done hys pylgrymage,
140 And maked all hys message
Wyth wordys that were not wy[kk],[n]
To fleme Jordan and to Bedlem,   *river, Bethlehem*
And to the borogh of Jerusalem,   *city*
There God was dede and qwykk,   *alive*

145 Then longed he at home to bene,
And for to speke wyth hys quene,
That hys thoght was ever upon.
And he gate schyppys prevay,   *private*
And to the schypp, on a day,
150 He thoght that he flewe anon.

So longe they dreve upon the fome   *sailed, sea*
That at the laste they come home
To hys owne lande.
When the kyng and the quene were togedur agayne,
155 They made mekyll yoye, gle and game.
Then tolde the kynge hur tythande.[n]   *news*

135 i.e. he acquired great fame.
141 wykk] wyckdd C.
144 i.e. where God died and rose again from the dead.
147 About whom he thought continually.
149–50 The sense appears to be that he felt that he could not get there quickly
enough.
155 They made great mirth, joy and sport.

The kynge behelde the quene mylde,   *gentle*
And sawe that sche was wyth chylde;
Then made he glad semland.   *he was (literally, looked) glad*
160 Twenty tymys he dud hur kysse;
Then made they game and blysse,
And he toke hur be the hande.

But sone aftur come tythynges:
Marrok mett hys lorde kynge,
165 And faste he can hym frayne: *question*
'Syr,' he seyde, 'for Goddys pyne,   *by God's suffering*
Of a thyng that now ys ynne   *going to happen*
Whare[for] be ye so fayne?   *Why, glad*
Ye wene the chylde yourys be;   *believe, is yours*
170 Hyt ys not so, so mote y the!   *as I hope to prosper*
The quene hath done the trayne: *betrayed you*
Another knyght, so mote y spede,   *as I hope to prosper*
Gat the chylde syth thou yede,   *Begot, after, departed*
And hath the quene forlayne.'   *lain with*

175 'Allas!' seyde the kyng. 'What may that be?
Betoke y not hur to the,   *Did I not entrust her to you*
To kepe hur in weyle and woo?
Sche was undur thy kepeyng:
Why letyst thou hur do that wyckyd thynge?
180 Allas, why dud sche soo?'
'Syr,' seyde Syr Marrok, 'wyte not me,   *blame*
For grete moone sche made for the,   *lamentation*
As sche had lovyd no moo.   *As if, none more*
Y trowed in hur no falsehedd
185 Tyll y fonde them wyth the dede,   *caught them in the act*
Togedur, betwene them two.

'In the fyrste fourtenyght that ye were went
Y fownde them togedur, verament,   *truly*
O[s] they ther wylle had done.[n]   *As*

168 Wharefor] Whare of C.
184 I did not believe there was any falseness in her.
189 Os] Or C.

190 To hym y ran wyth egur mode, *fierce heart*
And slewe the knyght there he stode, *where*
Be myn owne dome. *According to my own judgement*

'Then wende sche sche schulde be schente, *thought, ruined*
And me behett londe and rente, *promised, revenue*
195 And hyght me to do my wylle;
But y myselfe wolde noght –
Ye were evyr in my thoght,
Bothe lowde and stylle.'ⁿ *Under all circumstances*

'Allas!' seyde the kyng. 'Now y wondur! *I am astonished*
200 For sorowe my herte brekyth in sondyr. *apart*
Why hath sche done amys?
Y wot not to whom y may meene, *do not know, lament*
For y have loste my comely quene, *beautiful*
That y was wonte to kysse. *accustomed*
205 'Marrok,' he seyde, 'what ys thy rede: *advice*
Whether that sche be done to dedd, *put to death*
That was my blysse? *(She) who was my joy*
For, sythen sche hath forsaken me, *since*
Y wylle hur no more see,
210 Nor dwelle wyth hur, ywys.' *indeed*

'Syr,' seyde Marrok, 'ye schall not soo! *(do) so*
Ye schall hur nother brenne nor sloo,
For dowte of synne. *Lest that is sinful*
Bettyr hyt ys, syr, be my rede, *by my advice*
215 Owt of yowre londe sche be flemyd indede, *banished*
And faste ye schall hur comawnde to wynne.'ⁿ *firmly, depart*

'But take hur an oolde stede, *give*
And an olde knyght that may hur lede,
Tyll sche be paste yowre realme; *outside, kingdom*
220 And gyf them some spendynge, *money for expenses*
That them owt of thy londe may brynge –
Y can no bettyr deme. *judge*

195 And promised me that she would do as I wished.
212 You shall neither burn nor kill her.

'For, syr,' he seyde, 'hyt were not feyre   *proper*
A horcop to be yowre heyre,   *That a bastard should be*
225 But he ware of yowre kynne.'[n]   *Unless, kindred*
Then seyde the kynge, 'So mote y the,   *As I hope to prosper*
As thou haste seyde, so schall hyt bee.
Arste y schall not blynne.'
Then exylyd the kyng the quene;
230 Sche had wondur what hyt myght meene —
What made hym so to begynne.   *act*
No lenger he wolde gyf hur respyte,
Nor no worde he wolde speke hur wyth —
And that was grete synne!

235 He let clothe hur in sympull wede,
And set hur upon an olde stede,
That was bresyd and blynde;[n]   *decrepit, blind*
And toke to hur an olde knyght,   *assigned*
That Syr Roger hyght,   *was called*
240 That curtes was and kynde;   *courteous*
And gaf them twenty dayes to passe;
And ovyr that tyme hys wylle was,   *beyond, wish*
Yf men myght hur fynde,
Sche schulde be takyn and be brente,   *burned*
245 And the knyght, be there assente,[n]
Schulde wayve wyth the wynde.   *i.e. hang from the gallows*

Thretty florens to there spendynge
He gaf them, wythowte lesynge,   *truly*
And comawnded them to goo.
250 The qwene for sorowe wolde dye,   *wanted to*
For sche wyste not wherefore nor why   *knew*
That sche was flemed soo.   *banished*
Therfore sche had grete drede,   *fear*
And sche swownyd on hur stede —   *swooned*
255 Hyt was no wondur thogh sche were wo!   *sorrowful*
Syr Roger comfortyd the quene,

228 i.e. I shall not stop until that is done.
232 He would not allow her any further delay.
235 He had her clothed in plain garments.
241 i.e. in which to get outside the kingdom.
247 Thirty florins for their expenses.

And seyde, 'At Goddys wylle muste hyt bene.   *According to*
What helpyth hyt yow yf ye youreselfe sloo?'

Knyghtys, squyers and ladyes gente
260 Morned for the quene was wente.   *Lamented, because*
The kynge had no chesowne;   *(good) reason (for what he did)*
And the quene had grete care,   *sorrow*
For sche schulde fro hur lorde fare,
Wythowte ony resowne.
265 But then they wente fro that stede;   *place*
On ther way forthe they yede,   *went*
Ferre fro every towne,   *Far from*
Into a grete wyldurnes –
Full of wylde bestys hyt was,
270 Be dale and eke be downe.

Marrok thoght utturly   *altogether*
To do the quene a velanye,
Hys luste for to fulfylle.   *satisfy*
He ordeygnyd hym a companye
275 Of hys owne meynye,
That wolde assente hym tylle.   *do his bidding*
To a wode they wente in hye,   *haste*
There the quene schulde passe by,   *Where*
And there stode they all stylle.   *waited, quite quietly*
280 There had he thoght redyly   *quickly/easily*
To have do the quene a velanye –   *done*
Fayne he wolde hur spylle.   *Gladly, ruin*

The quene and Syr Roger come into the wode;
Wote ye wyll, thay thoght but gode –
285 To passe wythowtyn dowte.   *without fear/certainly*
Then were they war of the steward   *aware*
Come rydyng to them warde,   *towards them*
Wyth a grete rowte.   *crowd*

258 What good will it do you if you kill yourself?
263 Because she had to leave her husband.
270 By valley and also by hill (i.e. all around).
272 To commit a wicked action against the queen.
274–5 He furnished himself with a troop of men from his own household.
284 You may be sure that they expected nothing but good.

'Here ys treson!' seyde the quene.
290 'Allas!' seyde Roger. 'What may that bene?　　　　　　　*be*
We here be sett all abowte!
Syth we here schall dye,　　　　　　　　　　　　　　　*Since*
Oure dedys full sore they schall abye,
Be they nevyr so stowte!'　　　　　　　　　*However strong they are*

295 The steward Roger can ascrye,　　　　　　　　*challenged Roger*
And seyde, 'Yylde the, for thou schalt dye!　　　*Yield yourself*
To us thou haste no myght.'　　　　　*You are powerless against us*
Syr Roger seyde, 'Traytour, forthy　　　　　　　　*therefore*
My dethe schalt thou dere abye,
300 Yf that y wyth the fyght!'
There come they to hym in hye;　　　　　　　　　　*haste*
Syr Roger, wyth grete envy,　　　　　　　　　*very fiercely*
Kydd he was a knyght.　　　　　　　　　　　　　　*Showed*
They hewe on hym full boldely;　　　　　　　　*struck at*
305 Ther was none of all that company
So bolde nor so wyght.　　　　　　　　　　　　　*brave*

Syr Roger smote them on the hede,
That to the gyrdyll the swerde yede;　　　　　　　*waist*
Of hym were they qwyte.[n]
310 They hewe on hym faste, as they were wode,　　　*as if, mad*
On eche syde then sprong the blod<e>,　　　　　*flowed*
So sore on hym they dud smyte.　　　　　　*hard, strike*
Trewelove, hys hownde so gode,　　　　　　　　　　*dog*
Halpe hys maystyr and be hym stode;[n]　　*Helped, supported him*
315 Byttyrly he can byte.

Whyll they were togedur bestedd,
The quene passyd awey and fledd
On fote, and lefte hur stede.
Sche ranne to a thorne grene –　　　　　　　　*thorn tree*
320 Tyl sche come thedur sche wolde not blyn –
And daryth there for drede.　　　　　　　　*cowers, fear*
Syr Roger sche dydd beholde:

291 We are completely surrounded.
293 They shall pay dearly for our deaths.
316 While they pressed hard on each other.
320 She would not stop until she reached it.

He hewe on ther bodyes bolde;
Hys hownde halpe hym at nede. *in that necessity*
325 Os hyt ys in the story tolde, *As*
Fourti Syr Roger downe can folde — *threw down*
So qwyt he them ther mede!

Had he ben armyd, ywys, *fully armed, indeed*
All the maystry had byn hys — *victory, would have been*
330 Allas, why wantyd he hys wede? *lacked, armour*
As Syr Roger gaf a knokk, *blow*
Behynde hym come Syr Marrok —
Therfore evyll mote he spede![n]
He smot Syr Roger wyth a spere;
335 Thorow the body he can hym bere; *Through, pierce*
Faste then can he blede. *Heavily*

He hath an evyll wounde; *serious*
That dynte hath broght hym to the grounde, *blow*
And fellyd hym on the grene. *struck him down, grass*
340 Than he was slayne, certenly,
They rode forthe wyth grete envy; *malice*
To seke aftur the quene.
But they wyste not what they myght sey — [n] *knew*
Hur stede they fonde, sche was awey: *gone*
345 Then had that traytur tene. *anger*
Ther jurney then they thoght evyll sett:
But they wyth the lady not mett,
They wyste not what to mene.[n]
Ovyr all the wode they hur soght,
350 But, as God wolde, they fonde hur noght.
Then had they grete tene.

When he myght not the lady fynde,
He wente away, as knyght onkynde, *wicked*
To Syr Roger, there he lay. *where*

327 Thus he gave them their reward!
333 For that, may ill fortune be his!
346 They thought then that their undertaking (day's work) had failed/been ill-advised.

355 Thryes he styked hym thorowowt;
     Of hys dede he had no dowte –   *death, doubt*
     Allas that ylke day!   *same*
     When that traytur had done soo,
     He turnyd ageyne there he come fro,   *back where*
360 Unmanly for to say;[n]
     For hys company was all gon;
     Fourti he had chaunged for oon;
     Ther skaped but two away.   *escaped, only*

     The quene was aferde to be schente,   *afraid, ruined*
365 Tyl sche sye that they were wente,   *saw*
     And passyd owt of the slogh.   *ditch*
     Then rose sche up and come agayne   *back*
     To Syr Roger, and fonde hym slayne –
     Then had sche sorow ynogh!   *much sorrow*

370 'Allas!' sche seyde, 'Now am y spylte!   *destroyed*
     Thys false thefe, wythowtyn gylte,
     Why dyd he the to-slon?
     Syr Roger, thys haste thou for me.   *on my account*
     Allas that evyr y schulde hyt see!'
375 Wyth that sche felle in swowne.   *swoon*

     When sche myght ryse, sche toke hur stede;
     Sche durste no lenger dwell, for drede   *dared*
     That no man schulde fynde hur thore.   *Lest anyone*
     Sche seyde, 'Roger, y see the blede:
380 Allas, who may me wys and lede,   *guide*
     For, certen, thou mayst no more?'   *certainly*

     Hys gode hownde, for weyle nor woo,
     Wolde not fro hys maystyr goo,
     But lay lykyng hys woundys.
385 He wende to have helyd hym agayne;
     Therto he dyd all hys mayne –
     Grete kyndenes ys in howndys![n]

     355 Three times he stabbed him right through.
     362 i.e. he had lost forty men as against one (Sir Roger).
     371–2 Why did he kill you, who were innocent?
     385–6 He thought he could bring him back to health; he did all in his power to
     that end.

He lykkyd hym tyll he stanke,[n]
Than he began, and kenne hym thanke,[n]
390 To make a pytt of ston;   *grave*
And to berye hym was hys purpos,
And scraped on hym bothe ryn and mosse,   *bark*
And fro hym nevyr wolde gon.

Than levyd they stylle thare;   *remained*
395 The quene faste can sche fare,
For fere of hur foon.   *enemies*
Sche had grete mornyng in hur herte,   *sorrow*
For sche wyste not whedurwarde   *which way*
That sche was beste to goon.

400 Sche rode forthe, noght forthy,   *notwithstanding*
To the londe of Hongary,
Tyll sche come thedur wyth woo.
When sche come undur a wode syde,   *to the edge of a wood*
Sche myght no lenger abyde,   *wait*
405 Hur peynys were so throo.   *(labour) pains, fierce*
Sche lyghtyd downe, that was so mylde,   *dismounted, gentle*
And there sche travaylyd of a chylde —   *went into labour*
Hyrselfe allon, wythowtyn moo.   *more*
Forthe sche went, wyth sorowe ynogh,   *great sorrow*
410 And tyed hur hors to a bogh,   *branch*
Tyll the throwes were all ydoo.[n]   *labour pains, over*

A feyre sone had sche borne;
When sche herde the chylde crye hur beforn,
Hyt comfortyd hur full swythe.   *greatly*
415 So, when sche hurselfe myght styr,   *move*
Sche toke up hur sone to hur,
And lapped hyt full lythe.   *wrapped, softly*

What for febulnes, wery and woo,   *weariness*
Sche felle aslepe, and hur sone alsoo;
420 Hur stede stode hur behynde.
There come a knyght them full nere,
That hyght Syr Barnard, messengere,
Huntyng aftur an hynde;   *hind (female deer)*
And founde that lady, lovely of chere,   *face*

425 And hur sone, slepyng in fere,   *together*
    Lyeng undur a lynde.   *lime tree*
    He put upon that lady bryght,   *came towards*
    And sche loked upon that knyght,
    And was aferde full sore of hys comyng.

430 He seyde, 'What do ye here, madam?
    Fro whens come ye? What ys yowre name?   *From whence*
    Why lye ye here nowe?'
    'Syr,' sche seyde, 'yf ye wyll wytt,   *know*
    My name at home ys Margaret,
435 Y swere be God a vowe!

    'Here have y mekyll grefe: *great distress*
    Helpe me now, at my myschefe,   *in my predicament*
    At some towne that y were.'
    The knyght behelde the ladyes mode,   *observed, manner*
440 And thoght sche was of gentyll blode,   *noble birth*
    That in the foreste was bystadd there.   *beset (by trouble)*

    He toke hur up full curtesly,
    And hur sone, that lay hur by,
    And home he can them lede.
445 He let hur have wemen at wylle,   *at her pleasure*
    To tent hur – and that was skylle –   *attend, proper*
    And broght hur to bede.   *put*

    Whatsoevyr sche wolde crave,   *desired*
    All sche myght redyly hyt have: *quickly*
450 Hur speche was sone spedd.
    They crystenyd the chylde wyth grete honowre,
    And callyd hyt Tryamowre;[n]
    Of hyt they were full gladd.
    A norse they gatt hyt untyll.   *got a nurse for it*
455 Sche had mekyll of hur wyll:
    They dud as sche them badd.   *asked/commanded*
    Sche was bothe curtes and hynde;   *gracious*

    438 So that I can reach some town.
    450 i.e. her spoken wishes were soon fulfilled.
    455 i.e. she (Margaret) got whatever she wished.

Every man was hur frynde,
And of hur was full gladd.

460 There dwellyd that lady longe.
Moche myrthe was them amonge,
But ther gamyd hur no glewe.
Of hyr they were nevyr yrke;   *wearied*
Sche techyd hur sone for to wyrke,[n]
465 And taght hym evyr newe.   *continually(?)*
Hur sone, that than dwellyd hur wyth,
He was mekyll of boon and lyth,   *large, bone and limb*
And feyre of hyde and hewe.   *skin and complexion*
Every man lovyd hym, aftur ther estate;
470 They had no cheson hym to hate: *reason*
So seyde all that hym knewe.

Leve we stylle at the quene,
And of the greyhound we wyll mene,   *tell*
That we before of tolde.
475 Sevyn yere, so God me save,
Kepyd he hys maystyrs grave,   *Guarded*
Tyll that he wexyd olde.   *grew*

Evyr on hys maysty[r]s grave he lay;
Ther myght no man gete hym away,
480 For oght that they cowde do;   *anything*
But yf hyt were onys on the day,   *Except that once a day*
He wolde forthe to gete hys praye,   *go out, catch his prey*
And sythen ageyne he wolde goo.   *afterwards, back*

Sevyn yere he levyd there,   *remained*
485 Tyll hyt befell, agenste the Youle,   *as Yuletide approached*
Upon the fyrste day,[n]
The hounde, as the story says,
Ranne to the kyngys palays,
Wythowt ony more delay.

462 Cf. line 108.
469 All men loved him, according to their rank.
472 Let us say no more of the queen.
478 maystyrs] maystyes C.

490 As the kyng at the mete was than,   *dining*
    Into the halle the hound can ren,   *run*
    Amonge the knyghtys gay.   *finely dressed*
    All abowte he can beholde,   *look*
    And when he sawe not that he wolde   *what he wanted (to see)*
495 He dyd hym faste away.   *He took himself off quickly*

    The hound rennyth evyr, ywys,   *without stopping, indeed*
    Tyll he come there hys maystyr ys;
    He fonde not that he soght.   *what he was seeking*
    The kynge wondryth, in hys wede,[n]
500 Fro when he come and whedur he yede,   *From whence, whither*
    And who hym thedur broght.   *thither*
    He thoght that he had sene hym [y]are,   *before*
    But he wyste not when nor whare,
    Forthy then seyde he noght;   *Therefore*
505 But faste bethenkyth he hym then,   *he ponders earnestly*
    For he thoght he schulde hym kenne;   *recognize*
    So syttyth he in a thoght.   *thinking*

    The tother day, on the same wyse,   *next, in the same way*
    As the kynge fro the borde can ryse,   *table*
510 The hownde spedd not thoo.   *succeeded*
    All abowte the halle he soght,   *searched*
    But at that tyme he fonde hym noght;
    Than dyd he hym faste to goo.
    Then seyde the kyng, that ylke stounde,   *at that time*
515 'Methynkyth that was Syr Roger hounde,
    That wente wyth hym thoo   *then*
    When the quene was flemed owt of my londe.'   *banished*
    'Syr,' they seyde, 'we undurstonde,   *believe*
    Forsothe, that hyt ys soo.'   *Truly*

520 The kyng seyde, 'What may thys mene?   *mean*
    Y trowe Syr Roger and the quene   *suppose*
    Be comen to thys londe:
    For nevyr syth they went, ywys,   *since, indeed*

502 yare] þare C.
510 i.e. he still did not find what he was seeking.

Sawe y Syr Roger hounde or thys.   *before*
525 That ys wondur tythand!ⁿ   *strange news*

'When he goth, pursewe hym then,
For evyrmore he wyll renne
Tyll he come there hys maystyr ys.'   *without stopping*
The tothyr day, among them all,   *next*
530 To mete as they were sett in halle,   *food, seated*
Syr Marrok was there, ferre wythynne, ywys;

And the hounde wolde nevyr blynne,   *cease*
But ranne abowte faste wyth wynne,   *eagerly*
Tyll he wyth hym metyth.   *comes up to him*
535 He starte up verament;   *sprang, truly*
The steward be the throte he hente;   *seized*
The hownd wrekyd hys maystyrs dethe.   *avenged*
The stewardys lyfe ys lorne –   *lost*
There was fewe that rewyd theron,   *regretted it*
540 And fewe for hym wepyth!   *weep*

The greyhownde dyd hym sone to go,   *soon departed*
When hys maystyrs dethe he had venged soo
On hym that wroght hym trayne.   *did him treachery*
All they folowed hym in that tyde,   *at that time*
545 Some on horsys and some besyde,   *i.e. on foot*
Knyghtys, squyers and swayne.   *attendants*
Reste wolde he nevyr have
Tyll he come to hys maystyrs grave,
And then turned he agayne.   *back (to face them)*
550 They myght not gete hym therfro –   *away from there*
He stode at fence ageyn them tho –   *defence, against*
But they wolde hym have slayne.   *Unless*

When they sawe no bettyr bote,   *remedy*
They turned ageyne, on hors and fote,
555 Wyth grete wondur, y wene.   *I believe*
They tolde the kyng all thus.

---

531 i.e. a long way from the door (*literally*, far inside).
552 This line should be understood with line 550: they could not get him away
from there without killing him.
553 i.e. when they saw that there was nothing else to be done.

'Allas!' seyde Kyng Ardus.

'What may thys be to meene?   *What can this mean?*

Y trowe Syr Marrok, be Goddes payne,   *suppose*

560 Have slayne Syr Roger be some trayne,   *treachery*

And falsely flemyd my quene.   *wrongfully*

The hound had not Syr Marrok slayne,   *would not have*

Had not some treson byn,

Be dereworth God, as y wene!'   *precious*

565 They wente agayne, bothe knyght and knave,   *servant*

And founde Syr Roger in hys grave,

As hole as he was layde.[n]

They toke hym up, and leved hym noght.   *left*

The corse before the kyng was broght;   *body*

570 That made hys herte sory, as men sayde.

Hys hownde wolde not fro hym fare.[n]

'Allas!' seyde the kyng. 'Now have y care!

Thys traytur hath me betrayed:

For he hath slayn an awnturs knyght,[n]

575 And flemyd my quene wythowte ryght,

For false tales that he hath me telde.'   *On account of*

The steward, also tyte,   *forthwith*

The kyng let drawe hym, wyth grete dyspyte,

With horsys thorow the towne,

580 And hanged hym on the galowe tree,[n]

That al men myght hyt see,

That he had done treson.

Syr Rogers corse, wyth nobull [arr]ay,   *ceremony*

They beryed hyt the tothyr day,[n]   *next*

585 Wyth many a bolde baron.

Hys hownde wolde not fro hym away,

But evyr on hys grave he lay,

Tyll deth had broght hym downe.

The kyng let sende a messengere

590 Fro towne to towne, ferre and nere,   *far and near*

567 Physically as uncorrupted as when he was buried.

578–9 The king had him dragged, with great ignominy, by horses through the town.

583 array] delay C.

Aftur the quene to spye.   *To look for the queen*
For nothyng that they cowde spere,
They cowde nevyr of hur here: *hear*
Then was the kyng sory.
595 He seyde, 'Now can y no redd,   *I do not know what to do*
For well y wot that y am but dedd –   *know*
For sorowe y wyll now dye.
Allas that sche evyr fro me wente!
Owre false steward hath us schent   *destroyed*
600 Wyth hys false traytory.'   *lying treachery*

Thus leveth the kyng in sorowe;   *lives*
Ther may no blys fro bale hym borowe,
Tyll he be broght to grounde.
Soche lyfe he leved many a yere,
605 Wyth mekyll sorowe and evyll chere;   *bitter thoughts*
Nothyng may make hym sounde.
Hyt dothe the kyng mekyll payne   *causes*
When he thenkyth how Syr Roger was slayne,
And then halpe hys hownde;   *his hound helped (him)*
610 And of hys quene, that was so mylde,
How sche went fro hym grete wyth chylde;
He swownyd that ylke stownde.

And at Syr Roger yende we wyll dwelle,
And of the quene we wyll telle,
615 And of hur chylde, Tryamowre.
He was a moche man and a longe,   *large, tall*
In every lym styff and stronge,   *sturdy*
And semely of colowre.   *beautiful, complexion*
Men and wemen dwellyd he among,
620 Yyt wrethyd he never non wyth wrong –
That was hys owne honowre.

592 i.e. for all their enquiries.
602–3 No joy can deliver him from pain, until he is put in the ground (i.e. only
death can relieve his sorrow).
612 He swooned at the thought of it (*literally*, that same time).
613 We shall cease to speak of Sir Roger's death.
620 Yet he never angered anyone by wrongdoing/injustice.
621 That was (due to) his own (sense of) honour.

In that tyme, certaynly,
Dyed the kyng of Hungary
And was beryed, ywys.
625 He had no heyre hys londes to welde   *heir, rule*
But a doghtyr of sevyn yerys elde: *Except*
Hur name Helyn ys.
Sche was whyte os blossom on flowre,
Mery and comely of colowre,   *Sweet*
630 And semely for to kysse.

When hur fadur was dede,
Moche warre began to sprede
Yn hur lande all abowte.
Therfore sche ys gevyn to rede   *is advised*
635 To take a lorde, to rewle and to lede   *husband*
Hur londe wyth hys rowte: *army*
A nobull knyght, that cowde or myght
Rewle hur londe wyth gode ryght,   *properly*
That men myght drede and dowte.   *fear and respect*

640 Hur cownsell wyll that sche do soo,   *council wishes*
For grete nede cawsyth hur therto;   *impels*
And sche answeryd them there on hye   *in haste (i.e. at once)*
That they schulde faste hur wyth no fere,
But he were prynce or prynceys pere,   *Unless, equal*
645 Or ellys chefe of chyvalry.   *an outstanding knight*
Therfore that lady feyre and gente,
Wyth them wolde sche assente
A justyng for to crye;   *tournament, proclaim*
And at that justyng schall hyt bee
650 Whosoevyr wynneth the gree   *gains preeminence*
Schall wedde hur wyth ryalte.   *royal splendour*

A day of justyng was ther sett   *appointed*
Halfe a yere – no lenger they lett –   *delayed*
To be thore at that day;   *there*
655 That they myght have there a space,   *interval/opportunity*
Knyghtys of dyvers a place,   *various places*
And no lenger delay.[n]

643 That they should bind her to no husband.

Knyghtys of dyvers londys,
When they harde of these tythandys,
660 They gysed them full gay.   *arrayed, finely*

Of every londe the beste,
Thedur they rode, wythowten reste,   *Thither, delay*
Full wele arayed and dyght;   *attired, equipped*
Some therselfe for to assay,   *prove*
665 And some to wynne that feyre may,
That semely was in syght.   *beautiful to behold*
Mekyll was the chevalry   *Great was the number of knights*
That then come to Hungary,
To go juste wyth ther myght!   *joust*

670 When Tryamowre herde telle of thys tythand —
Of that justyng in that londe,
Schulde hastely begynne —   *(That it) should, soon*
Yf he wyste that hyt wolde gayne,   *thought, be of any avail*
He wolde purvey hym full fayne,   *prepare himself, gladly*
675 That lady for to wynne.
He had nothyr hors nor spere,
Nor no wepyn hym wyth to were —
That brake hys herte wythynne.
Faste he bethynkyth hym, bothe evyn and morow,
680 Where hym were beste to borowe;   *it would be best for him*
Arste wolde he not blynne.

To hys lorde he can meene,   *lament*
And preyed hym that he wolde hym leene   *lend*
Wepyn, armowre and stede;
685 'For at the justyng wolde y bene,
To kythe me wyth the knyghtys kene,
My body for to blede.'ⁿ

Syr Barnard seyde, 'What haste thou thoght?
Of justyng canste thou ryght noght,   *you know nothing*

677 Nor any weapon with which to defend himself.
679 He considers earnestly, both evening and morning (i.e. constantly).
681 Cf. line 228.
686 To prove myself among/against the bold knights.

690 For thou art not of age.'ⁿ
     'Syr,' he seyde, 'what wott ye
     Of what strenkyth that y bee,
     Or y be prevyd in felde wyth the sage?'

     Barnarde seyde, also hynde,   *very graciously*
695 'Tryamowre, syn ye wyll wynde,   *since you intend to go*
     Ye schall wante no wede: *lack, armour*
     For y schall lende the all my gere —   *equipment*
     Hors and harnes, schylde and spere —   *armour*
     And helpe the at thy nede.'

700 Then was Tryamowre full blythe;
     He thanked Bernard fele sythe   *many times*
     Of hys feyre proferynge.   *For his generous offer*
     Before the justyng schulde bee,
     The chylde wente to hys modur free,
705 And preyed hur of hur blessynge.   *asked her for*
     Sche wolde have had hym at home fayne,
     But ther myght no speche gayne —
     Ther myght be no lettynge.   *Nothing could stop him*

     Sone on the morne, when hyt was day,   *Early, morning*
710 Tryamowre was gysed full gay,   *attired, finely*
     Redyly armyd and dyght.   *Properly, equipped*
     When he was armed on a stede,
     He was a mykell man of brede,
     And also moche man of myght.   *a man of great strength*
715 Tryamowre to the felde rydeth;
     Barnard no lenger abydeth,
     But rode wyth hym full ryght.   *at once*
  . Ther was no prynce that day in felde
     That was so semely undur schylde   *splendid in his armour*
720 Nor bettur besemyd a knyght.

     691–3 How do you know how strong I am, before I have been proved on the field
     of battle among those who are experienced.
     707 But nothing she could say would avail.
     713 He was a man of great (physical) breadth.
     720 Or more knightly in appearance.

Then was that lady sett
Hye upon a garett,   *High, watch-tower*
To beholde that play.   *sport*
There was many a nobull knyght,
725 And prynceys proved in that fyght,
And themselfe to assay.[n]
Wyth helmes and armowre bryght
That felde schon as candull lyght,   *like*
So were they dyght gay.   *So splendidly were they attired*

730 There was mekyll pres in pryde   *throng, fine apparel*
When eche man began to ryde,
Knyghtys of grete renowne.
Hyt befelle Tryamowre, in that tyde,   *at that time*
To be on hys fadurs syde,   *father's*
735 The kyng of Arragon.
The fyrste that rode, noght forthy,   *nevertheless*
Was the kyng of Lumbardy,
A man of grete renowne;
And Tryamowre rode hym ageyn –   *against*
740 Thogh he were mekyll man of mayne,
The chylde broght hym downe.

The kyngys sone of Armony,   *Armenia*
On a stede, wyth grete envy,   *hostility*
To Tryamowre he ranne;
'45 And Tryamowre turnyd forthy,   *therefore*
And justyd wyth hym pertly,   *boldly*
And downe he bare hym than.   *thrust*

Then seyde Barnard, wyth gret honowre,
'A Tryamowre! A Tryamowre!'
50 That men myght hym kenne.   *know*
Maydyn Elyn, that was so mylde,
More sche behelde that chylde[n]
Then all othur men.   *Than*

Then was ther a bachylere,[n]   *young knight*
55 A prowde prynce, wythowtyn pere –   *equal*

740 Although he was a man of great strength.
750 i.e. to draw attention to him and let people know who he was.

Syr James he hyght,
The emperoure sone of Almayne —   *Germany*
He rode Syr Tryamowre agayne,   *against*
And he kepyd hym full ryght.   *defended himself at once*
760 Ayther on other sperys braste,   *Each, broke*
But neyther to the grounde was caste —
Bothe were they men of myght.
But Syr James had soche a chopp   *received such a blow*
That he wyste not, be my toppe,   *by my head*
765 Whethur hyt were day or nyght.

Thus they justyd tyll hyt was nyght,
Then they departyd — in plyght,   *assuredly*
They had nede to reste!
Sone on the morne, when hyt was day,
770 The knyghtes gysed them full gay,   *attired*
And proved them full preste.   *showed themselves very eager*
Then, wythowtyn more abode,   *delay*
Every knyght to odur rode,   *another*
And sykurly can they stryke and threste.   *surely, thrust*

775 Tryamowre rode forthe in haste,
And prekyd among the oost,   *rode, host*
Upon the tother syde.
The fyrste that rode to hym thon   *then*
Was the kynge of Arragon.
780 He kepeyd hym in that tyde;   *defended himself*
He gaf hys fadur soche a clowte   *blow*
That hors and man felle down, wythowt dowte,
And sone he was dystryed.   *discomfited*

Syr Asseryn, the kynges sone of Naverne,   *Navarre*
785 Wolde nevyr man hys body warne,   *protect*
He come hym ageyne.   *against him*
He hyt hym on the helme soo —   *i.e. Tryamowre hit him*
Soche a strokk he gaf hym tho,
That all men hyt syen.   *saw*
790 The blode braste owt at hys eerys,   *burst*

785 The sense is presumably that he would never hesitate to expose himself to
physical danger.

And hys stede to grownde he berys.   *thrusts*
Then was Syr Barnard fayne.   *glad*

Then that lady of grett honowre,
Whyte os lylly flowre,
795 Hur love was on hym lente.   *given to him*
They sesyd not tyll hyt was nyght,   *ceased*
And then they departyd them, in plyght,   *assuredly*
And to ther ynnys they wente.   *lodgings*

The nyght was paste, the day was come;
800 Every knyght hys hors hath nome;   *taken*
Some were wey and on wylde.[n]
The dewke of Sysell, Syr Sywere,   *Sicily*
He was the furste in that were   *fight*
That fared forthe to the felde.
805 Syr Tryamowre toke to hym a spere: *himself*
To the dowke he can hyt bere,   *At . . . thrust*
And hyt hym on the schylde.
And togedur they wente,   *i.e. they engaged in battle*
That hyt bowed and bente,
810 So ferse he was in felde.
And at that tyme, as y yow hente,   *tell (literally, teach)*
Many a lovely lady gente
Full faste them behelde.   *closely*

The dewke of Lythyr, Syr Tyrre,
815 He prekyd forthe full pertly,   *boldly*
Tryamowre to assayle.   *attack*
Tryamowre turned hym belyve;   *himself, quickly*
To the dewke can he dryve,   *aim*
But lothe he was to fayle.   *reluctant*
820 Soche a strokk he gaf hym then
That the dewke, bothe hors and man,
Turned toppe ovyr tayle.   *head over heels*
Then rode to hym the dewke of Aymere;
He servyd hym on the same manere —
825 Ther myght nothyng avayle.   *i.e. Nothing could prevent it*

Kyng Ardus rode forthe in pres;   *amongst the host*
The emperours sone, Syr James,

A spere spendyd he thare: *expended*
He prekyd to the kyng wyth fors,   *violently*
830 And bare hym downe of hys hors,   *thrust, off*
And hath hym hurted sare.   *grievously*

Then Tryamowre was fayne;
Then he pryked to James of Almayn,
As kene as ony bore.   *fierce, boar*
835 So harde to hym can he caste   *hurl (himself)*
That schylde and spere all to-braste: *broke in pieces*
Then myght James no more.   *could (do)*

Tryamowre wolde nevyr have reste,
But bare hym boldely to the beste,
840 That was moost of honowre.
To ylke a prynce he was preste: *every, ready*
Hors and man downe he caste,
So styrde he hym in that stowre.   *exerted, fight*
Ther was none so gode as he:
845 Therfore they grauntyd hym the gree   *preeminence/prize*
That hyght Tryamowre.[n]   *(To him) who*
Than hath that lady gente
Chosyn hym, wyth comyns assente,[n]
To be hur governowre.   *ruler*

850 Than began the justyng to cese,
And Tryamowre wened to have had pese,   *expected*
And onarmed hym also tyte.   *unarmed himself at once*
The emperours sone, Syr James,
Wyth grete pryde aftur hym can pres: *pursued him*
855 Of hym he had grete dyspyte.   *envy*
To Tryamowre can he crye:
'Yelde the, thefe, or thou schalt dye!   *Yield, villain*
Thou schalt not go qwyte.'   *unpunished*
Tho seyde Tryamowre, wyth grete envy,   *enmity*
860 'Syth y am demed to dye,   *Since, condemned*
Some stroke wyll y smyte!'

839–40 But conducted himself boldly towards the best and most honoured
(knights).
849 i.e. to be her husband and rule her land.

Ther was no lenger let: *delay*
On ylke a syde they hym beset,   *every, surrounded*
And gaf hym many a wounde.
865 Tryamowre sturde hym so there   *exerted himself*
That whosoever he come nere
He was nevyr aftur sownde.   *able-bodied*
Syr Barnard was of myght,
And halpe Syr Tryamowre to fyght,   *helped*
870 And styrde hym in that stownde.   *at that time*

Kyng Ardus of Arragon
Come rydyng to the towne,
And sawe them fyght in fere.   *together*
Hyt dud the kyng mekyll grefe   *caused*
875 When he sawe the chylde at myschefe,   *young man in trouble*
That was hym leve and dere.   *Who was beloved and dear to him*
Than halpe he Tryamowre,
And broght hym gode socowre –   *assistance*
Men that of myght were.
880 Then began a strong stowre;   *fierce battle*
Ther was no lenger socowre,
But every man to hys pere.[n]   *equal*

Syr James was prowde and preste;   *resolute*
Among the knyghtys can he thruste;
885 At Tryamowre had he tene.   *anger*
Styfly he stroke in that stownde,   *He struck hard*
And gaf Tryamowre a wyckyd wounde
Thorowowt the flanke, y wene.   *thigh, believe*

Then was Tryamowre owt of hys wytt: *maddened (by pain)*
890 Syr James on the hedd he hytt,
Tyll he felle downe at that stede.   *in that place*
When Syr James to the grownd was caste,
Hys men were aferde and fledd faste,   *afraid*
And morned for drede.   *lamented*
895 Tryamowre was hurte sore,
That fyght myght he no more,
So byttyrly can he blede.

879 i.e. in the shape of powerful warriors.

Tryamowre made no lenger lettyng,   *delay*
But takyth hys leve at the kyng,
900 And thankyd hym for hys feyre dede.   *noble action*
And nevyr wolde he blynne   *stop*
Tyll he come to Syr Barnardes town wythynne,
And to hys modur he yede.

That lady sorowed in hur wede^n
905 When sche sawe hur sone blede,
That all wan was hur blee and hur blode.   *pale, complexion*
Tryamowre kyssed hys modur in hye,   *at once*
And seyde, 'Modur, let be yowre crye —   *leave off, crying*
Me eylyth nothyng but gode!'
910 A leche was sent aftur in that stownde,   *physician*
For to serche the chyldys wounde,   *probe*
And for to stawnche the chyldys blode.   *staunch*
Tryamowre he undurtoke belyve,
To save hym, upon hys lyfe:
915 Then mendyd hys modurs mode.   *improved, spirits*

The tother knyghtys, the boke says,
Prekyd to the palays,
The lady for to here.
Knyghtys apperyd to hur preste:
920 Then myght sche chose of the beste
Whych that hur wylle were.   *Whichever she wished*
The knyghtys behelde that free,   *noble (lady)*
But Tryamowre can sche not see;
Then chaungyd hur chere.   *mood/expression*
925 Sche seyde, 'Lordynges, where ys hee
That yysturday wan the gree?   *preeminence/prize*
I chese hym to my fere.'   *consort*

All that stode there, thay soght,
But Tryamowre fonde they noght:

902 Until he came inside Sir Barnard's town.
906 Perhaps the sense is that the blood drained from her face.
909 *Literally*, there is nothing the matter with me but good.
913–14 He at once undertook, (swearing) upon his (own) life, to save Tryamowre.
919 Knights presented themselves to her eagerly.

930 Then was that lady woo.
    Hur barons were before hur broght;
    Sche prayed them to graunt hur hur thoght,   *what she wished*
    Respyte of yerys two.
    Sche seyde, 'Lordynges, so God me save,
935 He that me wan, he schall me have:
    Ye wot wele yowre crye was so!'   *know well, proclamation*
    The lordys assentyd wele thertylle,   *to that*
    For sche seyde nothyng but skylle,   *what was reasonable*
    And that sche wolde no moo.

940 When thys was grauntyd, verament,   *truly*
    Of all the folke the lady gente
    Wolde none but Tryamowre.   *Wanted*
    Every prynce in hys present,   *at that time*
    Home to mete there thay went;
945 There dyd they lytyll honowre.[n]
    Syr James men were not fayne,
    For ther lorde was slayne,
    That was so strong in stowre.   *battle*
    And in a chare they hym layne,   *chariot, laid*
950 And ladd hym home into Almayne,   *took*
    To hys fadur, the emperowre.

    The emperowre felle downe in swown
    When they hys sone broght hym beforn,
    And seyde, 'Who hath hym slayne?'
955 They seyde, 'We wott not what he ys,   *who*
    But Tryamowre he hyght, ywys;[n]
    Ther was none there so moche of mayne.   *so powerful*

    'The kyng of Arragon alsoo,
    He halpe hym yowre sone to sloo,   *kill*
960 And also all hys pres.'   *troops*
    'Allas!' seyde the emperowre.
    'Tyll y be venged of Tryamowre,   *have revenge on*
    Schall y nevyr cese.
    King Ardus and Tryamowre,

939 And because she would say nothing more.

965 They schall abye full sore   *pay for*
    The dethe of Syr James!'
    The emperowre, verament,
    Aftur helpe he hath sente —
    Prynces proved in pres.   *proven in battle*

970 The kyng then was sore adredd,   *i.e. King Ardus, afraid*
    For the emperowre soche power hadd,   *Because*
    And wolde hym batayle bede.   *offer*
    He sawe hys londe ovyrspradd;   *overrun*
    To a castell hymselfe fledd,
975 And vetaylyd hyt for drede.

    The emperowre was full stowte,   *strong*
    And beseged the castell abowte,
    And spradd hys baners in haste,[n]
    And gaf asawte to the holde.   *attacked the keep*
980 Kyng Ardus was stowte and bolde:
    And defendyd hym full faste.   *himself, strenuously*
    Kyng Ardus fendyd hys wonys;   *defended his dwellings*
    Wondur grete were the stonys
    That they thereowt cowde caste.[n]
985 They brake of some bothe back and bonys;
    So they farde every day onys;   *They did so once a day*
    The sawte dud six dayes laste.   *assault*

    The kyng thoght that full stronge,   *terrible*
    To be beseged so longe,
990 That he wyste not what to do.   *(So) that*
    Two barons on hys message he sente,   *as his messengers*
    And to the emperowre they went,
    And prayed hym of reste thoo.   *begged him for peace then*

    'Syr, ye wyte owre kyng wyth wronge: *blame, wrongfully*
995 For he never Syr James slowe, at none honde.   *at all*
    He wyll hymselfe qwyte, full fayne,   *clear (of the charge)*
    Nor he was not in present,[n]   *present*
    Nor wyth hys wylle nor wyth hys assent   *by his wish*
    Was not Syr James slayne —

    975 And stocked it with provisions for fear (of a siege).

1000 That wyll he do betwene yow two,
Yowreselfe and he, yf ye wyll soo,
Yf ye hyt on hym wyll say;
Or ellys to take yow a knyght,   *choose for yourself*
And he to take anodur to fyght,
1005 Be a certayne day.   *By an appointed day*
And yf owre knyght happyn soo
To be scowmfetyd or be sloo,   *discomfited*
Os hyt wyll be may,   *As may well be*
He wyll put hym yn yowre wylle
1010 To make yowre pees, as hyt ys skylle,
Wythowtyn more delay.

'And yf hyt so betyde   *happen*
That the knyght of owre syde
May sle yowrys, wyth chawnce,   *by chance*
1015 He preyeth yow that ye wyll cese,
And let owre londys be in pees,
Wythowtyn any dystawnce.'   *discord*
The emperowre, wythowt fayle,   *certainly*
Toke the day of batayle   *Agreed to*
1020 Wyth the kyng, at that chawnce: *risk*
For he had a champyon,
In every londe of moste renown –
In hym was hys fyawnce.   *trust*

When pese was cryed and day tan,   *proclaimed, (a) day set*
1025 Kyng Ardus was a yoyfull man:
He trystyd on Tryamowre.
He sende to seke hym, wythowtyn fayle,
Agayne the day of batayle,   *In readiness for*
For hys dere socowre.   *welcome assistance*
1030 The messengere ys come and gone,
But tydynges of Tryamowre herde he none:
The kyng began to lowre.   *frown*

1000–2 He will demonstrate that (in battle) between the two of you . . . if you will undertake that with him.
1006 owre] yowre C.
1009–10 He will submit to your will and make peace between you, as is reasonable.
1022 every] euery of C.

'Yf he be dedd,' he seyth, 'allas!
Who schall fyght wyth Moradas,
1035 That ys so styffe in stowre?'   *strong in battle*

Whan Tryamowre was hole and sownde,
And coverde of hys grevus wounde,   *recovered from*
He busked hym to fare.   *made himself ready to depart*
'Modur,' he seyde, wyth mylde chere,
1040 'Wyste y who my fadur were,   *If I knew*
The lasse were my care.'   *less would be*

'Sone,' sche seyde, 'wele schalt thou wytt
When thou haste done that thou hett,[n]   *what you promised*
Be God that for us dye can!'
1045 'Modur,' he seyde, 'yf ye wyll soo,
Have gode day, for y wyll goo,
And speke wyth my lemman.'   *sweetheart*

Tryamowre rode ovyr dale and downe,   *valley and hill*
Into the londe of Arragon,
1050 Awnturs to seke and see.   *Adventures*
As he come rydyng in a foreste,
He sawe many a wylde beste,
And had howndys thre.
To a herte he let renne;
1055 Twelve fosters dyscryed hym then,   *caught sight of him*
That were kepars of that fee.   *herd*
They lapped hym in on every syde;   *surrounded*
Ther was no bote but to abyde,
But loth was hym to flee.   *he was reluctant*

1060 He bad a wedd nevyrthelesse,   *offered a surety*
And preyed them that he myght passe,
Yf he had trespaste oght.   *committed any offence*
Then swere the fosters, all twelve,
They wolde no wedd but hymselfe: *wanted*
1065 Othurwes be hyt noght.   *It should not be otherwise*
'Soche ys the lawe of thys londe

1054 i.e. he let the hounds pursue a hart (a young male deer).
1058 There was nothing for it but to stand firm.

That ye muste lese yowre ryght honde;   *lose*
Othur may hyt be noght!'[n]   *It cannot be otherwise*
Then seyde Tryamowre, wyth herte throo,   *fearless*
1070 'That wedd ys me lothe to forgoo,
But hyt be dere boght!'

There was noght ellys to say,
But all the fosters to hym cun lay,   *set upon him*
Wyth sterne worde and mode.
1075 But sone of pees they hym pray;   *they beg him for peace*
Ther wente but oon on lyve away —   *only one alive*
There had they lytyll gode!

When they were betyn to the growndys,
Tryamowre wente to seke hys howndys —
1080 And wolde not leve them soo —
Tyll he come to a watur syde;
There he sawe the beste abyde,   *at bay*
And had slayn hys howndys twoo.   *(it) had*
The thrydd hownde fyghtyng he fyndys;
1085 The beste stroke hym wyth hys tyndys,   *struck, antlers*
And Tryamowre was full woo.
He stroke hys hors into the rever;   *spurred*
He socowrd hys hownde and slew the dere;   *rescued*
Hys bewgull blewe he tho.[n]   *bugle*

1090 The kyng soyournyd, in that tyde,   *was staying*
At a maner there besyde,   *manor*
And herde a bewgull blowe.
All that were in the halle
Wondurd, bothe gret and small,
1095 For no man dud hyt knowe.   *recognize*
Wyth that come a foster,   *Thereupon, forester*
Certenly wyth a fowle chere,   *gloomy expression*
Into the kyngys halle, y trowe.   *I believe*
The kyng at hym can frayne;   *enquire*
1100 'Syr,' he seyde, 'yowre men ar slayne,
All evyn, on a rowe.'   *Altogether, one by one*

1070–1 I am reluctant to give up that pledge, unless it is hard won.

Than he tolde a tale trewe:
'That was he that the horne blewe
That thys wondur hath wroght.
1105 Twenty men were full fewe
To take the knyght, he ys soche a schrewe,   *villain*
But hyt were dere boght!'   *Unless*
Kyng Ardus seyde then,
'Y have mystur of soche a man: *need*
1110 God hath hym hedur broght.   *God has brought him here*
Full well y am begone —   *I am very fortunate*
Y trowe God hath me sent won   *one*
That shall Moradas bryng to noght!'   *destroy*

The kyng callyd knyghtys fyve,
1115 And bad them go belyve,   *quickly*
And fynde hym at hys play: *sport*
'No evyll worde to hym ye nevyn,   *utter*
But sey to hym wyth mylde stevyn —   *speak, gentle voice*
He wyll not sey yow nay.'   *refuse you*

1120 Anon the knyghtys ther horsys hente,
And to the wode then they went,
To seke aftur the chylde.   *young man*
They fonde, be a watur syde,
He sate and fedd hys howndys in that tyde
1125 Wyth the beest so wylde.   *i.e. the hart*
They seyde, 'God be at yowre game!'
He seyde, 'Welcome, all same.'   *all (of you) together*
He lete hymselfe then be gylyd.   *persuaded(?)*
They seyde, 'Syr, ys hyt thy wylle
1130 To come and speke owre kyng tyll,   *to our king*
Wyth wordys meke and mylde?'

Tryamowre asked them, full hende: *courteously*
'Syr,' he seyde, 'what hyght yowre kyng,
And what hyght hys londe?'
1135 'Thys londe,' they seyde, 'hyght Arragon;
The kyng hyght Ardus wyth crowne;
Hys place ys nerehonde.'   *dwelling, nearby*

1103–4 He who blew the horn is the one who has done this terrible deed.
1126 God be with you in your sport!

When Tryamowre come into the halle,
He haylesed the kyng, and sythen all;
1140 He knewe hym at that syght.
The kyng toke hym be the hande,
And made hym glad semelande,   *looked pleased*
And asked hym what he hyght.
'Syr,' he seyde, 'y hyght Tryamowre.
1145 Ye halpe me onys in a stowre —   *once in a battle*
Ye feynyd yow noght to fyght.   *You did not shirk fighting*
Had ye not byn, y had be slayne
Wyth the emperowrs sone of Almayne;   *By*
Ye knewe wele that knyght.'

1150 The kyng wyste wele that hyt was he:
He kyssyd hym tymes thre,
And terys let he falle.
He seyde, 'Welcome ye bee!
Grete blame y have sofurd for the.'   *injury*
1155 And sythen he tolde hym all:
'Wyth the emperowre y have takyn a day,   *set*
To defende me, yf y may.   *defend myself*
To Jhesu wolde y calle,
Os y nevyr Syr James sloo,   *Inasmuch*
1160 He delyvyr me of woo —   *(That) he should*
And so y trowe he schall.'   *trust*

Tryamowre seyde, 'Y am full woo
That thou art for me anoyed soo.   *harassed*
Yf y m07ght hyt amende!   *Would that I could make amends!*
1165 At the day of batayll, forthy,   *therefore*
Ther schall no man fyght but y —
Take the grace that God wyll sende!'
Then was the kyng bothe blythe and gladd,
And seyde, 'For Moradas y am not adrad,
1170 To batayle when he schall wende.
Ofte y made men aftur yow to spere,   *enquire*

1139 He saluted the king, and afterwards all (his retinue).
1140 He (Tryamowre?) recognized him when he saw him.
1147 Had it not been for you, I would have been killed.
1167 i.e. let God's will be done.
1169 I am not afraid of Moradas.

But myght y not of yow here.
My ryght schall thou defende.'

Than dwellyd they togedur same,   *remained, in company*
1175 Wyth mekyll yoye and game —
Therof they wantyd ryght noght.   *They lacked none of that*
They went on hawkyng be the rever,
And otherwhyle to take the dere,   *at other times, catch*
Where that they gode thoght,   *Wherever they pleased*
1180 Tyll the day of batayll was comen,
That they had before nomen.   *appointed*
Then the emperowre thedur soght;   *came there*
Wyth hym he broght kyng and knyght,
And Moradas, that was so wyght,   *brave*
1185 To batayle was he broght.

Bothe the partys there were harde,   *resolute*
And sythen to the felde they farde;
The place was barryd and dyght.   *barred, made ready*
The kyng comfortyd Tryamowre;   *encouraged*
1190 Forsothe, or he went to the stowre   *Truly, before*
He made hym a knyght.ⁿ
The kyng kyste hym, and seyde hym full feyre,   *courteously*
'Tryamowre, y make the myn heyre,
And for me thou schalt fyght.'
1195 'Syr,' he seyde, 'have thou no drede!
Y tryste in God that he schall me spede —   *help me win*
He standyth wyth the ryght.'   *supports*

Then bothe the partyes swore
To holde the covenaunt they made before —
1200 To Jhesu can they calle.
Syr Tryamowre and Moradas
Wer[e] redy armed in that place,
And broght among them all.   *led out*
Ayther were armed on a stede;   *Each was*
1205 Of Tryamowre was grete drede —
Ther was non so hynde in halle.   *gracious*

1173 You shall defend the justice of my cause.
1199 To abide by the agreement they had made previously.
1202 Were] Wery C.

Moradas was so styff in stowre,
Ther myght no man hys dyntys dewre,   *withstand his blows*
But he made them to falle.

1210 Than rode they two togedur aryght;   *at once*
Wyth scharp sperys and swerdys bryght,
They smote togedur sore.
Ther sperys they spendyd and brake schyldys;   *expended*
The pecys flewe into the feldys;   *pieces*
1215 Grete dyntys dud they dele thore.   *They dealt mighty blows*

All had wondur, that there were —
Olde, yonge and chylde, y swere —
So sore they dud smyte.   *hard, strike*
Tryamowre thoght hyt schulde be qwytt;[n]
1220 He faylyd of hym, hys hors he hytt —   *missed him*
To hys herte hys spere can byte.
Moradas seyde, 'Hyt ys grete schame   *very shameful*
On a hors to wreke thy grame!'[n]
Tryamowre seyde, as tyte,
1225 'Levyr y had to have hyt the!   *I would rather*
Have my hors, and let me bee —
Y am lothe to flyte.'   *bandy words*

Moradas seyde, 'Y wyll hym noght,   *I will not (take) him*
Tyll thou have that strok boght,   *paid for*
1230 And wynne hym wyth ryght.'   *properly*
Than leved Tryamowre hys stede;   *left*
He lyghtyd downe and to hym yede;   *dismounted*
On fote can they fyght.[n]
Tryamowre sparyd hym noght,   *spared*
235 But evyr in hys hert he thoght,
'Today was y maked knyght.
Owthyr schall he sle me sone,   *Either, soon*
Or on hym y schall wynne my schone,   *win my spurs*
Thorow the grace of God Almyght!'

240 Grete wondur hyt was to see them two —
The strokys that were betwene them tho —

1223 To take out your anger on a horse.

So harde on helme they hewe.   *hacked*
Moradas was forfoghtyn and forbledd;
Therfore h[e] was nevyr so sore adredd –   *had never been*
1245 Hym gamed lytyll glewe!   *i.e. He was far from merry*
Tryamowre was then ferse;   *furious*
Thorowowt the armour, into the flesche,
He gaf hym a wounde newe.
Thorow hys herte the swerde ranne;
1250 The emperowre was then a sory man,
And Moradas asked trewe.[n]   *truce*

He kyssyd the kyng and was hys frende,
And toke hys leve for to wende –
No lenger wolde he dwelle.   *remain*
1255 Kyng Ardus and Tryamowre
Were ledd home wyth honowre,
Forsothe, as y yow telle.

All that yn that cyte were,   *city*
Bothe lesse and more,   *lesser and greater*
1260 Hym presed for to see.   *Crowded to see him*
There were they, wythowtyn care,   *anxiety*
Wyth glad semeland and welfare –   *looks, prosperity*
Ther myght no bettur bee!

Grete was the honowre and the renowne
1265 That he had in Arragon
For hys feyre dede.
The kyng profurd hym full feyre: *offered, graciously*
'Tryamowre, y make the myn heyre,
Of londe and of lede.'   *people*
1270 'Syr,' he seyde, 'gramercy, nay!   *thank you*
Efte togedur speke we may.   *Later*
Y aske yow but a stede;   *just a horse*
To other londys wyll y spere,   *travel*
More of awnturs for to here,   *adventures*
1275 And who dothe beste yn dede.'

1243 Moradas was exhausted from fighting and loss of blood.
1244 he] ho C.
1275 And (to find out) who does best in deeds (of prowess).

There he dwellyd, whyll he wolde;   *for as long as he wished*
The kyng gave hym bothe sylver and golde,
That ryche gyftys were.
Gode horsys wantyd he noght,   *lacked*
280 To take or to leve, whethur he thoght,
And all hys other gere.

He toke hys leve at the kynge,
And kyssed hym at hys partyng.
The kyngys herte was full sore;
285 He seyde, 'Tryamowre, all that ys myne,
When thou wylt, hyt schall be thyn —
My londe, lesse and more.'   *altogether*

Now ys Tryamowre wente;
Hymselfe ys in gode atente,   *well disposed*
290 For every man ys hys frende.
Ynto every londe, ferre and nere,
Where he myght of awnturs here,   *Wherever*
Thedur can he wende.   *Thither*
In all londys he had the gree: *preeminence*
295 Ther was none so gode as hee
Of all the knyghtys hende.
Therfore gate he grete name   *reputation*
Yn every londe there he came,   *where*
In all placys where he can wende.

300 Justyng and turnamentys let he bee,
And into Hungary wende wyll hee —   *he intends to go*
For no man wyll he lett.   *tarry*
Betwene two mowntayns was hys way;
He went forthe as the strete lay;   *path*
305 Wyth a palmer he mett.   *pilgrim*

He askyd hym gode for charyte;   *alms*
Tryamowre gaf hym, wyth hert free;   *generous*
The palmer for hym can grete.   *weep*
He seyde, 'Syr, turne agayne!   *turn back*

1280 At his disposal, however he wished.
1281 i.e. nor did he lack other equipment.

1310 For, or ye passe the mowntayne,   *before*
      Ye schall be slayne or bete.'   *injured*

      Tryamowre asked hym how soo;   *in what way*
      'Syr,' he seyde, 'for brethur twoo,
      That on thys mowntayn can dwelle.
1315 Therfore y prey yow, wyth herte fayne,   *eager*
      That ye wyll turne ageyne:
      For drede hyt ys wyth them to melle.'   *fearful, engage*
      Then seyde Tryamowre, 'But they were moo,   *Unless, more*
      Owt of my wey wyll y not goo,
1320 Yf they were devyls of helle!'   *Even if*

      He seyde, 'Palmer, have gode day!',
      And went forthe on hys way,
      Os faste os he cowde ryde.
      He had not redyn but a whyle,
1325 Not the mowntans of a myle,[n]
      Two knyghtys sawe he hove and abyde.   *tarry and wait*
      The toon rode hym untyll;   *The one rode up to him*
      The tother hovedd on an hylle,
      A lytull there besyde.   *A little way away*

1330 The toon hoved and behelde
      The strokys they gaf undur schylde –
      Gret wondur had hee.
      Betwene them can he ryde,
      And preyed them to abyde,   *desist*
1335 And sone then let they bee.   *they left off*
      To Tryamowre he seyde anon,
      'So strong a knyght sawe y never non.
      Thy name anon telle thou me.'   *soon*
      Seyde Tryamowre, 'Then wolde y fayn wytt   *gladly know*
1340 Why ye two kepe thys strett,   *guard, path*
      And sythen y schall telle the.'

      The tother brothur seyde, 'We schall yow tell:
      For thys cheson here we dwelle   *reason*
      And wroght all thys woo.   *done all this harm*

      1313 On account of two brothers.

1345 We had a brodur they callyd Moradas;
Wyth the emperowre he was –
A stalworth man ynogh.   *A very strong man*
In Arragon, for the emperowre,
A knyght they callyd Tryamowre
1350 In batayll dud hym sloo.
Yf we wyth hym mett,   *In the hope of meeting with him*
Therfore kepe we thys strett.'
And Tryamowre logh thoo.   *laughed*

'And also y say another: *tell you another (reason)*
1355 Burlonde, owre other brother,
The man moost of myght,   *The strongest of men*
He besegeth a lady,
The kyngys doghtyr of Hungary –
To wedd hur hath he hyght.   *sworn*
1360 And so well then hath he spedd   *succeeded*
That forsothe he schall hur wedd,
Syr Burlonde that knyght,
But yf sche fynde may   *Unless*
To defende hur, os y yow say,
1365 A man of armes bryght.
Therfore sche hath takyn a day –   *agreed on*
Certenly, os y yow say –
And waged hur glove for to fyght.[n]   *pledged*

And that same Tryamowre
1370 Loveth that lady peramowre,[n]   *passionately*
As hyt ys me tolde.
And sche hath aftur hym sente,
And we have waytyd hym, verament,   *lain in wait for him*
And slayne hur barons bolde.
1375 And yf he wyll to Hungary,
Thus forthe schall hys way lye,   *This will be his way forth*
And sle hym fayne we wolde!
He hath hur socowre hett;   *promised her help*
Yf we may, we schall hym lett –   *prevent*
1380 Y trowe hyt schall not holde!

1348 (When he was fighting) for the emperor in Arragon.
1380 i.e. his promise will not be kept.

And yf sche at hur day fayle,
Ther schall nothyng hur avayle,
But Burlonde schall hur wedd.
And Tryamowre noght we kenne:　　　　　　　　*we do not know*
1385　Wherefore there passyth here no men
Wyth strenkyth but they be kedd.
Now have we the cheson tolde,
Thy ryght name wytt fayne we wolde,　　　　　　　*true*
And be thou not adredd.
1390　Thou schalt dwelle here wyth us twoo;
And yf thou wylt not soo,
Evyll then haste thou spedd!'　　　　　　　*You have fared ill*

'Spede,' seyde Tryamowre, 'as y may,
Whyll y have behett yow for to say,
1395　My name schall y not layne.
Yowre jurnay may ye thynk well sett:
Wyth the man have ye mett
That yowre brothur hath slayne.
And ye wyll geve me leve to goo,　　　　　　　*If*
1400　Wyth Burlonde wyll y fyght soo,
For hur love that ye sayne.'
'Welcome,' they seyde, 'Tryamowre!
Hur love thou schalt bye full sore —
Nothyng may the gayne!'　　　　　　　*avail*

1405　They smote togedur, wyth hert throo,　　　　　　　*fierce*
And he allone ageyne them twoo,
To fyght he was full preste.　　　　　　　*eager*
Ther armowre myght not gayne:
Bothe thorowowt back and bone
1410　He made the blode to owt breste.　　　　　　　*burst*
Grete strokys they gaf amonge,　　　　　　　*continually*
And that lasted wondur longe,

1381　i.e. if she fails to produce a champion on the appointed day.
1382　She will have no help for it.
1386　i.e. without being proved in deeds of strength.
1393–5　However I may fare, since I have promised to tell you, I shall not conceal
my name.
1396　Cf. line 346.
1401　For love of her of whom you speak.

Wythowtyn any reste.
So faste abowte conne they goo
1415 That they wroght hym mekyll woo,
As y yow say, be Goddys est.   *grace*

Tryamowrs hors was sekur, ywys,   *trusty*
And hys schylde flewe all to pecys,
So harde to hym they yede.   *they came at him*
1420 In that tyme ther was not soche thre:
Gret wondur hyt was to see,
So doghty they were in dede.   *valiant, deeds of arms*
But Tryamowre, at the laste,
The too[n] brothur downe he caste.   *The one*
1425 Then had the tothur mekyll drede:
No lengur there then wolde he byde,
But rode forthe there a lytull besyde,   *a little way away*
And hovedd on hys stede.

Sone had Tryamowre slayn the tother;
1430 A sory man was hys brothur,
And wolde be venged fayne.   *have revenge*
'Take the grace that God wyll sende me,
Me ys levyr to dye then flee.'   *I would rather*
Wyth that he turned agayne.   *back*
1435 Wyth hys swerde to hym he yede,
And slew Syr Tryamowrs stede —
Full mekyll was hys mayne.   *strength*
Syr Tryamowre faght on fote.
What schall we more of hym mote? —
1440 The tothur brothur was slayne.

Tryamowre takyth the knyghtes stede;
For that lady he was in drede,   *apprehensive*
Forsothe besegedd lay.   *(Who) truly was under siege*
The lady had so grete thoght   *anxiety*
1445 For Tryamowre came noght,

1414 They pressed on him so hard.
1420 There were not three to equal them.
1424 toon] too C.
1432 Cf. line 1167.
1439 What more is there to be said about him? (i.e. to cut a long story short).

Sche wyste not what to say.
The day was come that was sett;
Lordus come, as they hett,   *promised*
Many oon, stowte and gay.   *strong, finely arrayed*
1450 Burlonde was there, redy dyght,
And bad hur brynge forthe hur knyght,
And sche seyde schortly, 'Nay!'   *curtly*

In the castell had sche hyt hyght
To defende hur wyth all hur myght,
1455 So as hur counsayle radd.
'Certys, yf Tryamowre be on lyfe,   *Certainly, is alive*
Wyth Goddys grace, he schall come belyve: *quickly*
Wyth enemyes y am bestadd.   *I am beset by enemies*

'For y trowe he loveth me wele,
1460 And trewe he ys as any stele,   *steel*
In worlde whereever he be bestedd,   *situated*
And he wyste of thys case,   *If*
Hyddur he wolde take hys pase –   *Hither, way*
My lyfe dar y lay to wedd!'

1465 And ryght wyth that come Tryamowre,   *at that very moment*
In the moost of that stowre –   *thickest*
Then gamed hym no glee!
He asked a man what hyt myght meene,
And he tolde hym all bedeene –
1470 How the batayle schulde bee.   *altogether*
He sawe Burlonde on hors hove;
He rode to hym and waged hys glove;[n]   *wait*
That lady chalenged hee.   *He claimed that lady as his*
Sayde Tryamowre, 'Whoso wyll fyght,   *Whoever*
1475 Y am redy in my ryght   *in (defence of) my right*
To slee hym, or he mee.'

The lady on a towre stode,
And sche wende that he had ben wode,   *mad*

1453–5 She had sworn to defend herself in the castle with all her might, as her council advised.
1464 I dare wager my life!
1467 Cf. line 1245.

For sche knewe not hys myght.[n]
1480 Sche asked Barnarde then,
   'Syr, can not ye a knyght kenne   *recognize*
   That ys to batayle dyght?   *Who is arrayed for battle*
   A kreste he beryth in blewe.'   *crest, wears*
   Syr Barnarde then hym knewe,
1485 And seyde, at that syght,
   'Madam, God hath sent yow socowre,
   For yondur ys Syr Tryamowre,
   That wyth Burlonde wolde fyght!'

   Then was that lady full fayne;
1490 Bothe to Jhesu can they prayne
   To gyf hym grace to spede.   *succeed*
   Tryamowre to hym berys,   *thrusts*
   And they all to-braste ther sperys,
   That bothe to the grownde they yede,
1495 That ylke metyng was so throo.   *same encounter, fierce*
   When bothe to the grownde conne goo,
   The rychest in wede,[n]
   They settyd strokes of mode.
   When they bothe to the grownde yode,
1500 They were bothe doghty in dede.

   They start up bothe wythyn a whyle   *sprang, in a moment*
   (Ther stedys on the grownde lay full styll);
   On fote they faght in fere.   *together*
   Ther was none in felde thoo
1505 That cowde chese the bettur of them twoo,   *choose*
   So boldely they them bere.   *acquitted themselves*
   The batayle lasted wondur longe;
   They seyde, 'Be Burlonde never so stronge,
   He hath fonde hys pere.'
1510 Wyth swerdys scharpe the[y] faght faste;
   At ylke stroke the fyre owt braste;   *each, burst*
   They nyghed wondur nere.

1493 And they altogether broke their spears in pieces.
1508–9 However strong Burlonde may be, he has found his equal.
1510 they] þe C.
1512 They drew very close to each other.

Tryamowre at hym conne mynte;   *strike*
Hys swerde felle fro hym at that dynte;   *blow*
1515 To the grownde can hyt goo.
Then was Burlonde full gladd,
And that lady was sore adradd;   *terribly afraid*
Knyghtys were full woo.
Tryamowre asked hys swerde agayne,
1520 But Burlonde faste can hym frayne;   *question*
Then seyde he to hym soo:
'Telle trewly what thou hyght,
And why thou chalangyst that lady bryght –   *you claim*
And take thy swerde the too.'   *And (then you may)*

1525 Sayde Tryamowre, 'On that covenaund,   *agreement*
My ryght name schall y not wande,
Ware thou the devyll of helle!   *Even if you were*
Men calle me Syr Tryamowre;
Y wanne thys lady in a stowre,
1530 Wyth tonge as y the telle.'
Then seyde Burlonde, 'Thou hyt was
That slewe my brodur, Moradas –
A feyre chawnce there the befelle!'
Tho seyde Tryamowre, wyth hert throo,
1535 'So y dud thy brethur twoo   *two brothers*
That dwellyd upon the yondur hylle!'

Then was Burlond all preste;   *most eager/resolute*
'Tryamowre, have thou no reste!
Now am y well bethoght,   *resolved*
1540 Thy swerde getyst thou never agayne,
Tyll y be venged or be slayne –
Sorowe haste thou soght!'
Tho seyde Tryamowre, 'Holde thou thy pese!
That schall the rewe or that we cese!
1545 Go forthe – y drede the noght.'
Burlond to fyght was bowne;   *ready*

1519 Tryamowre asked to be allowed to take back his sword.
1526 I shall not refuse (to tell) my true name.
1533 You were fortunate there.
1542 i.e. you have brought sorrow on yourself.
1544 You shall regret that before we finish!

Hys fote sc[len]t and he felle downe, *slipped*
And Tryamowre wylyly wroght. *acted craftily*

Tryamowre, hys swerde he hente,
1550 And agayne to Burlond he wente,
And servyd hym on the newe gyse:[n] *treated, manner*
He smote Burlond of þe the kneys,
And hewe hys leggys all in pecys, *hacked*
Ryght as he schulde ryse. *As he was about to rise*
1555 'A lytull lower, syr,' seyde hee,
'And let us small go wyth thee.
Now are we bothe at oon assyse.'[n] *the same size*
A lowde laghtur that lady logh; *laughed*
And Syr Barnard was prowde ynogh,
1560 And thanked God fele sythes. *many times*

Burlonde on hys stompus stode — *stumps*
Wyte hym not yf he were wode; *Blame, enraged*
Then faght he wondur faste.[n]
Tryamowre on the hedd he hytt;
1565 He had gevyn hym an evyll smytt, *blow*
But hys swerde braste.
Tryamowre seyde to hym full sone,
'Thy gode dayes are nere done: *nearly over*
Thy power ys nere paste.'
1570 Tryamowre at hym can stryke,
That hedd and fete lay bothe in lyke: *alike*
To grownde was he caste.

Now ys Burlonde slayne,
And Tryamowre, mekyll of mayne,
1575 To the castell ys he wente.
That lady, that was so mekyll of myght,[n]
At the yate she kepyd the knyght, *awaited/met*
And in hur armes hym hente. *took*
Sche seyde, 'Welcome, Syr Tryamowre!
1580 Ye have boght my love full sowre. *won at the cost of great pain*

1547 sclent] schett C.
1552 i.e. he cut off his legs at the knees.
1571 i.e. both head and feet lay severed from the body.

My love ys on yow lente.'   *given to you*
Then seyde all the barons bolde,
'Of hym we wyll owre londes holde,
Be the comyns assent.'ⁿ

1585 Then was ther no nother to say,   *nothing else to say*
      But takyn they have another day,   *agreed*
      That he schulde hur wedd.
      Tryamowre had aftur hys modur sente;
      Barnard aftur hur was went,   *to fetch*
1590 And to the cowrte hur ledd.
      Tryamowre seyde to hys modur then,
      'Now y wolde my fadur kenne,
      For now have we well spedd.   *succeeded*
      Telle me now, modur free,
1595 Who ys my fadur and what hy[gh]t hee?
      For nothyng be ye adredd.'

      Hys modur togedur hur fyngers can folde,
      And all togedur sche hym tolde,
      And mekyll sche can hym meene: *relate*
1600 'Kyng Ardus of Arragone,
      He ys thy fadur, and thou art hys sone,
      And y was hys weddyd qwene.
      And afturward y was delefully demydd,   *grievously condemned*
      And owt of that londe y was flemydd.   *banished*
1605 Y never wyste what hyt myght meene –
      Why hyt was nothur wherefore –   *nor*
      Nothur myght hyt wete lesse nor more,
      But y was broght in tene.'   *distress*

      When Tryamowre thys tale herde –
1610 How he wyth hys modur farde –
      Letturs he dud wryte.
      To the kyng he sente them tylle,

      1592 Now I wish to know who my father was.
      1595 hyght] hyt C.
      1607 i.e. nor did anyone know why.
      1610 What had happened to himself and his mother *or* How he and his mother
      had journeyed.
      1612 *tylle* (to) is tautologous.

And preyed hym, yf hyt were hys wylle,
That he faylyd hym not at that tyde;   *disappointed*

1615 But that he wolde come to Hungary,
For to worschyp that mangery –   *do honour to that feast*
Therof he hym besoght.   *He begged him to do that*
Then was the kyng wondur gladd:
The messengere gode gyftys hadd,[n]   *received*
1620 That the tythyngys broght.   *Who*

The day was come that was sett;
The kyng come, as he hadd hett,   *promised*
Wyth mekyll pres in pryde.   *a great and splendid retinue*
The lordys wolde no lenger lett;   *delay*
1625 The maydyn forthe was fett,   *brought*
And erlys on ylke a syde.   *every*
The lady to the churche they ledd;
A byschopp togedur them to wedd –
Yn herte ys not to hyde.

1630 And sone aftur the weddynge
They crowned Tryamowre kynge –
They wolde no lenger abyde.

Ye may well wytt, certeynly,   *You can be sure*
That there was a grete mangery   *feast*
1635 There as so many were mett.   *Where*
Qwene Margaret began the deyse;[n]
Kyng Ardus, wythowtyn lees,   *deceit*
Be hur was he sett.
The kyng behelde the qwene;
1640 Hym thoght that he schulde hur have seene;
Wyth glad chere he hur grett.   *countenance*
'Yf hyt be yowre wylle,' he seyde, 'madam,
Telle me what ys yowre name,
For nothynge that ye lett.'

1645 'Syr,' seyde the qwene then,
'Sometyme was ye cowde me kenne,   *There was a time when*

1629 i.e. there is no secret about it.
1636 Queen Margaret sat at the head of the dais.
1644 i.e. do not let anything stop you.

And ye were well bethoght.'   *If you considered well*
The kyng spake not oon worde   *one*
Tyll men had etyn and drawen the borde,   *cleared, table*
1650 But stylle he satt in thoght.   *silent*

Then the kyng toke the lady gente,
And to a chaumbur anon they went;
Syr Tryamowre dud they calle.
Sche seyde, 'Here ys yowre sone –
1655 Knowe hym, yf ye konne.'   *Recognize/Acknowledge*
And sythen sche tolde hym all:

Sche tolde how Marrok wowyd hur indede,   *wooed*
Aftur that hur lorde yede –
'For nothyng wolde he spare.   *desist*
1660 Y seyde he schulde be drawe   *torn apart*
For hys sory sawe,   *vile words*
And he seyde he wolde no mare.   *(do so) no more*
Aftur that, in that wode so wylde
He mett me – and y wyth chylde!
1665 To fordo me thoght he thare.   *ruin, intended*
And Syr Roger slewe of hys men fiftene;
And y went away full clene,   *And I got clean away*
They wyste nevyr whare.
Sone aftur, in a wode so wylde,
1670 Y was delyvyr of a chylde,
Wyth mekyll sorowe and care.
Then come Syr Barnard,
Aftur a dere full harde,   *(Chasing) after*
And of me he was ware.   *he noticed me*

1675 'He seyde, "Dame, what doyst thou here?"
And hym y tolde of my matere;   *predicament*
Then syghed he full sore.
He toke up my sone and mee,
And ledd us home, wyth herte free,   *generous*
1680 And evyr sythen have we byn thore.'   *ever since*

Then was there yoye and blys
To see them togedur kysse
Full ofte or they cowde cese.

Kyng Ardus was nevyr so blythe;
1685 He kyssyd Tyramowre twenty sythe,   *times*
And for hys sone he hym chese.   *acknowledged*
Then the qwene was full gladd
That sche soche a lorde hadd –
Ye wott, wythowtyn lees.   *deceit*
1690 Sche seyde, 'Y have well spedd   *I have been fortunate*
That soche a lorde hath me wedd,
That beryth the pryce in prees.'

Then dwellyd they bothe in fere,   *together*
Wyth all maner deynteys that were dere,
1695 Wyth solas on every syde.   *delight*
Kyng Ardus toke hys leve and wente,
And ledd wyth hym hys lady gente;
Home rychely conne they ryde.   *in great state*
All hys londe was full fayne
1700 That the qwene was come ageyn:
The worde spronge full wyde.   *The news spread afar*
Kynge Ardus and hys wyfe,
Wyth yoye and blys they ladd ther lyfe –
Yn hert hyt ys noght to hyde.

1705 Kyng Tryamowre and hys qwene,
Mekyll yoye was them betwene;
Man chylder had they twoo.
Aftur that hys fadur was dedd,
Then he cowde no nothur redd –
710 Ywys, he was full woo.   *Indeed*

Hys yongyst sone then ordeygned hee   *appointed*
Aftur hys fadur kynge to bee –   *i.e. Tryamowre's father*
God grawnt hym wele to reyoyse!

Here endyth Syr Tryamowre,
715 That was doghty in every stowre,

1692 Who is of preeminent renown in battle.
1694 With every sort of costly delicacy.
1704 Cf. line 1629.
1709 *Literally*, Then he did not know what else to do – perhaps with the sense
that he was distraught.
1713 May God grant him joy!

And evyr wanne the gree.   *won the prize/achieved preeminence*
God bryng us to that blys
That ever schall laste, wythowt mys.   *fail*
Amen, amen, for charytee!

1716 gree] gree as þe boke seys C.

SYR LAUNFAL

Be doughty Artours dawes,   *In the days of mighty Arthur*
That held Engelond yn good lawes,   *Who, maintained*
Ther fell a wondyr cas.   *befell, marvel*
Of a ley that was ysette,   *lay, composed*
5 That hyght 'Launval', and hatte yette,[n]
Now herkeneth how hyt was!
Doughty Artour somwhyle   *once*
Sojournede yn Kardevyle,[n]   *Was staying*
Wyth joye and greet solas;   *delight*
10 And knyghtes that wer profitable,   *worthy*
Wyth Artour of the Rounde Table –   *(Were there) with*
Never noon better ther nas:

Sere Persevall and Syr Gawayn,
Syr Gyheryes and Syr Agrafrayn,
15 And Launcelet du Lake;
Syr Kay and Syr Ewayn,
That well couthe fyghte yn playn,   *in full battle*
Bateles for to take;   *engage in*
Kyng Ban, Booght and Kyng Bos,
20 Of ham ther was a greet los –   *renown*
Men sawe tho nowher her make;
Syr Galafre and Syr Launfale,[n]
Wherof a noble tale   *Of whom*
Among us schall awake.   *i.e. be told*

---

5 Which was called 'Launval', and is still so called.
12 There were never any better.
21 At that time their equal was nowhere to be found.

25 Wyth Artour ther was a bacheler,[n]   *young knight*
   And hadde ybe well many a yer: *been*
   Launfal, forsoth, he hyght.   *truly, he was called*
   He gaf gyftys largelyche –   *generously*
   Gold and sylver and clodes ryche –   *clothes*
30 To squyer and to knyght.[n]
   For hys largesse and hys bounte   *generosity, bounty*
   The kynges stuward made was he[n]   *steward*
   Ten yer, y you plyght.   *assure*
   Of alle the knyghtes of the Table Rounde
35 So large ther nas noon yfounde,   *generous*
   Be dayes ne be nyght.   *i.e. At any time*

   So hyt befyll, yn the tenthe yer,
   Marlyn was Artours counsalere:[n]   *counsellor*
   He radde hym for to wende   *advised, go*
40 To Kyng Ryon of Irlond ryght,   *indeed*
   And fette hym ther a lady bryght,
   Gwennere, hys doughtyr hende.[n]   *i.e. Ryon's, noble*
   So he dede, and hom her brought;   *did, home*
   But Syr Launfal lykede her noght,[n]
45 Ne other knyghtes that wer hende:
   For the lady bar los of swych word
   That sche hadde lemmannys unther her lord,
   So fele ther nas noon ende.[n]   *many*

   They wer ywedded, as y you say,
50 Upon a Wytsonday,[n]
   Before princes of moch pryde.   *magnificence*
   No man ne may telle yn tale
   What folk ther was at that bredale,
   Of countreys fer and wyde.   *From, far and wide*
55 No nother man was yn halle ysette
   But he wer prelat other baronette –
   In herte ys naght to hyde.

41 And fetch for himself there a beautiful lady/wife.
46–7 For the lady had the reputation of taking lovers in addition to her husband.
52–3 No one can reckon how many people there were at that bridal feast.
55–6 There was no one seated in the hall who was not (at least) a bishop or a
baronet.
57 i.e. there is no secret about it.

Yf they satte noght alle ylyke,[n]   *Even if, alike*
Har servyse was good and ryche,
60 Certeyn, yn ech a syde.   *on every side (i.e. for them all)*

And whan the lordes hadde ete yn the halle
And the clothes wer drawen alle,   *removed*
As ye mowe her and lythe,   *may hear and listen*
  The botelers sentyn wyn   *cupbearers, served*
65 To alle the lordes that wer theryn,
Wyth chere bothe glad and blythe.   *countenance*
The quene yaf [g]yftes for the nones —   *indeed*
Gold and selver and precyous stonys —
Her curtasye to kythe.   *show*
70 Everych knyght sche yaf broche other ryng,   *gave, or*
But Syr Launfal sche yaf nothyng:
That grevede hym many a syde.[n]   *time*

And whan the bredale was at ende,
Launfal tok hys leve to wende
75 At Artour, the kyng;
And seyde a lettere was to hym come
That deth hadde hys fadyr ynome —   *taken*
He most to hys beryynge.   *must (go) to his burial*
Tho seyde Kyng Artour, that was hende,   *gracious*
80 'Launfal, yf thou wylt fro me wende,
Tak wyth the greet spendyng,   *money for expenses*
And my suster sones two —[n]   *sister's*
Bothe they schull wyth the go,
At hom the for to bryng.'   *To accompany you home*

85 Launfal tok leve, wythoute fable,
Wyth knyghtes of the Rounde Table,
And wente forth yn hys journe,
Tyl he com to Karlyoun,[n]
To the meyrys hous of the toune,[n]
90 Hys servaunt that hadde ybe.

---

59 The manner in which they were served was good and sumptuous.
67 gyftes] yftes MS.
74–5 Took leave of . . . Arthur.
85–6 Took leave . . . of the knights. The phrase *wythoute fable* could mean either
'without deceit' or, more probably, 'to cut a long story short'.
89–90 To the house of the mayor of the town, who had been his servant.

The meyr stod, as ye may here,
And sawe hym come ryde up anblere   *at an easy pace*
Wyth two knyghtes and other mayne.   *attendants*
Agayns hym he hath wey ynome,   *He set out to meet him*
95 And seyde, 'Syr, thou art wellcome!
How faryth our kyng? Tel me.'

Launfal answerede and seyde than,
'He faryth as well as any man –
And elles greet ruthe hyt wore!
100 But, syr meyr, wythout lesyng,   *deceit*
I am thepartyth fram the kyng,   *departed*
And that rewyth me sore!   *grieves*
Nether thar no man, benethe ne above,
For the Kyng Artours love,
105 Onowre me nevermore.   *Esteem*
But, syr meyr, y pray the, paramour,   *of your goodness*
May y take wyth the sojour?   *lodgings*
Somtyme we knewe us yore.'

The meyr stod and bethoghte hym there   *considered*
110 What myght be hys answere,
And to hym than gan he sayn,
'Syr, seven knyghtes han her har in ynom<e>,
And ever y wayte whan they wyl come,
That arn of Lytyll Bretayne.'   *Brittany*
115 Launfal turnede hymself and lowgh –   *turned round, laughed*
Therof he hadde scorn inowgh –   *great scorn*
And seyde to hys knyghtes tweyne,   *two*
'Now may ye se swych ys service   *what service is like*
Unther a lord of lytyll pryse,   *Under, renown*
120 How he may therof be fayn!'[n]   *glad*

Launfal awayward gan to ryde;   *away*
The meyr bad he schuld abyde,   *begged him to wait*
And seyde yn thys manere:
'Syr, yn a chamber by my orchard syd<e>,

99 Otherwise it would be a great sorrow!
103 Nor need any man, of whatever rank.
108 At one time previously we knew each other.
112 Have taken their lodgings here.

125 Ther may ye dwelle wyth joye and pryde,   *splendour*
      Yyf hyt your wyll were.'   *If it is your wish*
    Launfal, anoonryghtes,   *at once*
    He and hys two knytes,
    Sojournede ther yn fere.   *Took up lodgings, together*
130 So [l]argelych hys good he besette[n]   *wealth, spent*
    That he ward yn greet dette   *fell into great debt*
    Ryght yn the ferst yere.   *In the very first year*

    So hyt befell at Pentecost –[n]
    Swych tyme as the Holy Gost
135 Among mankend gan lyght –
    That Syr Huwe and Syr Jon[n]
    Tok her leve for to gon
    At Syr Launfal, the knyght.
    They seyd, 'Syr, our robes beth to-rent,   *tattered*
140 And your t[re]sour ys all yspent,   *wealth*
    And we goth ewyll ydyght.'   *ill-attired*
    Thanne seyde Syr Launfal to the knyghtes fre,   *noble*
    'Tellyd no man of my poverte,   *Tell*
    For the love of God Almyght!'

145 The knyghtes answerede and seyde tho
    That they nolde hym wreye nevermo,   *never betray him*
    All thys world to wynne.
    Wyth that word they wente hym fro
    To Glastyngbery, bothe two,[n]
150 Ther Kyng Artour was inne.   *In which King Arthur was*
    The kyng sawe the knyghtes hende,
    And ayens ham he gan wende,   *to meet*
    For they wer of hys kenne.   *kindred*
    Noon other robes they ne hadde
155 Than they owt wyth ham ladde,
    And tho wer to-tore and thynne.

    Than seyde Quene Gwenore, that was fel,   *evil*

    130 largelych] savargelych MS.
    134–5 The season in which the Holy Spirit descended upon mankind.
    140 tresour] tosour MS.
    154–5 They had no other clothes than those they had taken away with them.
    156 And those were tattered and threadbare.

'How faryth the prowde knyght Launfal?
May he hys armes welde?'   *wield his weapons*
160 'Ye, madame,' sayde the knytes than,   *Yes*
He faryth as well as any man –
And ellys God hyt schelde!'
Moche worchyp and greet honour   *esteem*
To Gonnore the quene and Kyng Artour   *Guinevere*
165 Of Syr Launfal they telde,   *told*
And seyde, 'He lovede us so
That he wold us evermo
At wyll have yhelde.

'But upon a rayny day hyt befel
170 Anhuntynge wente Syr Launfel,
To chasy yn holtes hore.[n]   *woods, grey*
In our old robes we yede that day,
And thus we beth ywent away,
As we before hym wore.'
175 Glad was Artour the kyng
That Launfal was yn good lykyng;   *health/prosperity*
The quene hyt rew well sore,   *regretted*
For sche wold, wyth all her myght,   *wished*
That he hadde be, bothe day and nyght,
180 In paynys mor and more.

Upon a day of the Trinite,[n]
A feste of greet solempnite
In Carlyoun was holde.[n]   *splendour*
Erles and barones of that countre,
185 Ladyes and boriaes of that cite,[n]   *burgesses*
Thyder come, bothe yongh and old.   *Thither*
But Launfal, for hys poverte,   *on account of*
Was not bede to that semble –   *invited, gathering*
Lyte men of hym tolde.
190 The meyr to the feste was ofsent;   *invited*
The meyrys doughter to Launfal went,
And axede yf he wolde   *asked*

162 God forbid that it should be otherwise!
167–8 That he would willingly have kept us with him always.
173–4 And we departed (dressed) as we were when we were in his presence.
189 He was held in low esteem.

In halle dyne wyth her that day.
'Damesele,' he sayde, 'nay!
195 To dyne have I no herte.   *inclination*
Thre dayes ther ben agon
Mete ne drynke eet y noon,
And all was for povert.
Today to cherche y wolde have gon,
200 But me fawtede hosyn and schon,   *I lacked hose and shoes*
Clenly brech and scherte;   *Clean breeches*
And, for defawte of clodynge,   *lack of clothing*
Ne myghte y yn wyth the peple thrynge —   *press*
No wonther dough me smerte!

205 'But o thyng, damesele, y pray the: *one*
Sadel and brydel lene thou me,   *lend*
A whyle for to ryde —   *So that I can ride for a while*
That y myghte confortede be —
By a launde unther thys cyte,   *clearing, beside, city*
10 Al yn thys underntyde.'   *morning*
Launfal dyghte hys courser;[n]   *harnessed, charger*
Wythoute knave other squyer,   *servant, squire*
He rood wyth lytyll pryde.   *pomp*
Hys hors slod and fel yn the fen,   *slipped, mire*
15 Wherfore hym scornede many men
Abowte hym, fer and wyde.[n][n]

Poverly the knyght to hors gan sprynge;
For to dryve away lokynge,   *escape notice*
He rood toward the west.
20 The wether was hot the underntyde;
He lyghte adoun and gan abyde   *dismounted, linger*
Under a fayr forest;   *At the edge of*
And, for hete of the wedere,   *heat*
Hys mantell he feld togydere   *cloak, folded*
25 And sette hym doun to reste.
Thus sat the knyght yn symplyte,   *without ostentation*
In the schadwe unther a tre,[n]
Ther that hym lykede best.

196–7 It is three days since I ate any food or drink.
204 It is no wonder that I smart!
217 Wretchedly – probably with overtones of humiliation.

As he sat yn sorow and sore,   *pain*
230 He saw come out of holtes hore[n]
Gentyll maydenes two.
Har kerteles wer of Inde sandel,[n]   *gowns, Indian silk*
Ilased smalle, jolyf and well —   *Laced, tight, fine*
Ther myght noon gayer go.
235 Har manteles wer of grene felwet,   *velvet*
Ybordured wyth gold, ryght well ysette,   *Adorned*
Ipelured wyth grys and gro.[n]   *Trimmed with fur*
Har heddys wer dyght well wythalle: *adorned, moreover*
Everych hadde oon a jolyf coronall,   *fine circlet*
240 Wyth syxty gemmys and mo.

Har faces wer whyt as snow on downe;   *Their, hill*
Har rode was red, her eyn were browne;   *complexion*
I sawe never non swyche.[n]   *any like them*
That oon bar of gold a basyn,
245 That other a towayle, whyt and fyn,
Of selk that was good and ryche.
Har kercheves wer well schyre,[n]   *bright/finely woven*
Arayd wyth ryche gold wyre.   *Adorned, thread*
Launfal began to syche.   *sigh*
250 They com to hym over the hoth;   *heath*
He was curteys and ayens hem goth,   *to meet*
And greette hem myldelyche.   *greeted, gently*

'Damesels,' he seyde, 'God yow se!'   *God keep you!*
'Syr knyght,' they seyde, 'well the be!
255 Our lady, Dame Tryamour,[n]
Bad thou schuldest com speke wyth here,   *Asked*
Yyf hyt wer thy wylle, sere,   *sir*
Wythoute more sojour.'   *further delay*
Launfal hem grauntede curteyslyche,
260 And wente wyth hem myldelyche;
They [wer] whyt as flour.[n]
And when they come in the forest an hygh,   *above*
A pavyloun yteld he sygh,   *pavilion/tent, pitched, saw*
Wyth merthe and mochell honour.   *i.e. Gay and splendid*

234 No one could be more splendidly attired.
254 May it be well with you!
261 wer] wheryn MS.

265 The pavyloun was wrouth, forsothe, ywys,   *made, indeed*
     All of werk of Sarsynys,[n]   *Saracens*
     The pomelles of crystall.   *finials*
     Upon the toppe an ern ther stod,   *eagle*
     Of bournede gold, ryche and good,   *burnished*
270 Iflorysched wyth ryche amall.   *Decorated, enamel*
     Hys eyn wer carbonkeles bryght;   *carbuncles*
     As the mone the[y] schon anyght,
     That spreteth out ovyr all.[n]   *Which shines*
     Alysaundre, the conquerour,[n]
275 Ne Kyng Artour yn hys most honour,[n]
     Ne hadde noon scwych juell!   *such*

     He fond yn the pavyloun
     The kynges doughter of Olyroun,[n]
     Dame Tryamour that hyghte.
280 Her fadyr was kyng of Fayrye,   *Faery*
     Of occient fer and nyghe,[n]   *the west, far and near*
     A man of mochell myghte.
     In the pavyloun he fond a bed of prys,   *splendid bed*
     Iheled wyth purpur bys,   *Covered, purple linen*
285 That semlye was of syghte.   *beautiful to behold*
     Therinne lay that lady gent,
     That after Syr Launfal hedde ysent;
     That lefsom lemede bryght.   *lovely creature, shone*

     For hete her clothes down sche dede,   *heat, put*
290 Almest to her gerdylstede;   *waist*
     Than lay sche uncovert.
     Sche was as whyt as lylye yn May,
     Or snow that sneweth yn wynterys day;
     He seygh never non so pert.   *openly/alluring(?)*
295 The rede rose, whan sche ys newe,
     Ayens her rode nes naught of hewe,
     I dar well say yn sert.   *with certainty*
     Her here schon as gold wyre;   *hair, like, thread*

272 they] þe MS.
287 Who had sent for Sir Launfal.
296 Was colourless by comparison to her complexion.

May noman rede here atyre,   *describe*
300 Ne naught well thenke yn hert.[n]

Sche seyde, 'Launfal, my lemman swete,   *beloved*
Al my joye for the y lete,   *have lost*
Swetyng, paramour!   *Sweetheart, lover*
Ther nys no man yn Cristente   *Christendom*
305 That y love so moche as the —
Kyng neyther emperour!'[n]   *nor*
Launfal beheld that swete wyghth —   *creature*
All hys love yn her was lyghth —   *was given to her*
And keste that swete flour,   *(he) kissed*
310 And sat adoun her bysyde,
And seyde, 'Swetyng, whatso betyde,   *whatever happens*
I am to thyn honour!'   *at your service*

She seyde, 'Syr knyght, gentyl and hende,
I wot thy stat, ord and ende: *situation, beginning*
315 Be naught aschamed of me!   *embarrassed, before*
Yf thou wylt truly to me take,   *devote yourself to me*
And alle wemen for me forsake,
Ryche I wyll make the.
I wyll the yeve an alner,   *give, purse*
320 Imad of sylk and of gold cler,   *Made, bright*
Wyth fayre ymages thre: *pictures*
As oft thou puttest the hond therinne,   *Whenever, your*
A mark of gold thou schalt wynne,[n]   *gain*
In wat place that thou be.   *Wherever you may be*

325 'Also,' sche seyde, 'Syr Launfal,
I yeve the Blaunchard, my stede lel,   *trusty horse*
And Gyfre, my owen knave.[n]   *servant*
And of my armes oo pensel,
Wyth thre ermyns y[p]eynted well,[n]
330 Also thou schalt have:
In werre ne yn turnement,   *war*
Ne schall the greve no knyghtes dent,

300 Nor properly imagine it.
328 And a pennon with my coat-of-arms.
329 ypeynted] yfeynted MS.
332 No knight's blow shall hurt you.

So well y schall the save!'[n]   *protect*
Than answerede the gantyl knyght,   *noble*
335 And seyde, 'Gramarcy, my swete wyght!   *Thank you*
No bettere kepte y have.'[n]

The damesell gan her up sette,   *sit*
And bad her maydenes her fette   *fetch*
To hyr hondys watyr clere.
340 Hyt was ydo wythout lette;   *done, delay*
The cloth was spred, the bord was sette;   *table*
They wente to hare sopere.   *their*
Mete and drynk they hadde afyn –   *in plenty*
Pyement, clare and reynysch wyn –[n]
345 And elles greet wondyr hyt wer.
Whan they had sowpeth and the day was gon,   *supped*
They wente to bedde, and that anoon,   *at once*
Launfal and sche yn fere.   *together*

For play, lytyll they sclepte that nyght,   *(amorous) sport*
350 Tyll on morn, hyt was daylyght,   *(when) it*
Sche badd hym aryse anoon.
[Sche] seyde to hym, 'Syr gantyl knyght,
And thou wylt speke wyth me any wyght,
To a derne stede thou gon: *secret place*
355 Well privyly I woll come to the –   *secretly*
No man alyve ne schall me se –
As stylle as any ston.'[n]   *quietly*
Tho was Launfal glad and blythe –
He cowde no man hys joye kythe –[n]
360 And keste her well good won.   *i.e. many times*

'But of o thyng, syr knyght, I warne the:
That thou make no bost of me,
For no kennes mede.   *For (the sake of) no sort of reward*
And yf thou doost, y warny the before
365 All my love thou hast forlore.'[n]   *lost*
And thus to hym sche seyde.
Launfal tok hys leve to wende;

345 Otherwise it would have been very strange.
352 Sche] Hy MS.
353 If you wish to speak to me at all.

Gyfre kedde that he was hende,   *showed*
And brought Launfal hys stede.
370 Launfal lepte ynto the arsoun,   *saddle*
And rood hom to Karlyoun
In hys pover wede.

Tho was the knyght yn herte at wylle;   *content*
In hys chaumber he hyld hym stylle   *remained quietly*
375 All that underntyde.
Than come ther thorwgh the cyte ten
Well yharneysyth men   *Richly armed*
Upon ten somers ryde: *pack-horses*
Some wyth sylver, some wyth gold —
380 All to Syr Launfal hyt schold,   *was to go*
To presente hym, wyth pryde,
Wyth ryche clothes and armure bryght.
They axede aftyr Launfal the knyght,   *enquired for*
Whar he gan abyde.

385 The yong men wer clodeth yn Ynde;[n]   *clad*
Gyfre, he rood all behynde
Up Blaunchard, whyt as flour.   *Upon*
Tho seyde a boy, that yn the market stod,
'How fer schall all thys good?
390 Tell us, paramour!'   *of your goodness*
Tho seyde Gyfre, 'Hyt ys ysent
To Syr Launfal yn present,[n]   *as a gift*
That hath leved yn greet dolour.'   *lived, sadness*
Than seyde the boy, 'Nys he but a wrecche!
395 What thar any man of hym recche?
At the meyrys hous he taketh sojour.'   *lodges*

At the merys hous they gon alyghte,
And presented the noble knyghte
Wyth swych good as hym was sent.
400 And whan the meyr seygh that rychesse,   *saw, wealth*

389 Where (*literally*, How far) is all this wealth going?
394 He is nothing but a wretch!
395 Why should (*literally*, What needs) anyone care about him?

And Syr Launfales noblenesse,
He held hymself foule yschent.   *considered, ill-used*
Tho seyde the meyr, 'Syr, par charyte,   *of your kindness*
In halle today that thou wylt ete wyth me.
405 Yesterday y hadde yment   *intended*
At the feste we wold han be yn same,   *together*
And yhadde solas and game;   *pleasure and sport*
And erst thou were ywent.   *already*

'Syr meyr, God foryelde the!   *requite*
410 Whyles y was yn my poverte,
Thou bede me never dyne.   *never invited me*
Now y have more gold and fe,   *property*
That myne frendes han sent me,
Than thou and alle dyne.'   *yours*
415 The meyr for schame away yede;
Launfal yn purpure gan hym schrede,   *clothe*
Ipelured wyth whyt ermyne.   *Furred*
All that Launfal hadde borwyth before,   *borrowed*
Gyfre, be tayle and be score,   *reckoning, tally*
420 Yald hyt well and fyne.[n]   *Repaid*

Launfal helde ryche festes;
Fyfty fedde povere gestes,   *(He) fed fifty*
That yn myschef wer;   *distress*
Fyfty boughte stronge stedes;
425 Fyfty yaf ryche wedes,
To knyghtes and squyere;
Fyfty rewardede relygyons;   *made gifts to, religious (noun)*
Fyfty delyverede povere prysouns,   *prisoners*
And made ham quyt and schere;
430 Fyfty clodede gestours —[nn]   *clothed, minstrels*
To many men he dede honours,
In countreys fer and nere.

Alle the lordes of Karlyoun
Lette crye a turnement yn the toun,   *Proclaimed*
435 For love of Syr Launfel —
And for Blaunchard, hys good stede —

429 Cf. *Amis and Amiloun* 8.13.

To wyte how hym wold spede,
That was ymade so well.   built
And whan the day was ycome
440 That the justes were yn ynome,   agreed
They ryde out also snell.   immediately
Trompours gon har bemes blowe;   Trumpeters, trumpets
The lordes ryden out arowe,   in due order
That were yn that castell.

445 Ther began the turnement,
And ech knyght leyd on other good dent,   laid, blows
Wyth mases and wyth swerdes bothe.   maces
Me myghte yse some therfore
Stedes ywonne and some ylore,
450 And k[n]yghtes wonther wroghth.   extremely angry
Syth the Rounde Table was,   Since
A bettere turnement ther nas,
I dar well say, forsothe!
Many a lord of Karlyou<n>
455 That day were ybore adoun,   thrust down
Certayn, wythouten othe.   doubt

Of Karlyoun the ryche constable   governor
Rod to Launfal, wythout fable —
He nolde no lengere abyde.   tarry
460 He smot to Launfal, and he to hym;   struck at
Well sterne strokes and well grym   fierce, grievous
Ther wer yn eche a syde.   on both sides
Launfal was of hym yware;   aware
Out of hys sadell he hym bar
465 To grounde that ylke tyde.   same time
And whan the constable was bore adoun,
Gyfre lepte ynto the arsoun,   saddle
And awey he gan to ryde.

The erl of Chestere therof segh;   saw that
470 For wreththe yn herte he was wod negh,   anger, nearly mad

437 To find out what success he would have.
448—9 As a result, some horses could be seen won and others lost.
450 knyghtes] kyȝtes MS.
458 Cf. lines 85—6.

And rood to Syr Launfale,
And smot hym yn the helm on hegh,   *on the top of the helmet*
That the crest adoun flegh —[n]   *flew*
Thus seyd the Frenssch tale.[n]
475 Launfal was mochel of myght;   *of great strength*
Of hys stede he dede hym lyght,   *dismounted*
And bar hym doun yn the dale.   *(the earl), on the ground*
Than come ther Syr Launfal abowte
Of Walssche knyghtes a greet rowte —[n]   *Welsh, crowd*
480 The numbre y not how fale.   *I do not know how many*

Than myghte me se scheldes ryve,   *one could, split*
Speres to-breste and to-dryve,
Behynde and ek before.   *i.e. On all sides*
Thorugh Launfal and hys stedes dent,
485 Many a knyght, verement,   *truly*
To ground was ibore.
So the prys of that turnay   *prize/preeminence*
Was delyvered to Launfal that day,
Wythout oth yswore.[n]
490 Launfal rod to Karl<youn>,
To the meyrys hou<s of> the toun,
And many a lord hym before.   *with him*

And than the noble knyght Launfal
Held a feste ryche and ryall,   *royal/splendid*
495 That leste fourtenyght.   *lasted*
Erles and barouns fale   *many*
Semely wer sette yn sale,   *Fittingly, seated, hall*
And ryaly wer adyght.
And every day Dame Triamour,
500 Sche com to Syr Launfal bour,   *bower*
A day whan hyt was nyght.   *Each day*
Of all that ever wer ther tho
Segh he[r] non but they two,
Gyfre and Launfal the knyght.

482 Spears shattered and split in pieces.
498 And were served/dressed with royal splendour.
502–3 None of all those who were there ever saw her except the two of them.
503 her] he MS.

505 A knyght ther was yn Lumbardye;
    To Syr Launfal hadde he greet envye;   *envy/malice*
    Syr Valentyne he hyghte.
    He herde speke of Syr Launfal,
    That he couth justy well
510 And was a man of mochel myghte.   *joust*
    Syr Valentyne was wonther strong;
    Fyftene feet he was longe;
    Hym thoghte he brente bryghte,   *would burst into flames*
    But he myghte wyth Launfal pleye   *Unless, joust*
515 In the feld, betwene ham tweye,   *i.e. in single combat*
    To justy other to fyghte.

    Syr Valentyne sat yn hys halle;
    Hys massengere he let ycalle,   *had called*
    And seyde he moste wende
520 To Syr Launfal, the noble knyght,
    That was yholde so mychel of myght;   *considered*
    To Bretayne he wolde hym sende.   *Britain*
    'And sey hym, for love of hys lemman –
    Yf sche be any gantyle woman,
525 Courteys, fre other hende –   *noble or gracious*
    That he come wyth me to juste,
    To kepe hys harneys from the ruste,[n]   *armour*
    And elles hys manhod schende.'

    The messengere ys forth ywent
530 To tho hys lordys commaundement;   *do*
    He hadde wynde at wylle.   *a favourable wind*
    Whan he was over the water ycome,
    The way to Syr Launfal he hath ynome,
    And grette hym wyth wordes stylle,   *greeted, quiet*
535 And seyd, 'Syr, my lord, Syr Valentyne,
    A noble werrour and queynte of gynne,
    Hath me sent the tylle;   *to you*
    And prayth the, for thy lemmanes sake,
    Thou schuldest wyth hym justes take.'

509 That] þᵉ þᵉ MS.
528 Or else he will bring his manliness into contempt.
536 A noble and skilful warrior.

540 Tho lough Launfal full stylle,   *softly*

And seyde, as he was gentyl knyght,
   Thylke day a fourtenyght   *A fortnight from that day*
He wold wyth hym play.   *joust*
He yaf the messenger for that tydyng   *news*
545 A noble courser and a ryng   *charger*
   And a robe of ray.   *striped cloth*
Launfal tok leve at Triamour,
   That was the bryght berde yn bour,[n]
And keste that swete may.
550 Thanne seyde that swete wyght,
   'Dreed the nothyng, syr gentyl knyght:
Thou schalt hym sle that day.'   *kill*

Launfal nolde nothyng wyth hym have
   But Blaunchard, hys stede, and Gyfre, hys kna<ve>,
555 Of all hys fayr mayne.   *retinue*
He schypede, and hadde wynd well good,   *took ship*
   And went over the salte flod   *sea*
Into Lumbardye.
Whan he was over the water ycome,
560 Ther the justes schulde be nome,   *held*
   In the cyte of Atalye,
Syr Valentyn hadde a greet ost,
   And Syr Launfal abatede her bost,   *subdued, arrogance*
Wyth lytyll companye.   *a small troop*

565 And whan Syr Launfal was ydyght
   Upon Blaunchard, hys stede lyght,   *nimble*
Wyth helm and spere and schelde,
   All that sawe hym yn armes bryght
Seyde they sawe never swych a knyght,
570 That hym wyth eyen beheld.   *(Those) who*
   Tho ryde togydere thes knyghtes two,
That har schaftes to-broste bo,   *spears, both*
   And to-scyverede yn the felde.   *splintered*
Another cours togedere they rod,

574 They charged at each other again.

575 That Syr Launfal helm of glod,   *slipped off*
In tale as hyt ys telde.

Syr Valentyn logh and hadde good game;
Hadde Launfal never so moche schame
Beforhond, yn no fyght.
580 Gyfre kedde he was good at nede,
And lepte upon hys maystrys stede;
No man ne segh wyth syght.[n]   *saw (him)*
And, er than thay togedere mette,   *before they encountered*
Hys lordes helm he on sette,
585 Fayre and well adyght.   *adjusted*
Tho was Launfal glad and blythe,
And donnkede Gyfre many syde   *thanked, times*
For hys dede so mochel of myght.

Syr Valentyne smot Launfal soo
590 That hys scheld fel hym fro,
Anoonryght, yn that stounde.   *At once, at that time*
And Gyfre the scheld up hente,   *caught*
And broghte hyt hys lord to presente   *present (it to him)*
Er hyt cam thoune to grounde.   *Before, down*
595 Tho was Launfal glad and blythe,
And rode ayen the thrydde syde,   *third time*
As a knyght of mochell mounde.   *valour*
Syr Valentyne he smot so there
That hors and man bothe deed were,   *dead*
600 Gronyng wyth grysly wounde.

Alle the lordes of Atalye
To Syr Launfal hadde greet envye   *enmity*
That Valentyne was yslawe,   *Because, slain*
And swore that he schold dye
605 Er he wente out of Lumbardye,
And be hongede and to-drawe.[n]
Syr Launfal brayde out hys fachon,   *drew, sword*
And as lyght as dew he leyde hem doune,
In a lytyll drawe.   *while*
610 And whan he hadde the lordes sclayn,   *slain*
He wente ayen ynto Bretayn,   *back*
Wyth solas and wyth plawe.[n]   *delight and enjoyment*

The tydyng com to Artour, the kyng,
Anoon, wythout lesyng,
615 Of Syr Launfales noblesse.
Anoon a let to hym [s]ende,   *he sent to him*
That Launfall schuld to hym wende
At Seynt Jonnys masse:[n]
For Kyng Artour wold a feste holde
620 Of erles and of barouns bolde,
Of lordynges more and lesse.
Syr Launfal schuld be stward of halle,   *steward*
For to agye hys gestes alle,   *direct*
For [he] cowthe of largesse.   *knew about generosity*

625 Launfal toke leve at Triamour,
For to wende to Kyng Artour,
Hys feste for to agye.
Ther he fond merthe and moch honour,
Ladyes that wer well bryght yn bour,
630 Of knyghtes greet companye.
Fourty dayes leste the feste,   *lasted*
Ryche, ryall and honeste —   *royal, seemly*
What help hyt for to lye?
And at the fourty dayes ende
35 The lordes toke har leve to wende,
Everych yn hys partye.   *direction*

And aftyr mete Syr Gaweyn,
Syr Gyeryes and Agrafayn,
And Syr Launfal also,
640 Wente to daunce upon the grene   *grass*
Unther the tour ther lay the quene,   *where*
Wyth syxty ladyes and mo.
To lede the daunce Launfal was set: *assigned*
For hys largesse he was lovede the bet,   *better*
45 Sertayn, of alle tho.   *by all those*
The quene lay out and beheld hem alle;   *leaned*
'I se,' sche seyde, 'daunce large Launfalle.   *generous*

616 sende] wende MS.
624 he] *om.* MS.
633 What is the point of lying?

To hym than wyll y go.
'Of alle the knyghtes that y se there,
650 He ys the fayreste bachelere:
He ne hadde never n[o] wyf.
Tyde me good other ylle,   *Whether good or ill comes of it*
I wyll go and wyte hys wylle —   *discover, inclination*
Y love hym as my lyf!'   *life*
655 Sche tok wyth her a companye —
The fayrest that sch[e] myghte aspye,   *see*
Syxty ladyes and fyf —   *five*
And wente hem doun anoonryghtes,   *(they) went down*
Ham to pley among the knyghtes,   *To disport themselves*
660 Wel stylle, wythouten stryf.   *quietly, dispute*

The quene yede to the formeste ende,
Betwene Launfal and Gauweyn the hende,
And after her ladyes bryght.
To daunce they wente, alle yn same;   *together*
665 To se hem play, hyt was fayr game,   *good sport*
A lady and a knyght.   *Ladies and knights alternately*
They hadde menstrales of moch honours,   *minstrels*
Fydelers, sytolyrs and trompours —[n]   *citole-players*
And elles hyt were unryght.   *wrong*
670 Ther they playde, forsothe to say,
After mete the somerys day,
All what hyt was neygh nyght.   *Until it was nearly night*

And whanne the daunce began to slake,   *slacken*
The quene gan Launfal to counsell take,
675 And seyde yn thys manere:
'Sertaynlyche, syr knyght,
I have the lovyd wyth all my myght
More than thys seven yere.
But that thou lovye me,   *Unless*

651 no] ne MS.
656 sche] sch MS.
661 The front end (i.e. the head of the dance).
663 And beautiful ladies after her.
674 i.e. she spoke to him privately.
675 manere] marnere MS.

680 Sertes, y dye for love of the,
      Launfal, my lemman dere!'[n]
      Thanne answerede the gentyll knyght,
      'I nell be traytour, thay ne nyght,[n]   *will not, day nor night*
      Be God, that all may stere!'   *guide*

685 Sche seyde, 'Fy on the, thou coward!   *villain*
      Anhongeth worth thou hye and hard.
      That thou ever were ybore,   *born*
      That thou lyvest hyt ys pyte.   *shame*
      Thou lovyst no woman, ne no woman the.[n]
690 Thow wer worthy forlore!'   *You deserve (to be) destroyed*
      The knyght was sore aschamed tho: *embarrassed*
      To speke ne myghte he forgo,   *refrain*
      And seyde the quene before,   *to the queen*
      'I have loved a fayr[er] woman
695 Than thou ever leydest thyn ey upon,
      Thys seven yer and more.

      'Hyr lothlokste mayde, wythoute wene,   *ugliest, doubt*
      Myghte bet be a quene   *better*
      Than thou yn all thy lyve!'   *life*
700 Therfore the quene was swythe wrogt[h];   *very angry*
      Sche taketh hyr maydenes and forth hy go<th>
      Into her tour, also blyve.   *at once*
      And anon sche ley doun yn her bedde;
      For wrethe syk sche hyr bredde,
705 And swore, so moste sche thryve,   *as she hoped to prosper*
      Sche wold of Launfal be so awreke   *avenged*
      That all the lond schuld of hym speke,
      Wythinne the dayes fyfe.

      Kyng Artour com fro huntynge,
710 Blythe and glad yn all thyng;
      To hys chamber than wente he.

      686 You deserve to be hanged high and hard.
      689 You love no woman, nor any woman you.
      694 fayrer] fayrye MS.
      700 wroghth] wrogt MS.
      704 She made herself ill with anger.

Anoon the quene on hym gan crye: *sought his help*
'But y be awreke, y schall dye! *Unless I am avenged*
Myn herte wyll breke a thre!
715 I spak to Launfal yn my game, *jokingly*
And he besofte me of schame,
My lemman for to be.
And of a lemman hys yelp he made, *boast*
That the lodlokest mayde that sche hadde *ugliest*
720 Myght be a quene above me.'

King Artour was well w[ro]th,
And be God he swor hys oth
That Launfal schuld be sclawe. *put to death*
He [s]ente aftyr doghty knyghtes, *valiant*
725 To brynge Launfal anoonryghtes
To be hongeth and to-drawe.[n]
The knyghtes softe hym anoon, *sought*
But Launfal was to hys chaumber gon
To han hadde solas and plawe.
730 He softe hys leef, but sche was lore, *sought his beloved*
As sche hadde warnede hym before –
Tho was Launfal unfawe! *unhappy*

He lokede yn hys alner, *purse*
That fond hym spendyng all plener,
735 Whan that he hadde nede;
And ther nas noon, forsoth to say,
And Gyfre was yryde away *had ridden*
Up Blaunchard, hys stede. *Upon*
All that he hadde before ywonne, *gained*
740 Hyt malt as snow ayens the sunne, *melted, in*
In romaunce as we rede.[n]
Hys armur, that was whyt as flour,
Hyt becom of blak colour.
And thus than Launfal seyde:[n]

716–17 And he begged me to do something shameful, that he might be my lover.
721 wroth] worþ MS.
724 sente] wente MS.
729 Intending to have delight and sport.
734 Which provided him with as much spending money as he wanted.

745 'Alas,' he seyde, 'my creature!
   How schall I from the endure,
   Swetyng, Tryamour?
   All my joye I have forlore,
   And the – that me ys worst fore,
750 Thou blysfull berde yn bour!'[n]   *delightful*
   He bet hys body and hys hedde ek,   *beat, also*
   And cursede the mouth that he wyth spek,   *spoke*
   Wyth care and greet dolour.
   And for sorow, yn that stounde,
755 Anoon he fell aswowe to grounde.   *in a swoon*
   Wyth that come knyghtes four,

   And bond hym and ladde hym tho   *bound, brought*
   (Tho was the knyghte yn doble wo)
   Before Artour, the kyng.
760 Than seyde Kyng Artour,
   'Fyle, ataynte traytour!   *Vile, attainted*
   Why madest thou swyche yelpyng?   *boast*
   That thy lemmannes lodlokest mayde
   Was fayrer than my wyf thou seyde –
765 That was a fowll lesynge!   *lie*
   And thou besoftest her befor than   *entreated*
   That sche schold be thy lemman –
   That was mysprowd lykynge!'   *presumptuous desire*

   The knyght answerede, wyth egre mode,   *angrily*
770 Before the kyng, ther he stode,
   The quene on hym gan lye: *was lying about him*
   'Sethe that y ever was yborn,
   I besofte her herebeforn
   Never of no folye.
775 But sche seyde y nas no man,
   Ne that me lovede no woman,
   Ne no womannes companye.
   And I answerede her, and sayde

746 How can I live without you?
749 And you – that is the worst thing to me.
752 i.e. because it was through breaking his promise of secrecy that he brought such distress upon himself.
773–4 I have never hitherto entreated her to do any rashness.

That my lemmannes lodlekest mayde
780 To be a quene was better wordye.   *worthy*

'Sertes, lordynges, hyt ys so.   *Certainly*
I am aredy for to tho   *ready, do*
All that the court wyll loke.'   *ordain*
To say the soth, wythout les –
785 All togedere how hyt was –
Twelf knyghtes wer dryve to boke.
All they seyde ham betwene,   *between themselves*
That knewe the maners of the quene,
And the queste toke,   *undertook the inquiry*
790 The quene bar los of swych a word   *(That) the*
That sche lovede lemmannes wythout her lord –
Har never on hyt forsoke.   *Not one of them denied it*

Therfor they seyden alle
Hyt was long on the quene and not on Launfal: *due to*
795 Therof they gonne hym skere.   *acquit*
And yf he myghte hys lemman brynge,
That he made of swych yelpynge,
Other the maydenes were   *Or*
Bryghtere than the quene of hewe,
800 Launfal schuld be holde trewe
Of that, yn all manere.   *Concerning that*
And yf he myghte not brynge hys lef,   *beloved*
He schu[l]d be hongede as a thef,   *rogue*
They seyden all yn fere.   *together*

805 Alle yn fere they made proferynge   *proposed*
That Launfal schuld hys lemman brynge;
Hys heed he gan to laye.
Than seyde the quene, wythout lesynge,
'Yyf he bryngeth a fayrer thynge,

779 Made to swear on the Bible.
790–1 Cf. lines 46–7.
799 More beautiful in colour/complexion than the queen.
800 Launfal should be considered innocent (perhaps with the implication that he
should be believed to be telling the truth).
803 schuld] schud MS.
807 He pledged his head (that he would do so).

810 Put out my eeyn gray.'
    Whan that waiowr was take on honde,   *condition, agreed*
    Launfal therto two borwes fonde,   *pledges/guarantors*
    Noble knyghtes twayn:
    Syr Percevall and Syr Gawayn,
815 They wer hys borwes, soth to sayn,
    Tyll a certayn day.[n]   *appointed*

    The certayn day, I yow plyght,   *assure*
    Was twelfmoneth and fourtenyght,
    That he schuld hys lemman brynge.   *By which time*
820 Syr Launfal, that noble knyght,
    Greet sorow and care yn hym was lyght;   *had descended on him*
    Hys hondys he gan wrynge.
    So greet sorowe hym was upan,
    Gladlyche hys lyf he wold a forgon,   *given up*
825 In care and in marnynge;
    Gladlyche he wold hys hed forgo.
    Everych man therfore was wo,
    That wyste of that tydyn[g]e.

    The certayn day was nyghyng.   *approaching*
830 Hys borowes hym broght befor the kyng;
    The kyng recordede tho,[n]   *called to witness (?)*
    And bad hym bryng hys lef yn syght.
    Syr Launfal seyde that he ne myght:
    Therfore hym was well wo.
835 The kyng commaundede the barouns alle
    To yeve jugement on Launfal,
    And dampny hym to sclo.   *condemn him to death*
    Than sayde the erl of Cornewayle,
    That was wyth ham at that counceyle,
840 'We wyllyd naght do so.   *will not*

    'Greet schame hyt wer us alle upon   *would be*
    For to dampny that gantylman,
    That hath be hende and fre.
    Therfor, lordynges, doth be my reed: *advice*

828 tydynge] tydynde MS.

845 Our kyng we wyllyth another wey lede;
    Out of lond Launfal schall fle.'ⁿ   *flee (i.e. be banished)*
    And as they stod thus spekynge,
    The barouns sawe come rydynge
    Ten maydenes, bryght of ble.
850 Ham thoghte they wer so bryght and schene   *fair of face*
    That the lodlokest, wythout wene,
    Har quene than myghte be.

    Tho seyde Gawayn, that corteys knyght,
    'Launfal, brodyr, drede the no wyght: *fear nothing*
855 Her cometh thy lemman hende.'
    Launfal answerede, and seyde, ywys,
    'Non of ham my lemman nys,
    Gawayn, my lefly frende.'   *dear*
    To that castell they wente ryght;   *straight*
860 At the gate they gonne alyght;   *dismount*
    Befor Kyng Artour gonne they wende,
    And bede hym make aredy hastyly   *begged*
    A fayr chamber for her lady,   *their*
    That was come of kynges kende.   *of royal birth*

865 'Ho ys your lady?' Artour seyde.   *Who*
    'Ye schull ywyte,' seyde the mayde,   *see*
    'For sche cometh ryde.'
    The kyng commaundede for her sake
    The fayryst chau[m]ber for to take
870 In hys palys that tyde.
    And anon to hys barouns he sente,
    For to yeve jugemente
    Upon that traytour full of pryde.
    The barouns answerede anoonryght,
875 'Have we seyn the madenes bryght,   *When we have seen*
    Whe schull not longe abyde.'

    A newe tale they gonne tho —   *discussion*
    Some of wele and some of wo —
    Har lord the kyng to queme.   *please*

869 chaumber] chaunber MS.

880 Some dampnede Launfal there,
And some made hym quyt and skere —
Har tales wer well breme.   *discussions, fierce/heated*
Tho saw they other ten maydenes bryght,
Fayryr than the other ten of syght,   *to behold*
885 As they gone hym deme.   *adjudge*
They ryd upon joly moyles of Spayne,   *fine mules*
Wyth sadell and brydell of Champayne;[n]
Har lorayns lyght gonne leme.

They were yclodeth yn samyt tyre: *clothed, silken garments*
890 Ech man hadde greet desyre
To se har clodynge.
Tho seyde Gaweyn, that curtayse knyght,
'Launfal, her cometh thy swete wyght,
That may thy bote brynge!'   *remedy*
895 Launfal answerede, wyth drery doght,   *thought*
And seyde, 'Alas, y knowe hem noght,
Ne non of all the ofsprynge!'[n]
Forth they wente to that palys,
And lyghte at the hye deys,[n]   *high dais*
900 Before Artour, the kynge,

And grette the kyng and quene ek;   *greeted*
And oo mayde thys wordes spak   *one*
To the Kyng Artour:
'Thyn halle agrayde, and hele the walles[n]   *prepare, cover*
905 Wyth clodes and wyth ryche palles,   *cloths, rich cloths*
Ayens my lady, Tryamour.'   *In readiness for*
The kyng answerede bedene,   *at once*
'Wellcome, ye maydenes schene,   *beautiful*
Be Our Lord, the Savyour!'
910 He commaundede Launcelot du Lake to brynge hem yn fere
In the chamber ther har felawes were,   *into, companions*
Wyth merthe and moche honour.   *revelry*

Anoon the quene suppose[de] gyle: *suspected a trick*
That Launfal schulld, yn a whyle,

881 Cf. line 429.
888 Their harness shone brightly.
913 supposede] suppose MS.

915 Be ymade quyt and skere,
      Thorough hys lemman that was commynge.   *By means of*
      Anon sche seyde to Artour, the kyng,
      'Syre, curtays yf [thou] were,
      Or yf thou lovedest thyn honour,
920 I schuld be awreke of that traytour,
      That doth me changy chere —   *makes, change countenance*
      To Launfal thou schuldest not spare.
      Thy barouns dryveth the to bysmare —   *humiliate you*
      He ys hem lef and dere.'

925 And as the quene spak to the kyng,
      The barouns seygh come rydynge
      A damesele alone,
      Upoon a whyt, comely palfrey;   *saddle-horse*
      They saw never non so gay   *finely attired*
930 Upon the grounde gone:[n]
      Gentyll, jolyf as bryd on bowe,   *merry, bird on bough*
      In all manere fayr inowe,   *Very beautiful in every respect*
      To wonye yn wordly wone.   *dwell, earthly dwelling*
      The lady was bryght as blosme on brere,   *blossom, briar*
935 Wyth eyen gray, wyth lovelych chere;   *face*
      Her leyre lyght schoone.   *countenance, brightly*

      As rose on rys her rode was red;   *rose on spray, complexion*
      The her schon upon her hed,   *hair*
      As gold wyre, that schynyth bryght.   *thread*
940 Sche hadde a croune upon her molde,   *head*
      Of ryche stones and of golde;
      That lofsom lemede lyght.   *beautiful (one) shone brightly*
      The lady was clad yn purpere palle,   *rich purple cloth*
      Wyth gentyll body and myddyll small,   *noble, slender waist*
945 That semely was of syght.[n]
      Her mantyll was furryth wyth whyt ermyn,   *furred*
      Ireversyd jolyf and fyn —   *Lined splendidly*
      No rychere be ne myght.

915 Cf. line 429.
918 thou] *om.* MS.
922 You should not spare Launfal.
924 He is beloved and dear to them.

Her sadell was semyly set; *splendidly adorned*
950 The sambus wer grene felvet, *saddle-cloths, velvet*
Ipaynted wyth ymagerye; *pictures*
The bordure was of belles,
Of ryche gold and nothyng elles
That any man myghte aspye; *see*
955 In the arsours, before and behynde, *saddle-bows, in front*
Were twey stones of Ynde,
Gay, for the maystrye. *Extremely brilliant*
The paytrelle of her palfraye *breast-trappings*
Was worth an erldome, stoute and gay, *magnificent*
960 The best yn Lumbardye.

A gerfawcon sche bar on her hond;[n] *gerfalcon*
A softe pas her palfray fond,
That men her schuld beholde.
Thorugh Karlyon rood that lady;
965 Twey whyte grehoundys ronne hyr by;
Har colers were of golde. *collars*
And whan Launfal sawe that lady,
To alle the folk he gon crye an hy,
Bothe to yonge and olde: *loudly*
970 'Her,' he seyde, 'comyth my lemman swete!
Sche myghte me of my balys bete,
Yef that lady wolde.'[n] *If, wished*

Forth sche wente ynto the halle,
Ther was the quene and the ladyes alle, *Where*
975 And also Kyng Artour.
Her maydenes come ayens her ryght, *to meet her at once*
To take her styrop whan sche lyght, *hold her stirrup*
Of the lady, Dame Tryamour.
Sche dede of her mantyll on the flet, *took, floor*
980 That men schuld her beholde the bet, *better*
Wythoute a more sojour. *further delay*
Kyng Artour gan her fayre grete, *greeted her courteously*

962 Her palfrey came at a gentle pace.
963 So that she could be seen.
971 She can cure me of my ills.
979 i.e. she let her cloak fall to the floor.

And sche hym agayn wyth wordes swete,   *in return*
That were of greet valour.   *worth*

985 Up stod the quene and ladyes stoute,   *stately*
     Her for to beholde all aboute,
     How evene sche stod upryght.   *straight*
     Than wer they wyth her also donne
     As ys the mone ayen the sonne
990 Aday, whan hyt ys lyght.   *By day*
     Than seyde sche to Artour, the kyng,
     'Syr, hydyr I com for swych a thyng,   *this purpose*
     To skere Launfal the knyght —   *clear*
     That he never, yn no folye,   *rash moment*
995 Besofte the quene of no drurye,   *lovemaking*
     By dayes ne be nyght.   *i.e. At any time*

     'Therfor, syr kyng, good kepe thou [nyme]:
     He bad naght her, but sche bad hym   *asked*
     Here lemma[n] for to be;
1000 And he answerede her, and seyde
     That hys lemmannes lothlokest mayde
     Was fayryr than was sche.'
     Kyng Artour seyde, wythouten othe,
     'Ech man may yse that ys sothe —   *see, true*
1005 Bryghtere that ye be.'   *That you are more beautiful*
     Wyth that Dame Tryamour to the quene geth,   *goes*
     And blew on her swych a breth
     That never eft myght sche se.ⁿ   *afterwards*

     The lady lep an hyr palfray,   *leapt on*
1010 And bad hem alle have good day —
     Sche nolde no lengere abyde.
     Wyth that com Gyfre, allso prest,   *immediately*
     Wyth Launfalys stede, out of the forest,
     And stod Launfal besyde.

988–9 Then they were as dark by comparison with her as the moon is by
comparison to the sun.
997 nyme] myne MS. Take good heed.
999 lemman] lemmam MS.
1003 wythouten othe] wᵗ oute noþe MS.

1015 The knyght to horse began to sprynge
     Anoon, wythout any lettynge,
     Wyth hys lemman away to ryde.[n]
     The lady tok her maydenys, achon,   *each one*
     And wente the way that sche hadde er gon,   *previously*
1020 Wyth solas and wyth pryde.   *delight, splendour*

     The lady rod dorth Cardevyle,   *through*
     Fer, ynto a jolyf ile,   *Far, delightful island*
     Olyroun that hyghte.[n]
     Every er, upon a certayn day,   *year*
1025 Me may here Launfales stede nay,[n]   *One, neigh*
     And hym se wyth syght.
     Ho that wyll ther axsy justus,   *Whoever wants to ask*
     To kepe hys armes fro the rustus,[n]
     In turnement other fyght,   *or*
1030 Dar he never forther gon —   *Need go no further*
     Ther he may fynde justes anoon,
     Wyth Syr Launfal the knyght.

     Thus Launfal, wythouten fable,   *doubt*
     That noble knyght of the Rounde Table,
1035 Was take ynto Fayrye.
     Seththe saw hym yn th[y]s lond no man;   *Since then*
     Ne no more of hym telle y ne can,
     Forsothe, wythoute lye.
     Thomas Chestre made thys tale[n]
1040 Of the noble knyght Syr Launfale,
     Good of chyvalrye.   *in knighthood*
     Jhesus, that ys hevene kyng,
     Yeve us alle hys blessyng,
     And hys modyr Marye!   **Amen.**

Explicit Launfal

1019 i.e. she went back the way she had come.
1036 thys] þus MS.

THE ERLE OF TOLOUS

Jhesu Cryste yn Trynyte,
Oonly God and persons thre,
Graunt us wele to spede!   *prosper*
And gyf us grace so to do   *give*
5 That we may come thy blys unto,
On rode as thou can blede.[n]
Leve lordys, y schall you telle   *Dear*
Of a tale, sometyme befelle   *once*
Farre yn unkowthe lede: *foreign nation*
10 How a lady had grete myschefe,   *was much wronged*
And how sche covyrd of hur grefe —   *recovered*
Y pray yow, take hede!

Sometyme ther was in Almayn   *Germany*
An emperrour of moche mayn —   *power*
15 Syr Dyaclysyon he hyght.   *was called*
He was a bolde man and a stowte;   *strong*
All Crystendome of hym had dowte,   *fear*
So stronge he was in fyght.
He dysheryted many a man,   *seized the inheritance of*
20 And falsely ther londys wan,   *won*
Wyth maystry and wyth myght;   *force*
Tyll hyt befelle, upon a day,
A warre wakenyd, as y yow say,   *broke out*
Betwene hym and a knyght,

25 The erle of Tollous, Syr Barnard.
The emperour wyth hym was harde,

6 By your death on the cross.

And gretly was hys foo.   *enemy*
He had rafte owt of hys honde   *seized*
Thre hundred poundys worth be yere of londe —
30 Therfore hys herte was woo.
He was an hardy man and a stronge,   *brave*
And sawe the emperour dyd hym wronge,
And other men also.
He ordeyned hym for batayle   *made himself ready*
35 Into the emperours londe, saunsfayle,   *without fail*
And there he began to brenne and sloo.   *burn and kill*

Thys emperour had a wyfe,
The fayrest oon that evyr bare lyfe,   *lived*
Save Mary, mekyll of myght;   *Except for*
40 And therto gode in all thynge,   *moreover*
Of almesdede and gode berynge,   *deeds of alms, conduct*
Be day and eke be nyght.   *also*
Of hyr body sche was trewe
As evyr was lady that men knewe,
45 And therto moost bryght.   *beautiful*
To the emperour sche can say,
'My dere lorde, y you pray,
Delyvyr the erle hys ryght.'   *what is rightfully his*

'Dame,' he seyde, 'let that bee:
50 That day schalt thou nevyr see,
Yf y may ryde on ryght,
That he schall have hys londe agayne —
Fyrste schall y breke hys brayne,
Os y am trewe knyght!   *As*
55 He warryth faste in my londe;   *keenly*
I schall be redy at hys honde   *to meet him (in battle)*
Wythyn thys fourtene nyght.'
He sente abowte everywhare,
That all men schulde make them yare   *ready*
60 Agayne the erle to fyght.   *Against*

29 Land worth £300 a year.
39 The phrase *mekyll of myght* is probably best translated here as 'full of grace'.
43 i.e. she was faithful to her husband.
51 i.e. For as long as I can sit upright in the saddle (*literally*, ride properly).

He let crye in every syde, · *had it proclaimed*
Thorow hys londe, ferre and wyde, *Throughout*
Bothe in felde and towne,
All that myght wepon bere –
65 Sworde, alablast, schylde or spere – *cross-bow*
They schoulde be redy bowne. *armed in readiness*
The erle on hys syde also,
Wyth fourty thousand and moo,
Wyth spere and schylde browne. *burnished*
70 A day of batayle there was sett; *appointed*
In felde, when they togedur mett,
Was crakyed many a crowne. *Many a head was split*

The emperour had bataylys sevyn; *battalions*
He spake to them wyth sterne stevyn, *voice*
75 And sayde, so mote he thryve, *as he hoped to prosper*
'Be ye now redy for to fyght?
Go ye, and bete them downeryght, *utterly*
And leveth non on lyve! *leave, alive*
Loke that none rau[n]somyd bee,
80 Nothyr for golde ne for fee, *Neither, property*
But sle them wyth swerde and knyfe.'
For all hys boste, he faylyd yyt; *Despite, still*
The erle manly hym mett, *manfully*
Wyth strokys goode and ryfe. *many*

85 They reryd batayle on every syde; *joined battle*
Bo[l]dely togedyr can they ryde,
Wyth schylde and many a spere.
They leyde on faste, as they were wode,
Wyth swerdys and axes that were gode –
90 Full hedeous hyt was to here.
There were schyldys and schaftys schakydd, *spears*
Hedys thorogh helmys crakydd, *through*
And hawberkys all to-tore. *coats of mail torn to pieces*
The erle hymselfe an axe drowe;
95 An hundred men that day he slowe,
So wyght he was yn were. *valiant, war*

79 raunsomyd] raumsomyd C.
86 Boldely] Bodely C.
88 They struck at one another hard, as if they were mad.

Many a stede there stekyd was;   *pierced*
Many a bolde baron in that place
Lay burland yn hys own blode.   *weltering*
100 So moche blode there was spylte,
That the felde was ovyr hylte,   *covered over*
Os hyt were a flode.   *As if*
Many a wyfe may sytt and wepe,
That was wonte softe to slepe,   *Who used to sleep soundly*
105 And now can they no gode.   *know of*
Many a body and many a hevyd,   *head*
Many a doghty knyght there was levyd,   *valiant, left*
That was wylde and wode.

The erle of Tollous wan the felde;   *won the battle*
110 The emperour stode and behelde.
Wele faste can he flee
To a castell there besyde;   *nearby*
Fayne he was hys hedd to hyde,   *Glad*
And wyth hym erlys thre.
115 No moo, forsothe, scapyd away: *more, truly*
But they were slayn and takyn that day
Hyt myght non othyr bee.
The erle tyll nyght folowed the chace,   *pursuit*
And sythen he thanked God of hys grace,   *then*
120 That syttyth in Trynyte.

There were slayne in that batayle
Syxty thousand, wythowte fayle,
On the emperours syde;
Ther was takyn thre hundred and fyfty
125 Of grete lordys, sekyrly,   *certainly*
Wyth woundys grymly wyde.   *grievously*
On the erlys syde ther were slayne
But twenty, sothely to sayne,   *truly*
So boldely they can abyde.   *stand their ground*
130 Soche grace God hym sende,   *sent*
That false quarell cometh to evell ende,[n]
For oght that may betyde.   *Whatever happens*

108 Who had been savage and enraged.
116–17 It could not be otherwise than that they were killed and captured that
day.

Now the emperour ys full woo: *very sorrowful*
He hath loste men and londe also –
135 Sore then syghed hee.   *sighed*
He sware be hym that dyed on rode
Mete nor drynke schulde do hym no gode
Or he vengedd bee.   *Before he was avenged*
The emperes seyde, 'Gode lorde,   *empress, Good husband*
140 Hyt ys better yeve acorde,   *make peace*
Be oght that y can see.   *For anything*
Hyt ys grete parell, sothe to telle,   *peril*
To be agayne the ryght quarell –   *against, cause*
Be God, thus thynketh me!'   *it seems to me*

145 'Dame,' seyde the emperoure,
'Y have a grete dyshonoure –
Therfore myn herte ys woo.
My lordys be takyn, and some dede;
Therfore carefull ys my rede –[n]
150 Sorowe nye wyll me sloo.'   *nearly, kill*
Then seyde Dame Beulybon,
'Syr, y rede, be Seynt John,   *advise*
Of warre that ye hoo.   *cease*
Ye have the wronge and he the ryght,
155 And that ye may see in fyght,
Be thys and othyr moo.'

The emperour was evyll payde: *ill-pleased*
Hyt was sothe the lady sayde –
Therfore hym lykyd ylle.
160 He wente awey and syghed sore;
Oon worde spake he no more,   *He spoke not another word*
But helde hym wonder stylle.   *kept, silent*
Leve we now the emperour in thoght –
Game ne gle lyked hym noght,
165 So gretly can he grylle –   *grieve*
And to the erle turne we agayn,   *let us return*
That thanked God wyth all hys mayn,   *might*
That grace had sende hym tylle.   *Who had sent him grace*

146 I have been greatly dishonoured.
156 By this (defeat) and others besides.
164 Neither sport nor amusement was pleasing to him.

The erle Barnard of Tollous
170 Had fele men chyvalrous   *men, knightly*
Takyn to hys preson.
[How] moche gode of them he hadd   *wealth, from*
Y can not telle, so God me gladd,
So grete was ther raunsome!
175 Among them had he oon
Was grettest of them, everychon,   *i.e. the highest in rank*
A lorde of many a towne –
Syr Trylabas of Turky;
The emperour hym lovyd, sekurly,   *certainly*
180 A man of grete renowne.

So hyt befelle upon a day,
The erle and he went to play   *disport themselves*
Be a rever syde.[n]   *river*
The erle seyde to Trylabas,
185 'Telle me, syr, for Goddys grace,
Of a thyng that spryngyth wyde: *is widely spoken of*
That youre emperour hath a wyfe,
The fayrest woman that ys on lyfe,
Of hewe and eke of hyde.   *colour, skin/complexion*
190 Y swere by boke and by belle,[n]
Yf sche be so feyre as men telle,
Mekyll may be hys pryde!'   *He may well be proud!*

Then sayde that lord anonryght,   *at once*
'Be the ordre y bere of knyght,
195 The sothe y schall telle the:
To seeke the worlde, more and lesse,
Bothe Crystendome and hethynnesse,   *heathendom*
Ther ys none so bryght of blee.   *beautiful, colour/face*
Whyte as snowe ys hur coloure,
200 Hur rudde ys radder then the rose floure,   *complexion, redder*
Yn syght who may hur see.   *Whoever may see her*
All men that evyr God wroght   *created*

172 How] *om.* C.
173 As (I hope that) God will make me rejoice.
194 By the order of knighthood that I bear.
196 i.e. in all the world, in every part.

Myght not thynke nor caste in thoght   *imagine*
A fayrer for to bee.'   *That there is any fairer*

205 Then seyde the erle, 'Be Goddes grace,
Thys worde in mornyng me mas,   *makes me grieve*
Thou seyest sche ys so bryght!   *You say, beautiful*
Thy raunsom here y the forgeve;   *remit*
My helpe, my love whyll y leve,   *live*
210 Therto my trowthe y plyght,
So that thou wylt brynge me   *Provided that*
Yn safegarde for to bee
Of hur to have a syght;
An hundred pownde, wyth grete honoure,
215 To bye the horses and ryche armoure,   *buy yourself*
Os y am trewe knyght.'

Than answeryd Syr Trylabas,
'Yn that covenaunt, in thys place,   *On that understanding*
My trowthe y plyght thee.
220 Y schall holde thy forward gode: *abide by, agreement*
To brynge the, wyth mylde mode,   *i.e. peaceably*
In syght hur for to see.   *Where you can see her*
And therto wyll y kepe counsayle   *maintain secrecy*
And nevermore, wythowte fayle,
225 Agayne yow to bee.   *Against*
Y schall be trewe, be Goddys ore,   *grace*
To lose myn own lyfe therfore –
Hardely tryste to mee!'   *Confidently trust*

The erle answeryd, wyth wordes hende,   *gracious*
230 'Y tryste to the as to my frende,
Wythowte any stryfe.   *dispute*
Anon that we were buskyd yare,
On owre jurney for to fare,
For to see that wyfe.   *woman*

209–10 I pledge my faith (that you shall have) my help and friendship for as long as I live.
212–13 i.e. where I can safely see her.
227 Even if I lose my own life as a result.
232 Let us make ourselves ready at once.

235 Y swere be God and Seynt Andrewe[n]
     Yf hyt be so y fynde the trewe,
     Ryches schall be to the ryfe.'   plentiful
     They lettyd nothyr for wynde nor wedur,   delayed, weather
     But forthe they wente, bothe togedur,
240 Wythowte any stryfe.

     These knyghtes never stynte nor blanne   stopped, ceased
     Tyll to the cyte that they wan   they reached the city
     There the emperes was ynne.   Where
     The erle hymselfe, for more drede,   fear
245 Cladd hym in armytes wede,[n]   hermit's garments
     Thogh he were of ryche kynne: noble family
     For he wolde not knowen bee.   did not want to be recognized
     He dwellyd there dayes three,
     And restyd hym in hys ynne.   lodgings
250 The knyght bethoght hym on a day   decided
     The gode erle to betray;
     Falsely he can begynne.   Treacherously

     Anone he wente in a rese   in haste
     To chaumbur, to the emperes,
255 And sett hym on hys knee.
     He seyde, 'Be hym that harowed helle,[n]
     He kepe yow fro all parelle,
     Yf that hys wylle bee!
     Madam,' he seyde, 'be Jhesus,
260 Y have the erle of Tollous –
     Oure moost enemye ys hee.'   greatest
     'Yn what maner,' the lady can say,
     'Ys he comyn? Y the pray,
     Anone telle thou me.'   At once

265 'Madam, y was in hys preson;
     He hath forgevyn me my raunsom,   remitted
     Be God, full of myght!
     And all ys for the love of the;
     The sothe ys, he longyth yow to see,

     257 May he guard you against all danger.

270 Madam, onys in syght.   *once*
       An hundred pownde y have to mede,   *in reward*
       And armour [and] a nobull stede.
       Forsothe, y have hym hyght   *Truly, promised*
       That he schall see yow at hys fylle,
275 Ryght at hys owne wylle –
       Therto my trowthe y plyght.

       'Lady, he ys to us a foo: *an enemy*
       Therfore y rede that we hym sloo –   *advise*
       He hath done us grete grylle.'   *harm*
280 The lady seyde, 'So mut y goo,   *i.e. Upon my life*
       Thy soule ys loste yf thou do so!
       Thy trowthe thou schalt fulfylle.
       Sythe he forgaf the thy raunsom,   *Since*
       And lowsydd the owt of preson,   *freed*
285 Do away thy wyckyd wylle!ⁿ   *Give up your wicked intentions!*

       'Tomorne, when they rynge the masbelle,
       Brynge hym into my chapelle,
       And thynke thou on no false sleythe.
       There schall he see me at hys wylle,
290 Thy covenaunt to fulfylle:
       Y rede the, holde thy trowthe!   *advise, preserve, loyalty*
       Certys, yf thou hym begyle,   *Certainly, deceive*
       Thy soule ys in grete peryle,
       Syn thou haste made hym othe.   *Since, sworn an oath to him*
295 Certys, hyt were a traytory   *treachery*
       For to wayte hym [wyth] velany –   *ensnare, wickedness*
       Methynkyth hyt were rewthe.'   *would be piteous*

       The knyght to the erle wente;
       Yn herte he helde hym foule schente

272 and] *thus* A L R; *for* C.
274 That he shall see you to his heart's content.
275 Fully in accordance with his own wishes.
282 You shall keep your promise.
286 Tomorrow morning, when they ring the bell for Mass.
288 And do not think of any treacherous trick.
296 wyth] *thus* L R; *om.* C.
299 He considered himself ill-used.

300 For hys wyckyd thoght.
He seyde, 'Syr, so mote y the,   *as I hope to prosper*
Tomorne thou schalt my lady see;
Therfore dysmay the noght.   *do not despair*
When ye here the masbelle,
305 Y schall hur brynge to the chapelle —
Thedur sche schall be broght.
Be the oryall syde stonde thou stylle;[n]
Then schalt thou see hur at thy wylle,
That ys so worthyly wroght.'   *Who, nobly formed*

310 The erle sayde, 'Y holde the trewe;
And that schall the nevyr rewe,   *you will never regret that*
As farre forthe as y may!'   *To the best of my ability*
Yn hys herte he waxe gladd: *grew*
'Fylle the wyne wyghtly,' he badd: *quickly*
315 'Thys goyth to my pay!'   *to my liking*
There he restyd that nyght;
On the morne he can hym dyght   *clothed himself*
Yn armytes array.   *attire*
When they ronge to the masse,
320 To the chapell conne they passe,
To see that lady gay.   *finely dressed*

They had stonden but a whyle,
The mowntaunse of halfe a myle,[n]
Then came that lady free.   *noble*
325 Two erlys hur ladd;
Wondur rychely sche was cladd,
In golde and ryche perre.   *jewels*
Whan the erle sawe hur in syght,
Hym thoght sche was as bryght
330 Os blossome on the tree.
Of all the syghtys that ever he sye   *saw*
Raysyd never none hys herte so hye,
Sche was so bryght of blee.

Sche stode stylle in that place,
335 And schewed opynly hur face,

310 I believe you are loyal.

For love of that knyght.
He behelde ynly hur face;   *attentively*
He sware there, be Goddys grace,
He sawe never none so bryght.
340 Hur eyen were gray as any glas;
Mowthe and nose schapen was   *were formed*
At all maner ryght;   *Properly in every respect*
Fro the forhedd to the too,   *toe*
Bettur schapen myght non goo,   *i.e. be*
345 Nor none semelyer yn syght.   *more beautiful to behold*

Twyes sche turnyd hur abowte,
Betwene the erlys that were stowte,   *valiant*
For the erle schulde hur see.   *So that*
When sche spake, wyth mylde stevyn,   *gentle voice*
350 Sche semyd an aungell of hevyn,[n]
So feyre sche was of blee:
Hur syde longe, hur myddyll small,   *waist, slender*
Schouldurs, armes therwythall –   *as well*
Fayrer myght non bee;
355 Hur hondys whyte as whallys bonne,   *whalebone*
Wyth fyngurs longe and ryngys upon,
Hur nayles bryght of blee.[n]   *colour*

When he had beholden hur welle,
The lady wente to hur chapell,
360 Masse for to here.
The erle stode on that odur syde;
Hys eyen fro hur myght he not hyde,
So lovely sche was of chere.
He seyde, 'Lorde God, full of myght,
365 Leve y were so worthy a knyght
That y myght be hur fere!
And that sche no husbonde hadd,   *If*
All the golde that evyr God made
To me were not so dere!'
370 When the masse come to ende,

362 i.e. he could not take his eyes off her.
365–6 Grant that I might be a knight worthy to be her consort!

The lady, that was feyre and hende,
To the chaumbur can sche fare.
The erle syghed and was full woo,
Owt of hys syght when sche schulde goo;
375 Hys mornyng was the mare.   *sorrow, greater*
The erle seyde, 'So God me save,
Of hur almes [y] wolde crave,   *alms, beg*
Yf hur wylle ware:
Myght y [oght] gete of that free
380 Eche a day hur to see,[n]
Hyt wolde covyr me of my care!'   *cure me*

The erle knelyd down anonryght,
And askyd gode, for God Allmyght,   *alms*
That dyed on the tree.
385 The emperes callyd a knyght:
'Fourty floranse that ben bryght   *florins*
Anone brynge thou mee.'
To that armyte sche hyt payde;   *gave*
Of hyr fyngyr a rynge she layde   *From*
390 Amonge that golde so free.   *fine*
He thankyd hur ofte, as y yow say.
To the chaumbyr wente that lady gay,
There hur was leveste to bee.

The erle wente home to hys ynnys,   *lodgings*
395 And grete yoye he begynnys
When he founde the rynge.
Yn hys herte he waxe blythe,   *grew joyful*
And kyssyd hyt fele sythe,   *many times*
And seyde, 'My dere derlynge,
400 On thy fyngyr thys was;
Wele ys me y have thy[s] grace,
Of the to have thys rynge!
Yf evyr y gete grace of the quene,

377 y] *thus* A L R; he C.
379 oght] *thus* L; *not*. C.
389 Of] *thus* A; Of on C; And of L.
393 Where it most pleased her to be.
401 thys] thy C. I am fortunate to have this blessing.

That any love betwene us bene,[n]
405 Thys may be oure tokenyng.'

The erle, also soone os hyt was day,   *as soon as*
Toke hys leve and wente hys way
Home to hys cuntre.
Syr Trylabas he thanked faste: *earnestly*
410 'Of thys dede thou done me haste,
Well qwyt schall hyt bee.'   *rewarded*
They kyssyd togedur, as gode frende;
Syr Trylabas home can wende –
There evell mote he thee![n]   *There may he prosper ill!*
415 A traytory he thoght to doo,   *treachery*
Yf he myght come thertoo,   *achieve it*
So schrewde in herte was hee.   *wicked*

Anon he callyd two knyghtys,
Hardy men at all syghtys;   *Valiant, in all respects*
420 Bothe were of hys kynne.
'Syrs,' he seyde, 'wythowt fayle,
Yf ye wyl do be my counsayle,
Grete worschyp schulde ye wynne.   *honour*
Knowe ye the erle of Tollous?
425 Moche harme he hath done us:
Hys boste y rede we blynne.
Yf ye wyll do aftur my redd,   *according to my advice*
Thys day he schall be dedd,
So God save me fro synne!'

430 That oon [h]yght Kamiturs, that odur Kaym;[n]   *was called*
Falser men myght no man rayme,   *find (?)*
Certys, then were thoo.   *those*
Syr Trylabas was the thrydde.   *third*
Hyt was no mystur them to bydd
435 Aftur the erle to goo!
At a brygge they hym mett;

426 I suggest that we put a stop to his arrogance.
430 hyght] *thus* A L R; knyght C.
434 There was no need to beg them.

Wyth harde strokes they hym besett,   *attacked him*
As men that were hys foo.
The erle was a man of mayn: *strength*
440 Faste he faght them agayne,   *Hard, against*
And soone he slew twoo.

The thrydd fledd, and blewe owt faste;   *panted*
The erle ovyrtoke hym at the laste;
Hys hedd he clofe in three.   *split*
445 The cuntrey gedyrd abowte hym faste,
And aftur hym yorne they chaste —   *eagerly, chased*
An hundred there men myght see.
The erle of them was agaste;   *terrified*
At the laste fro them he paste —   *he eluded them*
450 Fayne he was to flee!   *Glad*
Fro them he wente into a waste;
To reste hym there he toke hys caste;   *chance*
A wery man was hee!

All the nyght in that foreste
455 The gentyll erle toke hys reste —
He had no nodur woon.   *dwelling*
When hyt dawed, he rose up soone,   *dawn came*
And thankyd God, that syttyth in trone,   *on throne*
That he had scapyd hys foon.
460 That day he travaylyd many a myle —
And ofte he was in grete parylle
Be the way os he can gone —
Tyll he come to a fayre castell,
There hym was levyst to dwelle,
465 Was made of lyme and stone.

Of hys comyng hys men were gladd.
'Be ye mery, my men!' he badd.
'For nothyng ye spare!   *Do not abstain for anything*
The emperour, wythowte lees,   *deceit*
470 Y trowe, wyll let us be in pees,   *believe*
And warre on us no mare.'
Thus dwellyd the erle in that place,

464 Where it most pleased him to dwell – i.e. his own castle.

Wyth game, myrthe and grete solase,   *delight*
Ryght os hym levyst ware.   *Just as*
475 Let we now the erle alloon,
And speke we of Dame Beulyboon –
How sche was caste in care.   *brought into sorrow*

The emperour lovyd hys wyfe
Also so moche os hys own lyfe –
480 And more, yf he myght.
He chose two knyghtys, that were hym dere,
Whedur that he were ferre or nere,   *Whether*
To kepe hur day and nyght.   *guard*
That oon hys love on hur caste,   *fell in love with her*
485 So dud the todur at the laste: *other*
Sche was feyre and bryght.
Nothyr of othyr wyste ryght noght;   *knew*
So derne love on them wroght,   *secretly, worked*
To dethe they were nere dyght.   *brought*

490 So hyt befelle, upon a day,
That oon can to that othyr say,
'Syr, also muste y thee,
Methynkyth thou fadyste all away,
Os man that ys clongyn in clay,
495 So pale waxeth thy blee.'
Then seyde that other, 'Y make a vowe:
Ryght so, methynketh, fareste thou,
Whysoevyr hyt bee.
Telle me thy cawse, why hyt ys,
500 And y schall telle the myn, ywys –
My trouthe y plyght to thee!'

'Y graunte,' he seyde, 'wythowt fayle!
But loke hyt be trewe counsayle.'   *a secret faithfully kept*
Therto hys trowthe he plyght.
505 He seyde, 'My lady, the emperes,
For love of hur y am in grete dystresse –
To dethe hyt wyll me dyght!'   *bring*
Then seyde that othyr, 'Certenly,

494 *Literally*, shrivelled in earth (i.e. dead).

Wythowte drede, so fare y,   *doubt*
510 For that lady bryght.
Syn owre love ys on hur sett,   *Since*
How myght owre bale beste be bett?   *affliction, relieved*
Canste thou rede on ryght?'   *give good advice*

Then seyde that othyr, 'Be Seynt John,
515 Bettur counsayle can y noon,
Methynkyth, then ys thys:
Y rede that oon of us twoo
Prevely to hyr goo,   *Secretly*
And pray hur of hur blys.
520 Y myselfe wyll go hyr tylle;   *to her*
Yn case y may gete hur wylle,
Of myrthe schalt thou not mys!
Thou schalt take us wyth the dede: *catch us in the act*
Leste thou us wrye sche wyll drede,   *betray*
525 And graunte the thy wylle, ywys.'   *desire, indeed*

Thus they were at oon assent.   *in agreement*
Thys false thefe forthe wente   *treacherous villain*
To wytt the ladyes wylle.   *find out, inclination*
Yn chaumbyr he founde hyr so free;
530 He sett hym downe on hys knee,
Hys purpose to fulfylle.
Than spake that lady free:
'Syr, y see now well be the   *i.e. from your looks*
Thou haste not all thy wylle.
535 On thy sekenes now y see.
Telle me now thy prevyte —   *secret*
Why thou mornyst so stylle.'   *grieve, silently*

'Lady,' he seyde, 'that durste y noght,
For all the gode that evyr was wroght,
540 Be grete God invysybylle![n]
But on a booke yf ye wyll swere
That ye schull not me dyskere,   *expose*

519 i.e. beg her to gratify him sexually.
521–2 If I can get her to yield to me, you shall have your share of pleasure.
535 I now see that you are sick.

Then were hyt possybyll.'
They seyde the lady, 'How may that bee,
545 That thou darste not tryste to mee?
Hyt ys full orybylle!   *horrible*
Here my trowthe to the y plyght,
Y schall heyle the, day and nyght,   *keep your secret*
Also trewe as boke or belle.'[n]

550 'Lady, in yow ys all my tryste.
Inwardely y wolde ye wyste   *I earnestly wish that you knew*
What payne y suffur you fore:
Y drowpe, y dare nyght and day;   *droop, pine*
My wele, my wytt ys all away,   *well-being*
555 But ye leve on my lore.
Y have yow lovyd many a day,
But to yow durste y nevyr say —
My mornyng ys the more!   *grief, greater*
But ye do aftur my rede,
560 Certenly, y am but dede —
Of my lyfe ys no store!'   *My life is worthless*

Than answeryd that lovely lyfe,   *creature*
'Syr, wele thou wottyst y am a wyfe;
My lorde ys emperoure.
565 He chase the for a trewe knyght,   *chose*
To kepe me, bothe day and nyght,
Undur thy socowre.   *protection*
To do that dede yf y assente,   *If I agree to do that deed*
Y were worthy to be brente   *I would deserve to be burned*
570 And broght in grete doloure.   *grief*
Thou art a traytour in thy sawe,   *speech*
Worthy to be hanged and to-drawe,[n]
Be Mary, that swete floure!'

'A, madam,' seyde the knyght,
575 'For the love of God Almyght,
Hereon take no hede!   *Do not attach any importance to this*
Yn me ye may full wele tryste ay: *always*
Y dud nothyng but yow to a[ss]ay,[n]   *test*

555 Unless you believe what I tell you, *or* Unless you trust to my counsel.
571 i.e. what you say is treacherous.
578 assay] affray C.

Also God me spede!

580 Thynke, madam, youre trowthe ys plyght
To holde counsayle, bothe day and nyght,
Fully, wythowte drede.   *doubt*
Y aske mercy, for Goddys ore!   *grace*
Hereof yf y carpe more,   *speak*

585 Let drawe me wyth a stede!'

The lady seyde, 'Y the forgeve.
Also longe os y leve,
Counsayle schall hyt bee.   *A secret*
Loke thou be a trewe man,

590 In all thyng that thou can,
To my lorde so free.'
'Yys, lady: ellys dyd y wronge –
For y have servyd hym longe,
And wele he hath qwytt mee.'   *repaid*

595 Hereof spake he no mare,
But to hys felowe can he fare –
There evyll must they the!ⁿ

Thus to hys felowe ys he gon,
And he hym frayned anon: *asked*

600 'Syr, how haste thou spedd?'   *fared*
'Ryght noght!' seyde that othyr.
'Syth y was borne, lefe brothyr,   *dear*
Was y nevyr so adredd!   *afraid*
Certys, hyt ys a boteles bale   *pointless, trouble*

605 To hur to touche soche a tale,
At borde or at bedde.'ⁿ   *i.e. Under any circumstances*
Then sayde that odur, 'Thy wytt ys thynne!
Y myselfe schall hur wynne –
Y lay my hedd to wedde!'   *I wager my head*

610 Thus hyt passyd ovyr, os y yow say,
Tyl aftur, on the thrydde day,
Thys knyght hym bethoght:
'Certys, spede os y may,   *however I may fare*

605 i.e. to broach such a subject to her.
607 Your intelligence is meagre.

My ladyes wylle, that ys so gay,   *inclination*
615 Hyt schall be thorowly soght.'   *enquired into thoroughly*
When he sawe hur in beste mode,
Sore syghyng to hur he yode,   *went*
Of lyfe os he ne roght.
'Lady,' he seyde, 'wythowte fayle,
620 But ye helpe me wyth yowre counsayle,
Yn bale am y broght!'

Sche answeryd full curtesly:
'My counsayle schall be redy.
Tell me how hyt ys.
625 When y wott worde and ende,[n]
Yf my counsayle may hyt mende,   *remedy*
Hyt schall, so have y blysse!'
'Lady,' he seyde, y undurstonde,
'Ye muste holde up yowre honde
630 To holde counsayle, ywys.'
'Yys,' seyde the lady free.
'Thereto my trouthe here to the,
And ellys y dudd amys!'

'Madam,' he seyde, 'now y am in tryste,   *am confident*
635 All my lyfe thogh ye wyste,
Ye wolde me not dyskevere.   *expose*
For yow y am in so grete thoght,
Yn moche bale y am broght,
Wythowte othe, y swere!   *doubt*
640 And ye may full wele see
How pale y am of blee —
Y dye nere for dere!
Dere lady, graunt me youre love,
For the love of God, thatt sytteth above,
645 That stongen was wyth a spere!'   *pierced*

'Syr,' sche seyde, 'ys that youre wylle?
Yf hyt were myne, then dyd y ylle!

618 As if he cared nothing for (his) life.
627 As I hope to have (heavenly) joy.
632 Here I give you my word as to that.
642 I am nearly dead with affliction.

What woman holdyst thou me?   *What (sort of) woman*
Yn thy kepeyng y have ben:
650 What haste thou herde be me or sene   *regarding me*
That touchyth to any velanye,   *concerns, wickedness*
That thou in herte art so bolde,
Os y were a hore or a scolde?   *As if*
Nay, that schall nevyr bee!
655 Had y not hyght to holde counsayle,   *promised*
Thou schouldest be honged, wythowt fayle,
Upon a galowe tree!'

The knyght was never so sore aferde,
Syth he was borne into myddyllerd,[n]   *the world*
660 Certys, os he was thoo.
'Mercy,' he seyde, 'gode madam!
Wele y wott y am to blame —
Therfore myn herte ys woo.
Lady, let me not be spylte —   *destroyed*
665 Y aske mercy of my gylte!
On lyve ye let me goo.'
The lady seyde, 'Y graunte wele:
Hyt schall be counseyle, every dele;   *part*
But do no more soo!'

670 Now the knyght forthe yede,
And seyde, 'Felowe, y may not spede.   *succeed*
What ys thy beste redd?
Yf sche telle my lorde of thys,
We be but dedd, so have y blys!
675 Wyth hym be we not fedd.[n]
Womans tonge ys evell to tryste;[n]
Certys, and my lorde hyt wyste,   *if*
Etyn were all owre bredd.
Felow, so mote y ryde or goo,
680 Or sche wayte us wyth that woo,
Hurselfe schall be dedd!'

'How myght that be?' that othur sayde.
'Yn herte y wolde be wele payde,   *pleased*

675 i.e. he will no longer provide for us.
680 Before she inflicts that distress on us.

Myght we do that dede.'   *If we could*
85 'Yys, syr,' he seyde, 'so have y roo!   *as I hope for peace*
Y schall brynge hur wele thertoo —
Therof have thou no drede.   *doubt*
Or hyt passe dayes three,   *Before three days are passed*
In mekyll sorowe schall sche bee:
90 Thus y schall qwyte hur hur mede.'   *repay her*
Now are they bothe at oon assente,
In sorow to brynge that lady gente —
The devell mote them spede!

Sone hyt drowe toward nyght;
95 To soper they can them dyght,   *went*
The emperes and they all.
The two knyghtys grete yapys made,   *jests*
For to make the lady glade,
That was bothe gentyll and small.   *slender*
00 When the soper tyme was done,
To the chaumbyr they went soone,
Knyghtys cladd in palle.   *rich cloth*
They daunsed and revelyd, os they noght dredd,
To brynge the lady to hur bedde —
05 There foule muste them falle!   *Ill-fortune befall them!*

That oon thefe callyd a knyght,
That was carver to that lady bryght —[n]
An erleys sone was hee.[n]
He was a feyre chylde and a bolde;   *young man*
10 Twenty wyntur he was oolde;
In londe was none so free.
'Syr, wylt thou do os we the say?
And we schall ordeyne us a play,   *arrange, game*
That my lady may see.
15 Thou schalt make hur to lagh soo,
Thogh sche were gretly thy foo,
Thy frende schulde sche bee.'

The chylde answeryd anonryght,
'Be the ordur y bere of knyght,

703 As if they feared nothing.

720 Therof wolde y be fayne –
   And hyt wolde my lady plese,   *If*
   Thogh hyt wolde me dysese –   *inconvenience*
   To renne yn wynde and rayne!'
   'Syr, make the nakyd save thy breke,   *except, breeches*
725 And behynde the yondur curtayn thou crepe,
   And do os y schall sayne.
   Then schalt thou see a yoly play.'
   'Y graunte,' thys yonge knyght can say,
   'Be God and Seynte Jermayne!'[n]

730 Thys chylde thoght on no ylle;   *suspected no evil*
   Of he caste hys clothys stylle,   *Off, quietly*
   And behynde the curtayn he went.
   They seyde to hym, 'Whatso befalle,   *Whatever happens*
   Come not owt tyll we the calle.'
735 And he seyde, 'Syrs, y assente.'
   They revelyd forthe a grete whyle;
   No man wyste of ther gyle,   *deceit*
   Save they two, veramente.   *Except, truly*
   They voyded the chaumber sone anon; *left the room empty*
740 The chylde they lafte syttyng alone,
   And that lady gente.

   Thys lady lay in bedd on slepe;
   Of treson toke sche no kepe,
   For therof wyste sche noght.   *she had no suspicion*
745 Thys chylde had wonder ever among   *from time to time*
   Why these knyghtys were so longe –
   He was in many a thoght.   *much puzzled*
   'Lorde, mercy! How may thys bee?
   Y trowe they have forgeten me,
750 That me hedur broght.   *(Those) who brought me here*
   Yf y them calle, sche wyll be adredd –
   My lady lyeth here in hur bedde –
   Be hym that all hath wroght!'   *created*

   Thus he sate, stylle as any stone;
755 He durste not store nor make no mone,   *stir, sound*
   To make the lady afryght.[n]
   Thes false men – ay worthe them woo! –

   757 May they always be wretched!

To hur chaumbur can they goo,
And armyd them full ryght.   *properly*
760 Lordys owte of bedd can they calle,
And badd arme them, grete and smalle:
'Anone that ye were dyght!   *Arm yourselves quickly!*
And helpe to take a false traytoure,
That wyth my lady in hur bowre
765 Hath playde hym all thys nyght.'   *disported himself*

Sone they were armyd, everychone,
And wyth these traytours can they gone,
The lordys that there wore.
To the emperes chaumber they cam ryght,   *straight*
770 Wyth torchys and wyth swerdys bryght
Brennyng them before.   *Burning*
Behynde the curtayne they wente;
The yonge knyght, verrament,
Nakyd founde they thore.
775 That oon thefe, wyth a swerde of were,   *of war*
Thorow the body he can hym bere,   *thrust*
That worde spake he no more.

The lady woke and was afryght,
Whan sche sawe the grete lyght
780 Before hur beddys syde.
Sche seyde, 'Benedycyte!   *Bless us!*
Syrs, what men be yee?'
And wonder lowde sche cryedd.
Hur enemyes mysansweryd thore,   *answered abusively*
785 'We are here, thou false hore!
Thy dedys we have aspyedd.   *watched*
Thou haste betrayed my lorde:
Thou schalt have wonduryng in thys worde –[n]
Thy loos schall sprynge wyde.'   *(ill) fame, spread*

790 The lady seyde, 'Be Seynte John,
Hore was y nevyr none,
Nor nevyr thoght to bee!'
'Thou lyest!' they seyde. 'Thy love ys lorne.'[n]
The corse they leyde hur beforne: *body*

795 'Lo, here ys thy lemman free!   *sweetheart*
    Thus we have for the hym hytt.
    Thy horedam schall be wele quytte –
    Fro us schalt thou not flee.'
    They bonde the lady wondyr faste,   *bound*
800 And in a depe preson hur caste –
    Grete dele hyt was to see!   *sorrow*

    Leve we now thys lady in care,
    And to hur lorde wyll we fare,
    That ferre was hur froo.   *far*
805 On a nyght, wythowt lette,
    In hys slepe a swevyn he mett –   *he dreamed a dream*
    The story telleth us soo.
    Hym thoght ther come twoo wylde berys,   *bears*
    And hys wyfe all to-terys,   *tear to pieces*
810 And rofe hur body in twoo.[n]   *tore*
    Hymselfe was a wytty man,   *intelligent*
    And be that dreme he hopyd than   *supposed/expected*
    Hys lady was in woo.

    Yerly, when the day was clere,   *Early, bright*
815 He bad hys men, all in fere,   *together*
    To buske and make them yare.   *equip themselves, ready*
    Somer horsys he let go before,   *Pack-horses, ahead*
    And charyettys stuffud wyth store,   *wagons, provisions*
    Wele twelve myle and mare.
820 He hopud wele in hys herte   *supposed*
    That hys wyfe was not in querte;   *safety*
    Hys herte therfore was in care.
    He styntyd not tyll he was dyght,   *ceased, prepared*
    Wyth erlys, barons and many a knyght;
825 Homeward can they fare.

    Nyght ne day, nevyr they blanne,   *stopped*
    Tyll to that cyte they came
    There the lady was ynne.
    Wythowt the cyte lordys them kepyd;   *Outside, awaited/met*

805 The formulaic *wythowt lette* here appears to mean 'without doubt'.
819 The line should be understood with *before* in line 817.

830 For wo in herte many oon wepyd —
     There teerys myght they not blynne.   *check*
     They supposyd wele yf he hyt wyste,
     That hys wyfe had soche a bryste,   *was in such a plight*
     Hys yoye wolde be full thynne.   *meagre*
835 They ladden stedys to the stabyll,
     And the lorde into the halle,
     To worschyp hym wyth wynne.   *honour, joy*

     Anon to the chaumbur wendyth he:
     He longyd hys feyre lady to see,
840 That was so swete a wyght.   *creature*
     He callyd them that schoulde hur kepe:
     'Where ys my wyfe? Ys sche on slepe?
     How fareth that byrde bryght?'   *fair lady*
     The twoo traytours answeryd anon,
845 'Yf ye wyste how sche had done,
     To dethe sche schulde be dyght.'   *She should be put to death*

     'A, devyll!' he seyde. 'How soo?
     To dethe that sche ys worthy to go,
     Telle me in what manere.'
850 'Syr,' he seyde, 'be Goddys ore,   *grace*
     The yonge knyght, Syr Antore,
     That was hur kervere,   *carver*
     Be that lady he hath layne,
     And therfore we have hym slayne —
855 We founde them in fere.   *together*
     Sche ys in preson, verrament;
     The lawe wyll that sche be brente,[n]   *requires*
     Be God, that boght us dere!'   *redeemed us dearly*

     'Allas!' seyde the emperoure.
860 'Hath sche done me thys dyshonoure,
     And y lovyd hur so wele?
     Y wende for all thys worldys gode   *believed*
     That sche wolde not have turned hur mode —   *been fickle*
     My yoye begynnyth to kele.'   *cool*

848–9 Tell me in what way she deserves to die.
864 kele] kelee C.

865   He hente a knyfe wyth all hys mayn: *seized, strength*
     Had not a knyght ben, he had hym slayn
     And that traytoure have broght owt of heele.   *health*
     For bale hys armes abrode he bredd,
     And fell in swowne upon hys bedd –   *swoon*
870   There myght men see grete dele!   *grief*

     On the morne, be oon assente,   *unanimous agreement*
     On hur they sett a perlyament,
     Be all the comyn rede.[n]
     They myght not fynde in ther counsayle,   *deliberations (?)*
875   Be no lawe, wythowt fayle,
     To save hur fro the dede.   *death*
     Then bespake an olde knyght: *spoke out*
     'Y have wondur, be Goddys myght,
     That Syr Antore thus was bestedd.   *set upon*
880   In chaumbyr thogh they naked were,[n]
     They let hym gyf none answere,
     But slowe hym, be my hedd!

     'Ther was nevyr man, sekurly,
     That be hur founde any velany,   *certainly*
885   Save they two – y dar wele say   *concerning her*
     Be some hatered hyt may be.   *On account of*
     Therfore doyth aftur me,   *do as I advise*
     For my love y yow pray!
     No mo wyll preve hyt but they twoo;   *others, prove*
890   Therfore we may not save hur fro woo –
     Forsothe, os y yow say –
     In hyr quarell but we myght fynde
     A man that were gode of kynde,
     That durste fyght agayn them tway.'

895   All they assentyd to the sawe: *what he said*
     They thoght he spake reson and lawe.
     Then answeryd the kyng wyth crowne,
     'Fayre falle the for thyn avyse!'

866 Had it not been for a knight, he would have killed him (the traitor).
868 For anguish he stretched out his arms.
874–6 i.e. they could find nothing in the law to save her.
892–4 Unless we could find a man of noble nature who would dare fight in her
cause against the two of them.
898 May good fortune befall you for your advice!

He callyd knyghtys of nobyll pryce,   renown
900 And badd them be redy bowne   prepared
    For to crye thorow all the londe,   proclaim
    Bothe be see and be sonde,   by sea and sand (i.e. everywhere)
    Yf they fynde mowne   (To see) if they could find
    'A man that ys so moche of myght,
905 That for that lady dar take the fyght —
    He schall have hys wareson!'   reward

    Messangerys, y undurstonde,
    Cryed thorow all the londe,
    In many a ryche cyte,
910 Yf any man durste prove hys myght,
    In trewe quarell for to fyght,   just cause
    Wele avaunsed schulde he bee.   promoted
    The erle of Tullous harde thys telle,
    What anger the lady befelle —   enmity
915 Thereof he thoght grete pyte.
    Yf he wyste that sche had ryght,
    He wolde aventure hys lyfe to fyght   risk
    For that lady free.

    For hur he morned nyght and day,   grieved
920 And to hymselfe can he say
    He wolde aventure hys lyfe:
    'Yf y may wytt that sche be trewe,
    They that have hur accused schull rewe,
    But they stynte of ther stryfe!'   regret it
925 The erle seyde, 'Be Seynte John,
    Ynto Almayn wyll y goon,
    Where y have fomen ryfe.   many enemies
    I prey to God, full of myght,
    That y have trewe quarell to fyght,
930 Owt of wo to wynne that wyfe!'   rescue

    He rode on huntyng on a day;
    A marchand mett he be the way,   merchant
    And asked hym of whens he was.   where he came from
    'Lorde,' he seyde, 'of Almayn.'   from

924 Unless they cease their hostility.

935　Anon the erle can hym frayne　　　　　　　　*ask*
　　　Of that ylke case:
　　　'Wherefore ys yowre emperes　　　　　　　　*Why*
　　　Put in so grete dystresse?
　　　Telle me, for Goddys grace!
940　Ys sche gylte, so mote thou the?'　　　　　　*guilty*
　　　'Nay, be hym that dyed on tree,
　　　That schope man aftur hys face!'[n]

　　　Then seyde the erle, wythowte lett,　　　　*at once*
　　　'When ys the day sett,
945　Brente that sche schulde bee?'
　　　The marchande seyde, sekyrlyke,　　　　　　*certainly*
　　　'Evyn thys day thre wyke –　　　　　*Just three weeks from today*
　　　And therfore wo ys mee.'　　　　　　　　*I am sorrowful*
　　　The erle seyde, 'Y schall the telle:
950　Gode horsys y have to selle,
　　　And stedys two or thre.　　　　　　　　　*stud-horses*
　　　Certys, myght y selle them yare,　　　　　*quickly*
　　　Thedur wyth the wolde y fare,　　　　　　*Thither*
　　　That syght for to see.'

955　The marchand seyd wordys hende:
　　　'Into the londe yf ye wyll wende,
　　　Hyt wolde be for yowre prowe:　　　　*to your advantage*
　　　There may ye selle them at your wylle.'
　　　Anon the erle seyde hym tylle,　　　　　　*to him*
960　'Syr, herkyn me nowe:
　　　Thys yurney wylt thou wyth me dwelle,
　　　Twenty pownde y schall the telle　　　*pay (literally, count)*
　　　To mede – y make a vowe.'　　　　　　　　*In reward*
　　　The marchand grauntyd anon;
965　The erle seyde, 'Be Seynt John,
　　　Thy wylle y alowe!'[n]

　　　The erle tolde hym in that tyde　　　　*at that time*
　　　Where he schulde hym abyde,　　　　　　　*await*
　　　And homeward wente hee.

942　Who created man in his own image.
961　*Probably* If you will wait for me and accompany me on this journey (cf. line 968).

970 He busked hym, that no man wyste;
For mekyll on hym was hys tryste,
He seyde, 'Syr, go wyth mee.'
Wyth them they toke stedys sevyn –
Ther were no fayre[r] undyr hevyn

975 That any man myght see;
Into Almayn they can ryde.
As a coresur of mekyll pryde   *horse-dealer*
He semyd for to bee.

The marchand was a trewe gyde;
980 The erle and he togedur can ryde
Tyll they came to that place.
A myle besyde the castell   *away from*
There the emperoure can dwelle,
A ryche abbey ther was.

985 Of the abbot leve they gatt
To soyorne and make ther horsys fatt –   *lodge (there)*
That was a nobyll cas!   *That was a fine thing*
The abbot was the ladyes eme;[n]   *uncle*
For hur he was in grete wandreme,   *distress*
990 And moche mornyng he mase.   *makes*

So hyt befelle, upon a day,
To churche the erle toke the way,
A masse for to here.
He was a feyre man and an hye;   *tall*
995 When the abbot hym sye,   *saw*
He seyde, 'Syr, come nere.   *nearer*
Syr, when the masse ys done,
Y pray yow, ete wyth me at noone,
Yf youre wylle were.'

1000 The erle grauntyd, all wyth game;   *pleasure*
Afore mete they wysche, all same,   *Before, washed, together*
And to mete they wente in fere.

Aftur mete, as y yow say,
Into an orchard they toke the way,

970 He made himself ready in such a way that no one knew (of it).
971 For his trust in him was great.
974 fayrer] fayre C.

1005　The abbot and the knyght.
　　　The abbot seyde, and syghed sare,
　　　'Certys, syr, y leve in care,　　　　　　　　　　　*live*
　　　For a lady bryght.　　　　　　　　　　　　　*On account of*
　　　Sche ys accusyd – my herte ys woo;
1010　Therfore sche schall to dethe goo,
　　　All agayne the ryght.　　　　　　　　　　　　*contrary to*
　　　But sche have helpe, verrament,
　　　In fyre sche schall be brente,
　　　Thys day sevenyght.'　　　　　　　　　　　*A week from today*

1015　The erle seyde, 'So have y blysse,
　　　Of hyr methynkyth grete rewthe hyt ys,
　　　Trewe yf that sche bee.'
　　　The abbot seyde, 'Be Seynt Poule,[n]
　　　For hur y dar ley my soule　　　　　　　　　　*wager*
1020　That nevyr gylte was sche!
　　　Soche werkys never sche wroght,　　　　　　*deeds, performed*
　　　Neythyr in dede nor in thoght;
　　　Save a rynge so free,　　　　　　　　　　　*Except that*
　　　To the erle of Tullous sche gafe hyt wyth wynne,　　*gladly*
1025　Yn ese of hym, and for no synne –　　　　　*To comfort him*
　　　In schryfte thus tolde sche me.'　　　　　　*confession*

　　　The erle sayde, 'Syth hyt ys soo,
　　　Cryste wreke hur of hur woo,
　　　That boght hur wyth hys bloode!　　　　　　*avenge*
1030　Wolde ye sekyr me, wythowt fayle,　　　　*If you would promise me*
　　　For to holde trewe counsayle,　　　　*To keep a secret faithfully*
　　　Hyt myght be for yowre gode.'　　　　　　　*advantage*
　　　The abbot seyde, be bokes fele　　　　　　　*many*
　　　And be hys professyon, that he wolde hele,　　　*conceal*
1035　And ellys he were wode.　　　　　　　　　　*mad*
　　　'Y am he that sche gaf the rynge,
　　　For to be oure tokenynge.
　　　Now heyle hyt, for the rode!　　　　　*conceal, by the cross*

　　　'Y am comyn, lefe syr,　　　　　　　　　　*dear*
1040　To take the batayle for hyr,　　　　　　　　*undertake*
　　　There to stonde wyth ryght.　　　　　　　*support justice*

　　　1016　It seems to me that she is much to be pitied.

But fyrste myselfe y wole hur schryve,
And yf y fynde hur clene of lyve,   *to be of pure life*
Then wyll my herte be lyght!
1045 Let dyght me, in monkys wede,   *Take me, habit*
To that place that men schulde hyr lede
To dethe to be dyght.   *To be put to death*
When y have schrevyn hyr, wythowt fayle,
For hur y wyll take batayle,
1050 As y am trewe knyght!'

The abbot was never so gladd –
Nere for yoye he waxe madd;
The erle can he kysse.
They made mere and slewe care;   *merry*
1055 All that sevenyght he dwellyd thare
Yn myrthe, wythowt mysse.   *lack*
That day that the lady schulde be brent,
The erle wyth the abbot wente,
In monkys wede, ywys.[n]
1060 To the emperour he knelyd blyve,   *at once*
That he myght that lady schryve;   *(And asked) that*
Anon resceyved he ys.   *accepted*

He examynde hur: wyttyrly,   *certainly*
As hyt seythe in the story,
1065 Sche was wythowte gylte.
Sche seyde, 'Be hym that dyed on tree,
Trespas was never none in me
Wherefore y schulde be spylte;
Save oonys, wythowte lesynge,   *once, deceit*
1070 To the erle of Tollous y gafe a rynge.
Assoyle me, yf thou wylte.   *Absolve*
But thus my destanye ys comyn to ende,
That in thys fyre y muste be brende –
There Goddes wylle be fulfyllyt!'

1075 The erle assoyled hur wyth hys honde,
And sythen pertely he can up stonde,   *boldly*

1042 But first I will hear her confession myself.
1067–8 I was never guilty of any wrongdoing for which I should be destroyed.

And seyde, 'Lordyngys, pese!   *quiet*
Ye that have accused thys lady gente,
Ye be worthy to be brente!'
1080 That oon knyght made a rees: *rush*
'Thou carle monke! Wyth all thy gynne,   *churl, trickery*
Thowe youre abbot be of hur kynne,   *Though*
Hur sorowe schalt thou not cees!
Ryght so thou woldyst sayne
1085 Thowe all youre covent had be hyr layn,   *Even if, monastery*
So are ye lythyr and lees!'   *vile, liars*

The erle answeryd, wyth wordys free,
'Syr, that oon y trowe thou bee
Thys lady accused has.
1090 Thowe we be men of relygyon,
Thou schalt do us but reson.[n]
For all the fare thou mas,
Y prove on hur thou sayst not ryght:
Lo, here my glove, wyth the to fyght;[n]
1095 Y undyrtake thys case.
Os false men y schall yow kenne,   *make you known*
Yn redd fyre for to brenne –
Therto God gyf me grace!'

All that stoden in that place
1100 Thankyd God of hys grace,
Wythowte any fayle.
The two knyghtes were full wrothe;   *angry*
He schulde be dedd they swere grete othe –
But hyt myght not avayle.
1105 The erle wente there besyde,   *a little way off*
And armyd hym wyth mekyll pryde,   *splendour*
Hys enemyes to assayle.
Manly when they togedur mett,   *Boldly*
They hewe thorow helme and basenet,[n]   *basinet*
1110 And martyrd many a mayle.   *ruined much chain-mail*

1088–9 I believe you are one of those who have accused this lady.
1092–3 For all the fuss you make, I (shall) prove that what you say about her is untrue.
1103 They swore great oaths that he should die.

They redyn togedur, wythowt lakk,   *fail*
That hys oon spere on hym brakk;
That othyr faylyd thoo.   *missed (him)*
The erle smote hym wyth hys spere;
1115 Thorow the body he can hym bere;
To grounde can he goo.
That sawe that odyr, and faste can flee;
The erle overtoke hym undur a tre,
And wroght hym mekyll woo.   *caused*
1120 There thys traytour can hym yylde   *yielded himself*
Os recreaunt yn the fylde:
He myght not fle hym froo.

Before the emperoure they wente,
And there he made hym verrament
1125 To telle, for the noonys.   *indeed*
He seyde, 'We thoght hur to spylle   *intended, destroy*
For sche wolde not do oure wylle,
That worthy ys in wonnys.'   *habits*
The erle answeryd hym then:
1130 'Therfore, traytours, ye schall brenne
Yn thys fyre, bothe at onys.'
The erle anon hym hente,
And in the fyre he them brente,
Flesche, felle and boonys.

1135 When they were brent, bothe twoo,
The erle prevely can goo   *secretly*
To that ryche abbaye.
Wyth yoye and processyon,
They fett the lady into the towne,   *brought*
1140 Wyth myrthe, os y telle may.
The emperoure was full gladd;
'Fette me the monke anon!' he badd.
'Why wente he so awaye?
A byschoperyke y wyll hym geve,[n]   *bishopric*
1145 My helpe, my love whyll y leve,
Be God, that owyth thys day!'   *owns*

1112 So that the spear of one of them broke on him (the earl).
1121 As fighting in a wrong cause.

The abbot knelyd on hys knee,
And seyde, 'Lorde, gone ys hee
To hys owne londe.
1150 He dwellyth wyth the Pope of Rome;
He wyll be glad of hys come, *coming*
Y do yow to undurstonde.' *I assure you*
'Syr,' quod the emperoure,
'To me hyt were a dyshonoure: *would be*
1155 Soche wordes y rede thou wonde. *I advise you to cease*
Anone yn haste that y hym see,
Or thou schalt never have gode of me, *alms*
And therto here myn honde!'ⁿ *And here is my hand on it*

'Lorde,' he seyde, 'sythe hyt ys soo,
1160 Aftur hym that y muste goo,
Ye muste make me sewrte, *give me an assurance*
Yn case he have byn youre foo,
Ye schall not do hym no woo:
And then — also mote y thee! —
1165 Aftur hym y wyll wynde,
So that ye wyll be hys frende, *Provided that*
Yf youre wylle bee.'
'Yys,' seyde the emperoure, 'full fayne:
All my kynne thogh he had slayne,
1170 He ys welcome to mee!'

Then spake the abbot wordys free: *frank*
'Lorde, y tryste now on thee
Ye wyll do os ye sey.
Hyt ys Syr Barnard of Tollous,
1175 A nobyll knyght and a chyvalrous,
That hath done thys jurney.' *day's work*
'Now, certys,' seyde the emperoure,
'To me hyt ys grete dyshonoure!
Anon, syr, y the pray
1180 Aftur hym that thou wende:
We schall kysse and be gode frende,
Be God, that owyth thys day!'

The abbot seyde, 'Y assente.'

1156 Let me see him quickly at once.

Aftur the erle anon he wente,
185 And seyde, 'Syr, go wyth mee.
My lorde and ye, be Seynt John,
Schull be made bothe at oon, *at one*
Goode frendys for to bee.'
Therof the erle was full fayne;
190 The emperoure came hym agayne, *to meet him*
And sayde, 'My frende so free,
My wrath here y the forgeve;
My helpe, my love whyll y leve,
Be hym that dyed on tree!'

195 Togedur lovely can they kysse; *lovingly*
Therof all men had grete blysse –
The romaunse tellyth soo.[n]
He made hym steward of hys londe,[n]
And sesyd agayne into hys honde[n]
200 That he had rafte hym froo.
The emperoure levyd but yerys thre; *lived only*
Be alexcion of the lordys free, *choice*
The erle toke they thoo: *accepted*
They made hym ther emperoure,
205 For he was styffe yn stoure, *valiant in battle*
To fyght agayne hys foo.

He weddyd that lady to hys wyfe;
Wyth yoye and myrthe they ladd ther lyfe,
Twenty yere and three.
210 Betwene them had they chyldyr fiftene –
Doghty knyghtys, all bedene, *together*
And semely on to see. *handsome*
Yn Rome thys geste ys cronyculyd, ywys;
A lay of Bretayne callyd hyt ys,[n]
215 And evyrmore schall bee.
Jhesu Cryste to hevyn us brynge,
There to have owre wonnyng! *dwelling*
Amen, amen, for charytee![n]

Here endyth the Erle of Tollous

1199–1200 And gave back to him what he had taken from him.

COMMENTARY

King Horn

[References to the Anglo-Norman *Romance of Horn* (*RH*) are by *laisse* number, to facilitate reference to the translation in Judith Weiss, *The Birth of Romance* (*BR*); references to other verse texts are by line number. Translations are quoted from *BR*.]

1–2 Calls for attention, and the invocation of blessings upon the poet's 'audience', are commonplace in Middle English romance and have often been seen as evidence of a continuing tradition of oral performance; but see the counter-arguments in Dieter Mehl, *The Middle English Romances of the Thirteenth and Fourteenth Centuries* (London, 1968), p. 7. Many medieval romances emphasize the moral benefits to be derived from hearing tales of exemplary or heroic deeds; here, less traditionally, the emphasis is upon the pleasure they can give.

13–16 The terms in which Horn's physical beauty is described are paralleled in many descriptions of romance heroines (see *KHH*, note to lines 15 and 16), but it is not usual to find a male protagonist thus described. There is considerable emphasis in *RH* too on Horn's extraordinary beauty and its effect on all who see him, particularly women. In the Anglo-Norman, however, there is a more critical approach to the value of physical appearance as an index of moral worth: in *laisse* 147 Gudreche (the Anglo-Norman equivalent of Thurston) says of Horn: 'Jo·l diseië asez, quant bien l'oi esgardé,/ Ne pout estre malveis ki si fu figuré' ('I said as much when I first observed him: no one who looked like that could be bad'); but earlier in the poem (*laisse* 118) Horn counsels Lenbürc (= Reynild) against giving her love too lightly, on the strength of appearances alone, before he has proved his moral worth. See also notes to lines 87–8, 315–16.

19 In *RH* (1) Horn has fifteen companions, though one should be cautious of making too much of the biblical echo in *King Horn*. It was common practice in the Middle Ages for upper-class boys to be raised away from the parental home, in a royal or aristocratic household: see Shulamith Shahar, *Childhood in the Middle Ages* (London, 1990), pp. 209–13, 216–18, 220. Cf. *The Erle of Tolous* 708.

29–80 In *RH* we learn of the death of Horn's father (there called Aalof) and the invasion of his land in 'flashback' at a later stage, when Horn is recounting his experiences to Hunlaf (*laisse* 13). Godhild's Anglo-Norman counterpart, Samburc, is not mentioned until she and Horn are reunited at the end of the romance (*laisses* 230–3).

36 *Arived* means literally 'came ashore'; it is not used in *King Horn* in any looser sense.

38 *Sarazins*: a generic name for heathen peoples. For its use to denote Danes in particular, see *KHH*, note to line 38. Cf. Diane Speed, 'The Saracens of *King Horn*', *Speculum*, 65 (1990), 564–95 (especially p. 565).

87–8 Cf. *RH* 2:

> Si lui ot Deus dune par ses digne buntez
> Un eür: k'i ne fust pur nul hom esgardez,
> Ki sempres n'en eüst e merciz e pitez. (23–5)

(Out of His great kindness, God gave Horn this good fortune, that all seeing him would at once pity and have mercy on him.)

The word *children* denotes youths of gentle birth, not yet knighted.

89 *admirad*: an Arabic term denoting an emir or prince under the sultan. It is used loosely in romance for any heathen officer or commander.

101–10 In *RH* (3) the heathens' decision not to kill Horn and his companions outright is differently motivated:

Car tant en ot pitez reis Rodmund des enfanz,
K'il ne volt devant lui k'il seient perillanz.
Lors demandet cunseil, as entur lui estanz:
'Seignurs, cunseilliez mei, quei en pusse estre fesanz? . . .
Dites mei cum murunt, ke ne·l seie veanz:
Ne·l verai de pited: tel ai des enfanz.'   (40–3, 49–50)

(For King Rodmund pitied the children so much that he could not bear them to perish in his presence. Then he asked for advice from those around him: 'My lords, counsel me, what should be done with them? . . . Tell me how they may die so that I do not witness it. From pity, I cannot see it; I have such children myself.')

In *King Horn* the decision seems to stem more from a desire to avoid direct responsibility for the youths' deaths, and therefore possible nemesis: see especially lines 105–6. The motif of exposure in a boat occurs in the classical story of Perseus, in the Life of St Gregory and in Chaucer's Man of Law's Tale, to name but a few examples. It is also attested historically: see J. R. Reinhard, 'Setting adrift in medieval law and literature', *PMLA*, 56 (1941), 33–68. See also notes to lines 118 and 139–52.

114 The line probably means 'forthwith', 'without further discussion'.

118 In *RH* (3) we are specifically told that the boat is not equipped with oars.

131 The phrase *on lyve* (*literally*, 'alive') is often used as a virtually meaningless tag: see *KHH*, note to line 131. Here, however, the meaning may be 'Let us rejoice that we are still alive.'

138 *Suddene*: Horn's father is also king of Suddene in *RH*, where, according to Pope, 'it would appear that . . . Suddene denotes South Devon' (*RH*, II, 4). In *King Horn* it has been variously identified with Cornwall (*KHH*, p. lv), with the Isle of Wight (Sands, p. 16), and with the Isle of Man (French & Hale, p. 29 n. 43). (The last-named would accord well with *bi weste* in line 5.) In *Horn Childe* (see p. viii above), the action is given a much more precise location than in *King Horn*, where topography is perhaps deliberately vague, or of little concern to the poet or his audience. (On the geography of *Horn Childe*, see

Horn Childe and Maiden Rimnild, ed. Maldwyn Mills, Middle
English Texts 20 (Heidelberg, 1988), p. 8.) See also Speed,
'Saracens', p. 565.

139–52 Horn's address here has no parallel in *RH*, where we are
specifically told that the boat was destroyed by the storm that
drove Horn and his companions ashore (*laisse* 11). Helen Cooper
points out to me that the handling of the whole 'casting adrift'
episode in *King Horn* (as opposed to *RH*) is anomalous in certain
respects, and that the English Horn's boat seems to possess some
of the attributes of the magic ship, usually associated with saints
(see C. Grant Loomis, *White Magic*, Medieval Academy of
America Publications 52 (Cambridge, Mass., 1948), ch. 7) or
with Celtic goddesses or enchantresses (as in Marie de France's
Guigemar). I am much indebted to Dr Cooper for her help in this
matter.

153 *yede to tune* probably means no more than 'went their way':
see *KHH*, note to line 153.

155 In *RH* (6–10) they are found by the king's seneschal,
Herland, who conducts them to his master, King Hunlaf.

156 Invocations of divine blessing (or the reverse) upon the
characters in the story is a typical feature of medieval romance.
According to Mehl, *The Middle English Romances*, pp. 26–7,
such partisanship is among the traits that distinguish the authorial
attitude in romance from that in hagiography.

157 In *RH* (5) they are said to have landed in Brittany. Westir,
explicitly identified with Ireland (*laisse* 103), is the realm of
Gudreche (the Anglo-Norman counterpart of *King Horn*'s
Thurston). The Westernesse of *King Horn* may denote the Wirral
(French & Hale, p. 30 n. 1; Sands, p. 16); but cf. note to line 138
above.

181 *to-droghe*: the verb is usually applied to some form of legal
capital punishment (see note to line 1494); here, however, the
sense may be vaguer, since the people of Suddene were presumably not condemned to death by process of law.

185 *galeie*: a large rowing-boat (*MED*, s.v. 'galei(e', n., 1(b)).

209 The play on Horn's name is peculiar to *King Horn*. It is, of course, impossible in Anglo-Norman; though cf. note to line 1147.

225–6 Athelbrus' Anglo-Norman counterpart is Herland (cf. note to line 155 above). On stewards in romance, see note to *Amis and Amiloun* 205–16.

230–4 Tristan, *par excellence*, combines skill in the courtly accomplishments of hunting and harping: cf. notes 12 and 20 to Weiss's translation of *La Folie Tristan* (*BR*, pp. 127, 131). Carving was an important part of a squire's duties; and there are frequent references in *RH* to Horn's role as cupbearer (e.g. in *laisses* 23–4, 48; cf. note to *Amis and Amiloun* 188). In *RH* the king does not specifically instruct that Horn should be taught to play the harp, although his skill as a musician is given greater emphasis in the Anglo-Norman (see especially *RH* 137). Depiction of musical accomplishment in romance indicates a movement towards a more courtly and refined, and less exclusively martial, concept of chivalric behaviour. Christopher Page, *Voices and Instruments of the Middle Ages: Instrumental Practice and Songs in France 1100–1300* (London, 1987), p. 244 n. 2, states: 'Epic heroes never play instruments before the later thirteenth century, and even then only in a few isolated cases.' See also Christopher Page, 'Music and chivalric fiction', *Proceedings of the Royal Musical Association*, 111 (1984/5), 1–27. Cf. lines 1477–80.

237–8 In *RH* each of Horn's companions is assigned to a different one of the king's lords, except for Haderof (the equivalent of *King Horn*'s Athulf), whom Horn chooses as his special companion.

271–2 There is no pretence of sickness in *RH*, where Rigmel (= Rymenhild) goes through an elaborate attempt to bribe Herland (= Athelbrus), at first using her maiden Herselot as intermediary (*laisses* 25–35). The motif of the 'wooing woman' seems to derive from Celtic story (see H. R. Patch, 'The adaptation of Otherworld motifs to medieval romance', in *Philologica: The Malone Anniversary Studies*, ed. T. A. Kirby and H. B. Woolf (Baltimore, Md, 1949), pp. 115–23 (p. 116)); but behaviour such as is here portrayed is not generally seen in a favourable light in the Middle English romances: even where it is not implicitly condemned by being attributed to an evil character, the author's sympathy and approbation seem to be more with the man who rejects than with the woman who makes the advances. See Judith Weiss, 'The wooing woman in Anglo-Norman romance', in *Romance in Medieval England*, ed. Maldwyn Mills, Jennifer Fellows and Carol M. Meale (Cambridge, 1991), pp. 149–61. Cf. also *Amis and Amiloun* 571–88; *Syr Launfal* 301–6.

283–4 This is somewhat better motivated in *RH* (34):

> 'Deu!' fait il en sun quoer,   'si el l'ad enamé?
> Ele est fille le rei,   mun seignur avué:
> Si çoe ne fust par lui,   mut sereit avilé
> E si par mei est fait   mal avrai espleité;
> De mun seignur, le rei   en serreïë reté
> Ke j'en avreïë fait   vers lui desleauté,
> Si·n serrai en la curt   a tuz jorz mal noté.
> N'i serra ceste feiz   par mei Horn amené,
> Einz i merrai Haderof,   taunt qu'aïë espruvé
> Quel semblant el li fra   de mustrer amisté.
> Bien m'en aparcevrai,   quant serrunt asemblé,
> Par cestui, k'el fereit   de Horn, le pruz sené.'   (665–74)

('Lord!' he said inwardly, 'what if she has fallen in love with him? She is daughter to the king, my sworn lord: if this is not done through him, she will be greatly dishonoured, and if it is done through me, it will be a wicked act. I shall be accused by my lord the king of disloyalty and I shall be blamed in the court for ever afterwards. This time I will not take Horn; I will take Haderof instead, until I have tested what show of affection she makes to him. When they meet, I will discover from her behaviour how she would treat Horn, the brave and wise.')

297–8 It is clearer in *RH* (25) that Rigmel has fallen in love with Horn without ever having seen him.

305–6 On 'trothplight' and 'handfasting', see Michael J. Franklin, '"Fyngres heo haþ feir to folde": trothplight in some of the love lyrics of MS Harley 2253', *Medium Ævum*, 55 (1986), 176–87. Trothplight 'represented a binding union as irrevocable as marriage' (*ibid.*, p. 177).

312 In *RH* (44) it is Rigmel's nurse, Godswith, who reveals Rigmel's mistake to her.

315–16 An unparalleled, and problematic, expression. It may mean simply that Horn's beauty was equal to a woman's (cf. Genesis ii.21–2, which gave rise to the popular belief that a man has one less rib than a woman). Susan Dannenbaum, '"Fairer bi one ribbe/Þane eni man þat libbe" (*King Horn*, C315–16)', *Notes and Queries*, n.s. 28 (1981), 116–17, believes that we have here a reference to the physical perfection of Adam and of Christ. I would suggest, rather, that Horn's beauty is seen as being such that he seems not to be of human birth (i.e. descended from Adam): cf. *RH* 22: 'E si diënt par tut   ke c'est chose faéé/E ke onc mes de Deu   ne fu tiel figuréé' ('And all said he must be some enchanted being, who could never have issued from the hand of God').

370 Cf. note to lines 230–4.

410 Cf. note to lines 305–6.

417 In *RH* (56) Horn insists rather on his poverty than, as here, on lowly birth. In *RH* his true parentage is known to the king and his court.

427 Both Sands and French & Hale suggest that Rymenhild perhaps throws up her arms in a gesture of despair. It could be that she folds them in indignation, but that seems unlikely given that she swoons in the next line.

435–42 Whereas this appears to be a somewhat shameless piece of bargaining, in *RH* there is a much longer discussion between Horn and Rigmel of the hero's genuine unworthiness to accept Rigmel's love until he has proved himself (*laisses* 58–61).

449–62 In *RH* Rigmel is not instrumental in getting Horn knighted: see next note.

475–6 The crown was often worn on church festivals and it was customary to confer knighthood on such occasions (especially at Easter and Whitsun): see Richard Barber, *The Knight and Chivalry* (London, 1974), p. 39. In *RH* (69–73) Horn is knighted and armed so that he can resist an invasion of heathens.

488 The unemended reading of MS C suggests that Aylmar intends to give Rymenhild to Horn. It is clear subsequently, however, that he has no such intention; and it is unlikely that he would refer to Rymenhild in such terms or with such a degree of allusiveness.

499–500 In the light of lines 503–4, which clearly refer to the conferring of the accolade, 'dubbede . . . With swerd' must mean 'girded with a sword': cf. Barber, *The Knight and Chivalry*, p. 38.

541 The word *stille* might be rendered 'silent', but it seems more likely that Horn is advocating emotional restraint and patience.

544–60 In *RH* Horn has already proved himself in battle against heathen invaders (cf. note to lines 475–6).

571–4 Rings with magical, and particularly protective, properties are common in romance and folktale (see *Ywain and Gawain*, ed. Albert B. Friedman and Norman T. Harrington, EETS, OS 254 (London, 1964), note to line 737) and are perhaps eastern in origin (see M. A. Owings, *The Arts in the Middle English Romances* (1952; repr. New York, 1971), p. 150). Cf. *Florys and Blauncheflour* 375–8.

585–644 Not in *RH* (cf. note to lines 544–60). Horn's encounter here has certain similarities to Murri's in lines 29ff.

598 *hethene honde*: the term 'hound' is often used as a term of opprobrium by the members of one religion for those of another, occurring most frequently in Middle English romance in the phrase 'heathen hound', as here. It seems to reflect a genuine attitude towards adherents of alien creeds as being in some way sub-human – an attitude which finds extreme expression in *Richard Coer de Lion*, where the eponymous hero is quite prepared to have Saracens served as meat at table, but is unlikely to have been regarded by the romancer in the light of a cannibal (see *Der mittelenglische Versroman über Richard Löwenherz*, Wiener Beiträge zur englischen Philologie 42 (Vienna and Leipzig, 1913), lines 3537–62).

623–4 The carrying on a sword or spear of the head of an enemy, human or animal (and especially draconic), is frequent in medieval romance: see *KHH*, note to lines 623–4.

632 The sense of the line as it stands is unclear. Most editors adopt the reading of MS L: 'Mid watere al byflowe' ('completely surrounded by water'), though that gives a rather weak sense.

650 As it stands, the line can only mean something like 'To see what the outcome would be'. Hall tentatively suggests emendation of *sen* to *seie*: i.e. Horn goes to tell Rymenhild of the previous day's adventures (*KHH*, note to line 649). MSS C and L, however, both read *sen*.

658–64 Rymenhild's dream is not in *RH*; but the erotic imagery of fish and net occurs later, in *laisse* 192. See *BR*, p. 93 and n. 39.

665 Possibly Horn is invoking the aid of St Stephen of Hungary (*c.* 975–1038), because of his advocacy of marriage for all except the clergy. If Rymenhild's dream comes true, her marriage to Horn will be prevented.

676 Sands renders this 'And Horn stilled her tears'; but cf. line 892. It was not at that time considered shameful for a man to weep.

685 Hall, French & Hale, and Sands all interpret *sture* (the reading of MSS C and H) as a proper noun, and French & Hale gloss it as 'the Mersey'. Allen, however, convincingly argues for the interpretation 'by the river' (*KHA*, note to line 695). MS L reads: 'Þe king rod bi his toure'.

687–8 In *RH* (90) the malice of Fikenhild (there called Wikele) is motivated by Horn's refusal to give him a horse already given to Haderof.

690 In *RH* (92) Wikele's accusation includes:

> Pus dist la u li plout: 'Ja ne l'espuserai,
> Mes taunt cum me plarra   si l'asoignanterai.
> A cel fol, cel vieillart,   sun rëaume toudrai,
> E par cesti mut bien   mun regne cunquerrai.'   (1891–4)

(Afterwards he said, whenever he pleased, 'I shall never wed her, but make her my paramour for as long as I like. I'll seize the kingdom from that old fool and with that I'll certainly reconquer my realm.')

692 i.e. he swore on his naked sword. See *KHH*, note to line 692 on the antiquity of this practice, particularly among northern nations.

705–6 It is clear here that Horn and Rymenhild's love has been consummated, although Horn subsequently denies it (lines

1275–8). This is not the case in *RH*, where Horn's banishment is due to his refusal to take an oath to that effect, since he regards this as dishonourable for a man of his rank (*laisses* 93–6).

716 This perhaps denotes that he arms his horse. However, Allen proposes emendation to *he him gan schrede* ('he armed himself'), the reading of MS L (see *KHA*, note to line 728).

722 *wyve*: cf. note to lines 305–6.

733–6 The motif of spouses or lovers being free to remarry or choose new partners after a period of seven years occurs several times in medieval romance: see, e.g., *The Romance of Sir Beues of Hamtoun*, ed. Eugen Kölbing, EETS, ES 46, 48, 65 (London, 1885–4), lines 3834–8. By the thirteenth century the seven-year period was a feature of canon law with regard to remarriage: see James A. Brundage, *Law, Sex, and Christian Society in Medieval Europe* (Chicago, 1987), p. 374. I am grateful to Dr Richard Smith for supplying me with this reference.

754 In *RH* (103) Horn deliberately chooses to go to Westir (cf. note to line 157).

767 Cf. *RH* 104:

Ki Gudmod des or mes   sera il apelé:
Pur çoe turna sun num,   dunt ainz esteit nomé,
Qu'il ne fust koneü   en estrange regné,
Desque pruesce oust fait   dunt doust estre preisié.   (2160–3)

(He will now be called Gudmod. He changed his name from what it was at first, so that he should not be recognized in a foreign land until he had performed valiant deeds that deserved praise.)

774 In *RH* (108) Horn becomes the retainer of Egfer (= Berild) as the result of an agreement between the two brothers.

794 Among the possible interpretations of this line is that Horn should be used as Berild's messenger in courtship (just as Cesario/ Viola is used in Shakespeare's *Twelfth Night*), for messengers sometimes carried their sender's glove by way of credential. For discussion of the range of possible meanings here, see *KHH*, note to lines 793–7. Wissmann (cited *ibid.*) draws a contrast between Horn's furthering Berild's cause in wooing but hindering it when Berild actually comes *to wyve*. *RH* (112) has: 'dont seiez purgardez,/Si alez donneier k'(e) ove vus ne·l menez' ('you should be careful not to take him with you if you go courting').

801–2 In *RH* (144) the messenger (Rollac) enters the king's hall without dismounting – a deliberate insult. As Hall notes (*KHH*, note to line 801) messengers usually appear when the king is at meat. These lines in *King Horn* inevitably recall the appearance of the Green Knight in Arthur's hall in *Sir Gawain and the Green Knight*.

849 When the time of day is specified at all in medieval romance, it is frequently expressed in terms of the canonical hours. 'The hour of Prime' is 6 a.m.

889–90 In *RH* the king is not actually present at the battle, which extends over twenty *laisses* (151–70), and in which a whole army fights on the same side as Horn.

897 A mistake: Thurston does not, of course, know Horn's true identity yet.

905 Reynild is a shadowy figure by comparison with her Anglo-Norman counterpart, Lenburc, who cherishes a hopeless passion for Horn and makes advances to him, though she is less imperious and more timid that Rigmel/Rymenhild. On the contrast between the two, see Weiss, 'The wooing woman', p. 155.

935–60 In *RH* (176–9) the son of Herland (= Athelbrus) arrives to tell Horn that Wikele (= Fikenhild) has driven his father out of the land, and incidentally reveals that Rigmel is to be married to Modin.

964–82 In *RH* (179) Horn at first conceals his identity from the messenger. He sends no message to Rymenhild, and the incident of the messenger's drowning and Rymenhild's discovery of his body is completely absent.

968 Cf. note to line 849.

997–8 In *RH* (183) Horn simply promises to find good husbands for Gudreche's daughters. Cf. note to lines 1517–18. He subsequently dissuades Lenburc from taking the veil upon learning that he is lost to her, and Gudreche from entering a monastery (*laisses* 184–5).

1003–8 In *RH*, of course, they are in Westir/Ireland (cf. note to line 157); Gudreche tells Horn (*laisse* 181) that he can take with him 'del païs le barné' ('the country's nobles').

1010 Cf. note to line 185.

1017 Cf. line 968.

1028 Hall cites several parallels to this expression elsewhere in Middle English literature and refers to a Teutonic legend according to which the first men sprang from trees and rocks (*KHH*, note to line 1026). Note also that Adam was created from 'the dust of the ground' (Genesis ii.7). The sense appears, therefore, to be that Horn was as alone as if he were the first and only man on earth.

1037–8 In *RH* (188) the palmer says: 'E ui deit espuser   Rigmel al vis riaunt. / Trestuit cil del païs   en sunt lez e joant' ('today he is to marry Rigmel, with her smiling face. Everyone in the land is happy and joyful').

1043–4 The significance of these lines as they stand is unclear. In MS H the corresponding couplet applies to the palmer himself: 'Ich wes in þe halle / Wiþ inne þe castel walle'. MS L reads: 'Modi myd strencþe hyre hadde / And in to toure ladde / In to a stronge halle / Whit inne kastel walle'. There is no corresponding passage in *RH* to throw light on the matter.

1054 For the frequency in Middle English romance of comparable episodes, see *KHH*, note to line 1052; *Sir Beues of Hamtoun*, ed. Kölbing, note to A 2067f. There are particularly close correspondences here between *King Horn* and *Beves*, and it seems probable that *Beves* was influenced by *King Horn*.

1056 *sclavyne*: a pilgrim's cloak or 'more probably a long robe of shaggy woollen stuff' (*KHH*, note to line 1052).

1069–70 Hall notes: 'The churlish porter is a stock character in the romances' (*KHH*, note to lines 1067–8) and provides numerous parallels to this passage. In *RH* the episode with the porter is preceded by an encounter between Horn and King Modin, who comes riding along with Wikele (*laisses* 190–3).

1076 The wicket was a small gate or door within the main gate of the castle.

1081–2 Cf. note to *Amis and Amiloun* 686.

1089–1106 There is no corresponding passage in *RH*.

1107–12 Cf. *RH* 197:

> Costume iert a idonc   en icele cuntréé
> Ke quant aveneit si   ke dame iert espuséé,
> Si el(e) pucele fust,   k'el ne fust essaiéé,
> Ke del beivre servist . . .
> E quant oüst çoe fait,   apres sa reposéé,
> Armes deveit porter   cil, a qui fust donéé,
> Pars defors la cité,   u en champ u en préé.   (4137–44)

(It was then the custom in that land that when a lady was to be married, if she were a virgin, she was put to the test of serving the drink . . . And when she had done this, the man who married her had, after his rest, to bear arms outside the city, in meadow or field.)

1121–2 In *RH* (198) Horn delivers a brief sermon, replete with biblical allusion, on the Christian duty of giving to the poor, and the spiritual dangers presented by riches.

1124 Presumably this is a brown, wooden bowl.

1128 The line is unclear as it stands; in MSS H and L Rymenhild tells Horn to drink up the contents of the cup.

1135–45 Not in *RH*, though there is a very similar passage in *laisse* 192, in Horn's exchange with Wikele and Modin: see note to lines 1069–70.

1147 Here a degree of wordplay is achieved even in the Anglo-Norman: as Horn says (*laisse* 199), 'Mes "corn" apelent "horn" li engleis latimier' ('But "horn" is the English word for what you took round just now'). Cf. note to line 209.

1157–60 In *RH* (197) Rigmel does not ask for tidings of Horn until after she has found the ring, which she does immediately, without retiring to her bower.

1177 It is appropriate that Horn, in his guise as pilgrim, should swear by St Giles, whose shrine was an important pilgrimage centre. Numerous churches and hospitals were dedicated to him in England.

1181-92 In *RH* Horn does not tell Rigmel this story of his own death, but he tests her loyalty in *laisse* 203, by pretending to be poverty-stricken.

1193-1212 None of this is in *RH*, where Horn and Rigmel are still in the hall. The motif of a reluctant bride killing her husband on her wedding-night occurs also in *Beves* (see *Sir Beues of Hamtoun*, ed. Kölbing, lines 3219-24) and in the *Nibelungenlied* (see *The Nibelungenlied*, trans. A. T. Hatto (Harmondsworth, 1965; repr. 1978), pp. 87-8), though in neither case does she also kill herself.

1213-22 In *RH* (204) Horn tells Rigmel to urge Modin to observe the ancestral custom of going out to joust after the wedding-feast: see note to lines 1107-12.

1225-30 In *RH* (206) Rigmel tests Haderof's loyalty by saying that he will see someone to love as much as Horn; he in turn momentarily doubts her loyalty (*laisse* 207) until she enlightens him as to Horn's return.

1233-6 In *RH* (209) Haderof leads Rigmel to see the jousting.

1237-48 In *RH* (210-12) Horn overcomes Modin in the jousting but does not kill him.

1249 This is usually interpreted as 'Horn took no terrible vengeance': see, e.g., *KHH*, note to line 1422. We should probably assume that both Horn and Rymenhild are still unaware of Fikenhild's treachery — though that is certainly not the case in *RH* (see, e.g., *laisse* 204).

1251 All the Middle English manuscripts have a plural pronoun here; but in *RH* (214) it is Wikele who swears, having abased himself before Horn and been pardoned.

1256 Cf. *RH* 214:

> Pus si vont al muster   pur prendre beneiçon
> De Rigmel espuser   od la gente façon,
> Kar de Modin fud fait   e de l(u)i parteisun.   (4545-7)

(Then they went to the abbey to receive a blessing on the marriage to Rigmel with the lovely face, for a divorce was made between Modin and her.)

1262 The word *gle* can mean entertainment/merrymaking or music/song. It is not used to denote a specific form of song until the seventeenth century.

1266 At this point the Cambridge MS of *RH* breaks off; the Oxford MS resumes the story at the point where Horn and his knights are planning their attack on Rodmund: see note to lines 1373–80.

1267 Horn is apologizing for the harshness of what he has to say: 'Forgive me for saying so, but . . .'.

1273 It is possible that *fleme* is a noun meaning 'exile' (see *KHH*, note to line 1271), but syntactically the couplet is smoother if it is taken as an infinitive.

1275–8 Cf. note to lines 705–6.

1298 *arive*: cf. note to line 36.

1311 After line 1304, MS H reads: 'L þe shelde wes ydrawe / A croyӡ of Ihesu Cristes lawe'; MS L has a comparable reading.

1345–6 The lines are undoubtedly corrupt as they stand. It is possible to read *stere* as an adjective, meaning 'stiff', 'strong', or as a noun meaning literally 'steersman' and hence perhaps 'guardian'. But neither gives a wholly satisfactory sense.

1373–80 *RH* picks up the story at this point: the knight, Hardré, leads Rodmund and his men into a trap, where they are destroyed by Horn and his forces (*laisses* 219–29).

1376 Horn's banner would serve as his standard in battle and as a rallying-point for his men.

1385–6 In *RH* (230–3) the episode of Horn's reunion with his mother, Samburc, is treated at some length. She hears of his return and seeks him out, and there is much emotion on both sides.

1397–1402 In *RH* (237) we are told that Wikele builds a castle 'in an impregnable spot' ('En un fort liu'), but the Anglo-Norman text does not convey the sense of isolation and claustrophobia found here. Cf. note to lines 1432–6.

1406 In *RH* (237–9) Wikele coerces the king by threatening to besiege him; the king is warned of this plan by Wikele's brother, Wothere.

1408 A startling image, perhaps related to the more common notion of sweating blood – in its turn apparently a literalistic distortion of the simile employed in Luke xxii.44.

1409–18 Cf. note to *Amis and Amiloun* 1015–16.

1418 In *RH* (234) Wikele uses an iron fork, a more obviously diabolical instrument.

1424 Cf. note to line 1249. Here the general sense is 'And done some terrible thing to Rymenhild'.

1425 The oath by the five wounds of Christ in times of adversity is relatively common in Middle English literature. *KHH*, note to line 1423, furnishes some examples. Cf. *Amis and Amiloun* 1653.

1432–6 The allusions to night and darkness, with their infernal connotations, are absent from *RH*. Cf. note to lines 1397–1402.

1445–8 In *RH* (241) Horn is met by Wikele's brother, Wothere, who swims out to meet his ship.

1467 Most editors interpret *gravel* as 'sand' or 'beach'. It is clear from lines 1397–1402, however, that Fikenhild's castle can be reached at low tide by a causeway, and that there is no landing place for a ship. The sense is probably, therefore, that they cross to the castle on foot over the causeway.

1471–86 There is no corresponding passage in *RH*.

1474 On the *gigue*, see Page, *Voices and Instruments*, pp. 145–7.

1478 It is possible that *clenche* here means 'grasp', but 'pluck' gives a better sense. See note to lines 230–4.

1494 *to-draghe*: this could mean either that he was torn apart by horses or that he was dragged to the place of execution on a hurdle. The latter sense is the more likely here: cf. *RH* 243: 'Pus l'ad fet fors sacher cum un mastin pullent / E pendre as querefu[r]s' ('Then he had him dragged out like a stinking cur and hung at the cross-roads'); in *RH*, though not so unambiguously in *King Horn*, he is already dead.

1495–1500 Not in *RH*.

1500 Though 'tribute' is the proper sense of *trewage*, it may be used here to denote homage.

1509 In *RH* (244) Gudreche has entered a monastery: cf. note to lines 997–8.

1511–12 The lines do not apparently yield any satisfactory sense.

1516 'Where he experienced sorrow'. It is not clear, however, what this refers to. Allen (*KHA*, note to line 1550) suggests emendation of *wo* to *wonung* ('dwelling-place').

1517–18 In *RH* (244) Horn marries Lenburc to Modin (see notes to lines 1237–48, 1256) and her sister to Haderof (= Athulf).

1523–4 The sense of these lines is unclear. Allen (*KHA*, lines 1557–8) suggests emendation to: 'Al folk hit iknewe / Þat hi hem loueden trewe' ('Everyone knew that they loved each other faithfully'). Other interpretations are discussed in Allen's notes to the lines.

1525–32 *RH* ends (245) with the poet, who names himself as Thomas, looking forward to the careers of Horn's sons, Hadermod and Wilmot, and praying for God's mercy. The blessing invoked at the end of *King Horn* is a traditional way of ending a romance.

Florys and Blauncheflour

The beginning of the romance is lacking in all Middle English manuscripts. We learn from the French version that a heathen king captures a Christian noblewoman, who gives birth to a daughter (Blanceflor) on the same day as his queen bears a son (Floire). The two children are reared together.

6 In *Floire* (197) the children are five years old.

18–20 The rhetorical repetition of Blauncheflour's name is not so pronounced in *Floire* (211–16).

25–8 *Floire* (217–61) gives a much more extended account of their schooling and their mutual love.

75–8 In *Floire* (329–44) both the children's tutor and Blanceflor's mother are to feign sickness. This may account for the reading *that other resoun*.

116–17 Again, the rhetorical repetition is absent from *Floire* (377–8). Cf. note to lines 18–20.

119 *Galyngale* denotes the 'aromatic root of certain East Indian plants . . . formerly much used in medicine and cookery' (*OED*, *s.v.* 'galingale').

140–1 In *Floire* (407–8) the king suspects Blanceflor of having won Floire's love through witchcraft. G. C. Britton, 'Three notes on "Floris and Blaunchefloor"', *Notes and Queries*, n.s. 17 (1970), 366–7, suggests that the threat of decapitation implies an accusation of treason against Blaunchefloure.

147 *Babyloyn* is the old Cairo, not the biblical Babylon.

155 *burgeise*: a magistrate or city official.

162 A mark was worth 13s 4d (i.e. two-thirds of a pound).

167–70 In *Floire* (457–90) there is a much longer description of the cup, on which the Judgement of Paris is also depicted. The story of the Trojan war was of enduring fascination during the Middle Ages: see C. David Benson, *The History of Troy in Middle English Literature* (Cambridge, 1980), esp. pp. 3–31. In the most general way, there is a correspondence between Florys's subsequent attempt to recover Blaunchefloure and Menelaus' attempt to recover Helen; in this light, the basket in which Florys later enters the emir's tower (lines 737–42) might be seen as his answer to the Wooden Horse.

171–5 Cf. note to line 584.

176 This line must refer to the cup generally, though the syntax is unsatisfactory.

180 Aeneas' *amy*, Lavinia, is named in *Floire* (506).

181 This probably refers to Julius Caesar, one of the Nine Worthies, who were a popular theme in medieval literature: see, e.g., *The Alliterative 'Morte Arthure'*, ed. Valerie Krishna (New

York, 1976), lines 3406–37; *The Parlement of the Thre Ages*, ed. I. Gollancz (London, 1915), lines 300–583. His appearances in medieval literature often show scant knowledge of, or regard for, historical chronology.

185–6 These lines are puzzling – unless they are to be read ironically as suggesting that the cup did not have the history claimed for it.

195 The significance of *as she stood upryght* is unclear.

209–18 De Vries (p. 64) notes a parallel to the device of the sham tomb in the story of Ghanim in the *Arabian Nights*. In *Floire* (551–666) there is a long and elaborate description of the tomb, on which the two lovers are depicted.

218 *paramoure* denotes passionate love between the sexes.

231–4 It remains unclear just how much of the king's plan is known to Blauncheflour's mother.

269–70 The repetition (cf. lines 255–6) does not occur in *Floire*.

286 Probably *woldest* here should be emended to *noldest*: cf. *Floire* 772: 'et jou t'apel, ne veus venir' ('and [when] I call you, you do not wish to come').

296 In *Floire* (1017–44) the queen admonishes Floire, telling him of the infernal punishment that awaits him if he takes his own life.

301 The number twelve is not specified in *Floire* (1057).

323 This must refer to a stone which they lift off the tomb.

351 The *chamburlayn* would be an official in charge of the running of the king's household.

370 *vertu*: this may denote monetary worth or, perhaps, magical properties.

375–8 Cf. note to *King Horn* 571–4.

390 He seats Florys near the upper end of the table. Cf. note to *Amis and Amiloun* 686.

429 *wylde flood* may mean no more than the open sea: it is clear from the next line that their voyage is not stormy.

438 i.e. all who held land as his vassals.

457–8 Cf. lines 393–4; again, the repetition is not in *Floire*.

478 The precise nature of miniver is uncertain, but it was probably a squirrel fur, perhaps white.

502 *senpere* denotes a man of high rank. *Floire* (1557) reads *pontenier* ('bridge-keeper').

523 In *Floire* (1606–44) he here debates with himself at length as to whether he should reveal his identity.

535–8 Cf. lines 465–8.

540 MSS A and V read *helpe*, and MS C gives a sense nearer to theirs. The reading of MS S is defensible, however, as meaning that he will find a remedy for Florys's grief.

551 *justinges* ('jousting') may be an error for *gestninge*, the reading of MS C (cf. line 436). *Floire*, however, reads *justise* (line 1783).

555 The word *amyral* here seems to be regarded as a proper noun: see also lines 1001, 1074.

556 Cf. note to *King Horn* 1494. The significance of *in his owne londe* is unclear.

557 There is an awkward transition here to description of the city.

571 i.e. about 600 feet. A fathom is the length covered by the outstretched arms.

584 A belief prevailed in the Middle Ages that precious stones, particularly carbuncles, shone with a light of their own. It has been suggested that descriptions of buildings surmounted by such refulgent gems may represent an attempt to interpret the lighthouse of Alexandria: see E. Faral, *Recherches sur les sources latines des contes et romans courtois du moyen âge* (Paris, 1913), pp. 81–5. Descriptions of brilliant and bejewelled cities and palaces occur frequently in Middle English romance – a fact probably due to the popularity and influence of the Alexander legend in the Middle Ages: see Owings, *The Arts in the Middle English Romances*, p. 152.

598 *Floire* (1910) describes him as 'fel et deputaire' ('cruel and ill-natured').

602 An apparently meaningless line in the context.

608 *mydlerd* ('middle-earth') denotes the world, situated between heaven and hell.

610 This may suggest a kind of Earthly Paradise, where people do not grow old (cf. Chaucer's *Parlement of Foulys*, lines 304–7), or mean simply that no one would want to leave that place.

618 Cf. note to line 370.

623–4 *Floire* (2072) says only that the water is very much agitated ('tote meüe').

630 *daungere*: the word is commonly used in medieval poetry to denote a lady's resistance to the advances of a lover — her haughtiness or 'hard-to-get-ness'. The meaning in this line seems to lie somewhere between that sense and 'danger' in its modern acceptance.

644 The use of *herkeneth* in this context is unusual. It could be taken fairly literally, as indicating that the emir is always asking questions about Blauncheflour or seeking news of her; but one would expect a sense nearer to that of 'yearns'.

647–8 Cf. lines 255–6, 269–70; not in *Floire*.

658 *free mason*: a mason not attached to a guild. It is curious that the detail of the hero's posing as a builder or architect is also present in the related story of Mozart's *Die Entführung aus dem Serail*.

660 Cf. note to line 598.

676 Cf. note to line 162.

698 This line may mean, loosely, 'Hoping that he will have better luck in play'. If *the* is taken as a pronoun, it could mean something like 'If you think it will make him help you the more readily'.

705–6 In the ceremony of homage, the man offering homage would place his hands between those of his lord: see Marc Bloch,

Feudal Society, trans. L. A. Manyon, 2nd edn, 2 vols (London, 1961–2; repr. 1975), I, 145–6.

737–42 De Vries (p. 65) notes that the device of the basket is found several times in *Arabian Nights* tales. Cf. also note to lines 167–70.

774 *OED* explains the unemended reading of MS S, *otter*, as short for 'otter-moth'. However, it is more probably a scribal error originating from the similarity of *fleye* (perhaps written as a separate word) and *fleygh*. MS A reads: 'A boterfleȝe toȝain me fluste'; MS C has: 'Þer fliste vt a buterfliȝe'; *Floire* reads: 'Des flors sali uns paveillon' ('A butterfly sprang out from the flowers').

794 MSS A and C both read here: 'So doþ Floris in his contreie'. De Vries (note to line 792) notes that this detail is not in the French, but does occur in Icelandic and Swedish versions of the story.

813–14 This may imply that anyone would need to be possessed of magical arts to win Florys away from Blauncheflour.

831 Note that the heathen Florys gives thanks to Jesus.

877 The reference to the *pyler* is puzzling; it is also in *Floire* (2557).

903 In *Floire* (2593–2603) the chamberlain, not realizing that Gloris (= Claris) was with the emir, had thought that it was she who was sharing a bed with Blanceflor.

928–33 Cf. lines 195–200, 485–90.

952 *more and lasse*: this may either mean 'altogether', 'the whole of the matter', or denote that any defence should be heard by (*of*) all present.

994–5 The sense appears to be that they did not show their sorrow; but we have just been told (line 982) that they come *wepyng*.

1009 The sense of the line as it stands would be something like 'You will achieve nothing by killing this maiden'. MSS A and C read 'Þou ne auȝtest nowt', and De Vries (line 1007) emends accordingly.

1042–3 These lines, omitted from MS S, are necessary to the sense of what follows and correspond to lines 3043–6 of *Floire*.

1048–53 Cf. lines 541–6, 715–20.

1086–7 The ending of the romance is very abrupt in MS S. In MSS A and C, as in *Floire* (3301), Florys embraces Christianity; in *Floire* (3309–26) he also obliges his subjects to do so. In MSS A and C the romance also ends with the traditional blessing (cf. note to *King Horn* 1525–32).

Amis and Amiloun

1–3 Cf. note to *King Horn* 1–2.

25–180 *AA* (1–38) gives a very much briefer introductory account of the two heroes, with no mention of their parents or of how they came to be at the duke's court.

25 Cf. note to line 2488. The action is not specifically localized at this point in *AA*.

27 Middle English romances often contain such appeals to authority; the device goes back to late classical antiquity and, more directly, links the techniques of Middle English romance with those of early English hagiography: see H. L. Levy, '"As myn auctor seyth"', *Medium Ævum*, 12 (1943), 25–39 (pp. 26–7).

29–30 The phrases *free to fond* and *worthy . . . in wede* are both conventional tags typical of tale-rhyme romance. Literally, the former means 'noble in the proving', the latter 'worthy in garments', but both have lost much of their meaning.

63 Another conventional epithet: cf. line 9.

65 The phrase *fre and bond* cannot qualify *erles, barouns*, but must refer to another class of people. It probably means little more here than 'all and sundry', since its literal sense would appear to be inapposite: it is unlikely that the duke would invite bondmen to his feast.

66 Cf. note to line 434.

110 The phrase *comly of kende* is another conventional epithet.

120 Cf. note to line 168.

134 Cf. note to *King Horn* 87–8.

138 Cf. note to lines 29–30.

139–56 Most texts of *AA* (17–18) say simply 'Tant s'entreamerent durement, / Ke freres se firent par serment' ('They loved each other so dearly that they swore to be brothers'), though MS C has a longer passage descriptive of their loyalty (*AA*, pp. 114–15).

142 The phrase *blod and bon* literally denotes the body; here it seems to be without any real meaning.

144 Cf. note to line 27.

145 *war and wight*: yet another alliterative tag typical of the tail-rhyme romances.

156 The hand played an important part in solemn promises of many kinds: cf. notes to *King Horn* 305–6; *Florys and Blauncheflour* 705–6.

163–5 Fifteen is the usual age for the conferring of knighthood in both romances and *chansons de geste*: see *KHH*, note to L, O 17, 18. The conferring of knighthood, and thereby of the right to bear arms, at a period roughly contemporaneous with the attainment of puberty reflects the origins of chivalry in the initiation rituals by which the coming of age of adolescents was marked in primitive societies: see Barber, *The Knight and Chivalry*, p. 38.

168 This is the more common form of a stock phrase also found in line 120.

188 As Weiss notes (*BR*, p. 159 n. 1), this was one of the most important offices in the royal household in late eleventh-century France.

191 Cf. *AA* 41–3:

> Amillun ne vout oblier,
> De sun ost le fist justiser,
> Mestre e marescal sur tuz.

(He did not neglect Amilun but made him administer justice among his soldiers as governor and marshal of them all.)

Weiss (*BR*, p. 160 n. 3) notes that the office of steward at first carried 'no more than catering duties', and such might be the significance of *in halle*; the 'wicked' steward (also described as *chef steward*, line 206) might then be supposed to have wider powers such as those assigned to Amilun in the passage from *AA* quoted above. Cf. note to lines 205–16.

196–8 Cf. *AA* 21–4:

> Ceus de la curt avoint envie
> De l'estre e de la compaignie,
> K'aveint entre eus tant fermement,
> E s'en coroucent bien sovent.

(The courtiers were jealous of their situation and the firm friendship between them, and it very often made them angry.)

205–16 In *AA* we learn of the steward through Amilun's words to Amis at their parting (lines 77–84). Stewards in romance are typically envious and treacherous (see, e.g., *Syr Tryamowre* 19–24; *Sir Beues of Hamtoun*, ed. Kölbing, lines 837–40, 4305ff.; *Ywain and Gawain*, ed. Friedman and Harrington, lines 2159–66 and p. xxix), perhaps because in actuality they were the objects of envy on account of their considerable power: see note to line 188. 'Good' stewards occur in *King Horn* 225–6, in *Syr Launfal* 32, and in *The Erle of Tolous* 1198.

218–19 MS D here reads: 'To Syre Amylyon there com thoo / A mesanger hende in hond'. This gives a slightly more satisfactory sense, *hende* here meaning 'skilful'.

244–52 The two cups are not mentioned in *AA* until the scene of Amis and Amilun's reunion at the gate of Amis's castle.

256–76 There is no equivalent to these lines in *AA*, except in MS C, where, however, Amys himself refuses to be disloyal to his lord by accompanying Amilun (*AA*, pp. 116–18).

281–2 The lines make little sense as they stand. Emendation of *That* to *Non* would give a satisfactory meaning, but there is no justification for that among any of the extant manuscript readings.

301–12 In *AA* (93) Amilun also advises: 'A tote gent bel responez!' ('Make fair answer to everyone'); cf. note to lines 367–84.

332 Cf. note to line 1508.

344–5 The word *him* (line 344) should probably be emended to *hem* so that the sense would be that people blessed his parents for producing such a son – a common enough formula. All Middle English manuscripts, however, read *him*; MS A does not elsewhere use that form for the plural pronoun.

367–84 In *AA* (137–40) Amis adds:

> Mes de tant me poez crere,
> Ke si vuz aiez de moi afaire,
> Je le vus frai a grant doçur,
> Sauve chescuni honur!

(But this much you may believe of me: if you need my help I'll do it most cordially, providing it's to the honour of us both!)
  Cf. note to lines 301–12.

373 The precise sense, though not the general drift, of this line is obscure.

389–96 There is no equivalent to these lines in *AA*; on the contrary, we are told that the steward 'atant se tint' ('held his tongue').

395 *nought a slo*: a common expression to denote contempt.

420 The line seems to be no more than an alliterative 'filler', with little apparent sense.

434 *birddes*: there is nothing derogatory in the use of this term, which often occurs in alliterative formulas: cf. lines 469, 560, 578, 661, 692, 776.

443 Cf. note to lines 29–30.

444 *semliest in sale*: yet another stock alliterative epithet.

459 *Seyn Savour*: by our Holy Saviour. The oath not infrequently occurs in this form, as though *Savour* were the name of a saint.

460 *swain*: a young man attendant on a knight; a squire.

474 Two related such expressions occur in *Amis and Amiloun*, and elsewhere in Middle English poetry: cf. line 548, where *kithe* means 'express' – a common usage. There may be overtones of that sense in the present context.

490 The phrase *withouten wrong* is probably a part of what she says: i.e. 'she answered that, without doubt, her pains . . .'.

503–4 In *AA* (243) also Amis remains behind because of illness. But see lines 508–10 below, where he seems to have stayed behind on account of his official duties. In the Middle English romance, as against the Anglo-Norman, there are two clearly defined encounters between Amis and Belisaunt, each of which begins with the duke going out hunting (cf. lines 721ff.). In *AA* the first encounter between Florie (= Belisaunt) and Amis occurs in his lodgings, as does the second in the Middle English (lines 724–6). Probably this inconsistency has been introduced as a result of the Middle English version's expansion of its source.

507 *holtes hare*: a common phrase; *hare* may denote the greyness of bare branches or of lichen-covered trees. Cf., however, *Syr Launfal* 171, where it is high summer.

512–16 The garden scene does not occur in *AA* (see note to lines 503–4), though in MS C Florie does announce her intention of going out into the garden (*AA*, p. 128, lines 19–21).

548 Cf. note to line 474.

571–88 On the motif of the 'wooing woman', see note to *King Horn* 271–2.

600 *fe*: a heritable property or office, held in return for homage to an overlord. On the whole line, cf. note to *King Horn*, line 417.

605–9 Not in *AA*. The emphasis on different kinds of *trewthe* (to God, to overlord, etc.) is greater in the Middle English than in the Anglo-Norman.

614–27 Not in *AA*. In the twelfth century at least, it was regarded as a great insult to call a knight a cleric: see Nigel de Longchamps, *Tractatus Contracurialis*, ed. A. Boutemy (Paris, 1959), p. 222. (I am indebted to Dr Ad Putter for this reference.) Such a notion may also lie behind the grim jokes in *chanson de geste* and romance when a knight, scalping an opponent in battle, declares that he has given him a tonsure: see, e.g., *Sir Beues of Hamtoun*, ed. Kölbing, lines 1869–74.

631 *kerchef*: this probably denotes here a covering for the bosom; its tearing would then have a symbolic value.

640–67 Amis's inner thoughts are described in *AA* only in MS C (*AA*, p. 130). The other Anglo-Norman texts state simply (lines 304–7):

> Tant li ad dit, tant ad parle,
> Ke sunt a un de cel afaire
> E unt devise la manere,
> Coment e kant s'assemblerunt.

(She said and spoke so much to him that they were agreed on the matter and devised how and when they could meet.)

642 This must mean 'before she has done with me', rather than referring to the present occasion.

645 Cf. note to *King Horn* 1494.

656 *rape wil rewe*. A proverbial expression: see Bartlett Jere Whiting, *Proverbs, Sentences, and Proverbial Phrases from English Writings mainly before 1500* (Cambridge, Mass., and London, 1968), R 32.

676–720 Not in *AA*, where (309–10) Amis and Florie's assignation has been overheard by a member of the steward's household, who reports it to his master.

686 The distinction between the *des*, on which the 'high table' was set, and the other tables in the hall was based on social standing. Amiloun's subsequent degradation as a beggar is underlined by the fact that he must no longer eat at the *heighe bord* (line 1580). See also *Sir Gawain and the Green Knight*, ed. J. R. R. Tolkien and E. V. Gordon, 2nd edn, rev. Norman Davis (Oxford, 1967), lines 112–15.

705 The treacherous stewards of romance are often motivated by sexual jealousy: see, e.g., *Syr Tryamowre* 22–4; *Sir Tristrem*, ed. E. Kölbing, Die nordische und die englische Version der Tristan-Sage, 2 (Heilbronn, 1882), lines 1492–8. There may be a hint of such a sense here.

720 Cf. note to *King Horn* 156.

725 Cf. note to lines 503–4.

727–32 We are not told in *AA* that the steward actually spies on the couple.

735–62 Not in *AA*.

758 *Seyn Tomas of Ynde*: i.e. St Thomas the Apostle, who, according to apocryphal tradition, preached and performed many marvels in India, where he was eventually martyred (see *The Apocryphal New Testament*, ed. and trans. M. R. James (Oxford, 1924; repr. 1969), pp. 364–438. The oath also occurs in, e.g., *Sir Beues of Hamtoun*, ed. Kölbing, line 3775; and in Chaucer's *Merchant's Prologue*, line 1230.

766–8 Cf. *AA* 318–22:

> Lors s'assemblent a grant delit;
> Par grant desir s'entrebaiserent,
> D'amur parlerent e juwerent.
> D'autre chose ne dirrai mie,
> Ne crei pas k'il eust vilainie.

(they came together with great pleasure, exchanging kisses of desire, indulging in the words and the sport of love. I shall say no more, but I think there was no harm in it.)

This probably does not mean, however, that their love remains technically unconsummated: one might compare what Malory says of Lancelot and Guinevere: 'And whether they were abed other at other maner of disportis, me lyste nat thereof make no mencion, for love that tyme was nat as love ys nowadayes' (*The Works of Sir Thomas Malory*, ed. Eugène Vinaver, 2nd edn, 3 vols (Oxford, 1967; repr. 1973), III, 1165). MS C of *AA* has no equivalent to line 322 above, but simply says that it would take too long to tell of their doings (*AA*, p. 132).

781 In *AA* (325) the steward does not tell the duke until the following morning.

793–4 Cf. *AA* 341–2: 'Est ceo veirs, sire senescal? / Jeo quid ke l'avez dit pur mal!' ('Is this true, seneschal? I think you've said it out of malice?')

796 *Seyn Jame*: St James the Greater, patron saint of Spain, whose shrine at Compostella was one of the great pilgrimage centres of the Middle Ages.

805–19 None of this occurs in *AA*: cf. note to line 781.

838 Cf. note to line 766–8.

845 The delivery of a glove was common practice in the Middle Ages as a way of offering or accepting a challenge. Cf. *Syr Tryamowre* 1368; *The Erle of Tolous* 1094.

870 Cf. note to lines 877–97.

877–97 In *AA* it is only Florie's mother who offers herself as Amis's surety: Florie has already been condemned to be burned if he is proved guilty (line 364). On the subject of sureties, who during certain periods were liable to suffer the punishment proposed for the accused if he defaulted, see *BR*, p. 165 n. 7.

880 Belisaunt here offers herself as surety: see previous note. Cf. also line 897.

886–8 In *AA* Amis has been condemned to hang unless he can prove his innocence, whereas Florie will go to the stake (line 364; cf. lines 1216–17 below). Burning was in fact a more common punishment for women than for men in the Middle Ages – perhaps on grounds of modesty, which may also have dictated the use of the *tonne* (line 1217). See also note to *King Horn* 1494.

910 This may mean either that he cared nothing for his life or that he reckoned his chances of survival to be very slim.

925–72 In *AA* (432–46) Amis simply asks leave of the countess to go and see Amilun; neither she nor her daughter is aware of the planned deception.

952 Cf. note to *King Horn* 1177.

956 Perhaps Amis swears here by St John as 'the disciple whom Jesus loved' (John xxi.7). The oath would be appropriate in reference to his loving friendship with Amiloun.

982 Not in *AA*.

1015–16 In *AA* (467) Amilun dreams that Amis is attacked by a lion. Premonitory dreams of this sort are common in romance: cf. *King Horn* 1409–18; *The Erle of Tolous* 805–10.

1114 Perhaps *aright* here means 'with a clear conscience'.

1120–2 In *AA* (498–9) Amilun likewise promises to take the oath on Amis's behalf, but in fact it never takes place.

1153–8 It is not entirely clear to whom the various pronouns in these lines refer.

1163–4 Cf. the episode alluded to in *La Folie Tristan* (*BR*, p. 137).

1165–76 *AA* (540) says simply that the lady 's'enmerveilla' ('was astonished'). Amis offers no explanation of his behaviour. His excuse here is ironic in view of the punishment that later befalls his friend.

1217 Cf. note to lines 886–8.

1234–5 These lines have a close parallel in *AA* (566–8).

1249–72 In *AA* there is no warning at this point, but later (708–17) a voice (not explicitly that of an angel: cf. line 1543 below) utters a similar warning against his giving a false name at his marriage to Florie. On the medieval view of leprosy as a punishment for sin, see *Amis and Amiloun*, ed. MacEdward Leach, EETS, OS 203 (London, 1937), pp. lxi–lxv; Saul Nathaniel Brody, *The Disease of the Soul: Leprosy in Medieval Literature* (Ithaca, NY, and London, 1974). There was a consequent belief that, like sin, leprosy could be washed away by the water of baptism, as Amiloun's leprosy is cleansed by the blood of his friend's children: see Brody, *The Disease of the Soul*, p. 132 n. 8; and cf. L. Thorndike, *A History of Magic and Experimental Science*, 8 vols (New York, 1923–58), I, 390.

1279 Cf. note to lines 1249–72.

1289–90 i.e. they take the oath that Amis had so feared.

1325–6 Cf. note to *Syr Tryamowre* 1220–3.

1341–4 Cf. *Syr Tryamowre* 1231–3.

1351–6 Cf. lines 2119–21. In *AA* (675–7) we are explicitly told that Amilun is not wounded in the battle.

1372 Cf. note to *King Horn* 623–4. In *AA* (661–4) Amilun has killed the steward by cleaving his head.

1402–4 Cf. *AA* 671: 'Les uns chantent, les autres plurent' ('some rejoiced, others wept'). In *AA* (697–770) we are given an account of Amilun's wedding to Florie and of their chaste wedding-night: Amilun explains the latter to Florie by telling her the truth.

1423–53 There is no direct equivalent to this passage in *AA*, though MS C does give some account of their reunion and their sorrow at parting again (*AA*, pp. 160–1).

1425 *forest plain*: this perhaps denotes a clearing in the forest.

1439–40 The more usual formula would have been for Amis to thank God for Amiloun's birth: cf. note to lines 344–5.

1474–1500 In *AA* (807–8), when asked by his wife to explain his conduct of the past weeks, Amilun replies: 'Dame, jeo ne le dirrai mes: / A ceo ne me fai jeo confes' ('My lady, I shan't tell you; I won't confess it'). Note how the Middle English poet seeks to disarm potential criticism of the somewhat dubious morality of his romance by putting this perfectly valid (and, indeed, 'correct') appraisal of the situation into the mouth of a character elsewhere described as 'unkende' (line 1456), 'wicked and schrewed' (line 1561).

1508 *sesed*: related to *seisin*, the freehold possession of landed property. The construction used here is the normal one; but cf. line 332, which probably has overtones of the same technical sense.

1512 Cf. line 1456, where Amiloun's wife is described as 'unkende'.

1525–36 In this instance, the Middle English agrees with other Anglo-Norman manuscripts *against* MS C in telling of the duke's death. In C, where his lord is the king, Charlemagne, Amys simply enjoys the land he has been given (*AA*, pp. 161–2). There is no mention of Amis's children at this point in *AA*.

1564–9 Not in *AA*; cf. note to lines 1474–1500.

1567 *Seyn Denis of Fraunce*: bishop of Paris in the third century. He was finally beheaded and, according to tradition, picked up his head and walked away. His cult received added impetus in the ninth century through confusion with the Neoplatonist pseudo-Dionysus the Areopagite, and many English churches were dedicated to him: see David Hugh Farmer, *The Oxford Dictionary of Saints* (Oxford, 1978), *s.n.* DENYS.

1573–1602 *AA* (815–18) says simply:

> La dame le tint trop en despit,
> Ne voleit entrer en son lit,
> Ne ne voleit od li parler,
> Ne od li beivre ne manger.

(The lady held him in great contempt and would not enter his bed, nor talk to him, nor eat or drink with him.)

MS C treats the episode more fully (*AA*, pp. 163–4) but without use of direct speech.

1579–82 Cf. note to line 686.

1608 For the sake of holy charity; cf. note to line 459.

1612–14 Only MS C of *AA* says that the lady has the *chambre* built herself (*AA*, p. 164, line 20). In other Anglo-Norman manuscripts it is described as a *bordel*, which, as Weiss points out (*BR*, p. 172 n. 13), 'means both hut and whorehouse'. Cf. lines 2465–9.

1619–20 Romance heroes quite frequently thank God in adversity: cf., e.g., *Sir Beues of Hamtoun*, ed. Kölbing, p. 74, lines 77–8.

1628 *AA* (829) says that the boy is 'Fiz d'un conte, son parent' ('a count's son, his relative'). In the Middle Ages the relationship with a maternal uncle (*eme*) was supposed to be of special significance.

1634–7 Cf. *AA* 888–9: 'La gent l'apellent Amiraunt, / Mes Owein esteit son dreit noun' ('people called him Amiraunt, but Owein was his real name'). MS A, alone among the Middle English versions, contains this detail; cf. note to line 2416.

1640 I am not entirely satisfied that MS A in fact reads *livere*, which is very unclearly written: cf., however, *levere* in MS C of *AA* (p. 164) and line 1659 below; these justify this reading.

1642 Cf. note to *King Horn* 1262.

1653 Cf. note to *King Horn* 1425.

1661–2 MS C of *AA* contains a long passage, not found else-where, in which Amilloun's wife punishes her son, Florentyn, so severely for visiting Amilun that the child dies (*AA*, pp. 166–8).

1681–1752 Most of this is not in *AA*; there (lines 909–12) they encounter famine *after* they have left with the donkey.

1809–12 Not in *AA*.

1825–63 This episode is much more briefly treated in *AA* (913–26), without any description of the hardships they suffer on account of the weather.

1867–79 Not in *AA*.

1882–4 Not in *AA*.

1885–2016 Again, this whole episode is treated much more briefly in most texts of *AA* (935–60), without use of direct speech; but cf. MS C (*AA*, pp. 174–5).

1900 *semly* probably denotes here 'in accordance with their status': cf. note to line 686.

1931 The sense is probably 'ask for alms (*gode*) on our behalf'; though it may be 'bring our errand to a successful conclusion'.

1946 *fole sage*: i.e. a professional fool, who is given licence to offer sound advice or comment in satirical form (like the Fool in *King Lear*). See also *BR*, p. 132 n. 25.

2014 *Seyn Martin*: a fourth-century officer in the Roman army, who embraced Christianity. The most famous story about him is that he divided his cloak to share it with a beggar and that Christ subsequently appeared to him in a dream wearing the cloak. The oath here, then, is particularly apposite.

2043 This may refer to the fact that in the Middle Ages lepers were often deprived of their property: see *Amis and Amiloun*, ed. Leach, note to line 2043.

2046 Cf. note to *King Horn* 1494.

2077–2100 Not in *AA*, where the count orders that the leper be thrown into prison, saying that he will question him later. Amilun begs him not to put him in prison, but to kill him outright.

2107–12 In *AA* Owein identifies Amilun more directly. At this point MS D of the Middle English text includes an extra stanza:

> [He] ys thi brother, Sir Amylioun,
> That whilom was a noble baroun
> Bothe to ryde and go,
> And now with sorwe ys dreue adoun.
> Nowe God, þat suffred passioun,
> Breng him oute of his wo!
> For the of blysse he ys bare,
> And thou yeldyst him all with care
> And brekest his bones atwo.
> That he halp the at thi nede,
> Well euell aquitest thou his mede.
> Alas, whi farest thou so?

Leach includes this stanza in his edition, which is based on the text of MS A (see *Amis and Amiloun*, ed. Leach, lines 2113–24); but if we assume Amis to have been fairly quick on the uptake, it is not strictly necessary to the sense.

2119–20 Cf. note to lines 1351–6.

2143–66 Not in *AA*.

2167–72 In *AA* (1056–65) Amis carries him to a chamber. We are told, however, that the lady often visits him: 'Com mes que ele fust sa suer / Plus n'i pout fere compaignie' ('Had she been his sister, she could not have showed him more friendship').

2174 Three years in *AA* (1070).

2188 Again, it is a voice, rather than an angel, that speaks to Amis in *AA* (1677); cf. note to lines 1249–72.

2191 *AA* contains no mention of Christmas.

2193–6 On the belief that leprosy could be cured by the application of children's blood, see Brody, *The Disease of the Soul*, pp. 72, 152. See also note to lines 1249–72.

2197–2202 There is no repetition of the dream in *AA*.

2203–8 Cf. *AA* 1086–92:

> 'A, deu,' dist il,' 'ke ne menti,
> Doint ke veirs seit mon sunge.
> Mes ore seit voir ou mensunge,
> Al meins la voiz voil esprover,
> Por mes enfanz ne voil lesser.
> Mult avroie fait bone jornee,
> Si par lur sank fust sane!'

('Oh God,' he said, 'who has never lied, grant my dream be true. But whether it's true or false, at least I want to test the voice, not ignore it on account of my children. I'll have done a very good day's work if he is healed by their blood!')

2209–38 Neither Amiloun's dream nor Amis's soul-searching is in *AA*.

2222 This perhaps means that they speak of their past adventures.

2239–68 None of this has any parallel in *AA*.

2257–2310 The furtiveness and secrecy of Amis's doings in this passage are entirely absent from *AA*. Amis himself seems to doubt that what he is doing is right, despite the angelic messages that have prompted him. His subterfuges, particularly with regard to the keys, also seem somewhat pointless: cf. lines 2362–70.

2275–95 Cf. *AA* 1103–4: 'Le piere des fiz n'out nule pite / Ambedou ad le chief trenche' ('The children's father had no pity, but cut the heads off them both').

2296–2328 Not in *AA*.

2329–34 In *AA* (1105–6) Amis wraps Amilun in the blood-stained sheets.

2336–64 Amis's prayer is not in *AA*, though he does go to church to pray *before* he kills the children (lines 1093–6). In *AA* (lines 1111–18) Amis takes the fully recovered Amilun to church, where the lady is overjoyed to see him.

2367 Cf. *AA* 1119–20: '"Dame," dist il, "bien vus dirraie, / Mes trop vus desconforteraie"' ('"My lady," he said, "I shall tell you indeed, but it will grieve you terribly"').

2377–9 Cf. *AA* 1123–4: 'La dame a deu ses mains tendi / E gre e graces li rendi' ('The lady stretched her hands up to God and gave Him thanks').

2386–8 Not in *AA*.

2389–2400 Not in *AA*: cf. note to lines 2336–64.

2402 Cf. note to line 474; here the sense seems to be that no one could appreciate the full extent of their joy.

2409 In *AA* (1142) they are playing with a sunbeam, a symbol of Christ: see *BR*, p. 176 n. 15.

2413–60 Amilun's preparations are not described in *AA*, where we are told that his wife hears of his recovery and becomes anxious and afraid. Although she has planned to remarry (line 1158), she has not done so, and thus there is no wedding-feast in progress when Amilun returns.

2416 This part of the text is taken from MS S, which does not give Amiloun's attendant the alternative name of Amoraunt: see note to lines 1634–7.

2462 The reference to *broun and blake* is puzzling, and may mean, vaguely, 'all and sundry'; *broun*, however, is usually applied to swords, in the sense 'burnished' (cf. line 2453).

2468 In *AA* (1227) it is a *garce* ('harlot') who feeds her, through a window.

2476–7 Cf. notes to lines 1508, 1634–7.

2488 On the tradition that Amis and Amiloun were venerated at Saint-Albin in Lombardy, see *BR*, p. 178 n. 16. *AA* (1247–8) states: 'deu fait pur eus grant vertuz, / Evegles veer e parler mutz' ('God performs great miracles through them: the blind see, the mute speak').

Syr Tryamowre

1–12 Cf. note to *King Horn* 1–2.

19–24 Cf. notes to *Amis and Amiloun* 205–16, 705.

27 Schmidt (*STS*, note to line 27) interprets this as meaning 'faithful, as e.g. the spearpoint is to the shaft', *tree* here meaning 'wood'. Cf. the more usual simile in line 17.

31–6 The motif of a childless couple's offering something to God in return for a child occurs more than once in Middle English romance: cf., e.g., *Octavian* 76–81 (in *Six Middle English Romances*, ed. Maldwyn Mills (London, 1973), p. 77).

38 On papal preaching of the crusade, and the wearing by crusaders of a red cross sewn on to the surcoat, see Steven Runciman, *A History of the Crusades*, Vol. I: *The First Crusade and the Foundation of the Kingdom of Jerusalem*, Penguin edn (1965; reissued Harmondsworth, 1978), p. 109.

80 *For specyall tryste* may mean either that he consigned the queen to Marrok's keeping as a special trust, or that he did so because he especially trusted Marrok.

103–4 Cf. *Sir Percyvell of Gales* 931–2 (in *Ywain and Gawain [etc.]*, ed. Maldwyn Mills (London, 1992), p. 126).

105–7 The sense of these lines is inextricably entangled in the syntax. MS P reads 'If I may knowe ever after this, / That thou tise me to doon amis', which has the advantage of being intelligible.

111 Cf. *The Erle of Tolous* 578.

116 Cf. note to line 27.

132 *in Goddys grace* probably means 'on God's behalf'. MS P treats the line as part of the next stanza, and reads: 'To fight gains goddes foos'.

140–1 These lines presumably refer to his prayers for a child, if we assume from the previous line that he has also gone on pilgrimage, as distinct from his crusading.

156 The line may be corrupt; one would expect the king to enquire, or to be told, the queen's news.

189 The unemended reading *Or* ('Before') makes nonsense of the steward's accusation and is inconsistent with lines 185–6.

198 This is a stock expression but may have here more than a conventional significance, denoting that the steward proclaimed his loyalty as well as maintaining it inwardly (or so he says).

211–16 On the notion that it is less sinful if one avoids direct responsibility for a person's death, cf. note to *King Horn* 101–10.

223–5 Noblemen often acknowledged their own illegitimate sons, who might also have rights of inheritance: see Shahar, *Childhood in the Middle Ages*, pp. 209, 321 (n. 3).

237 *bresyd* here may mean 'shaggy': see *STS*, note to line 237.

245 *be there assente* suggests that some sort of judicial body has decided these sentences.

309 The sense is probably that he paid them back, or gave as good as he got (cf. lines 327, 1219).

313–14 Bevis of Hampton is similarly aided in battle by his horse, Arundel: see *Sir Beues of Hamtoun*, ed. Kölbing, lines 4447–50.

333 Cf. note to *King Horn* 156.

343 This perhaps means that Marrok's men did not know what they could tell him.

348 The sense is similar to that of line 343, but its significance at this point is more obscure.

360 Marrok's conduct in defacing the body of a fallen adversary is condemned here as unbecoming in a knight.

382–7 On the motif of the faithful hound who avenges his master's death, particularly in relation to the Sebilla story (see p. xvii above), see Laura A. Hibbard, *Mediæval Romance in England: A Study of the Sources and Analogues of the Non-Cyclic Metrical Romances* (New York, 1924), pp. 286–7.

388 Cf. line 567, where we are told that the body remained uncorrupted.

389 This may mean that the hound demonstrated his own gratitude to his master, or that we should be grateful to him for his loyalty. In the latter case, a pronoun is missing.

406–11 It is not uncommon for 'calumniated queens' in romance to give birth alone in the forest: see, e.g., *Valentine and Orson*, ed. Arthur Dickson, EETS, OS 204 (London, 1937; repr. 1971), p. 33.

452 The name occurs as that of Launfal's fairy mistress in *Syr Launfal* (255). It does not occur elsewhere.

464 According to certain didactic writers, it was the main function of mothers to rear their sons up to the age of seven: see Shahar, *Childhood in the Middle Ages*, p. 209. It is not clear, however, what sort of 'work' Margaret teaches Tryamowre. In *Emaré* 731 we are told that the heroine 'tawghte her sone nortowre [i.e. courtesy]' (see *Six Middle English Romances*, ed. Mills, p. 66).

472–571 Cf. note to lines 381–7.

486 i.e. the first day of the Christmas festivities.

499 Cf. note to *Amis and Amiloun* 29–30.

525 This must refer back to lines 521–2.

567 It was a sign of special sanctity if a corpse remained uncorrupted: cf. *St Erkenwald*, ed. Sir Israel Gollancz (London, 1922), lines 86–96. Cf., however, line 388 above.

574 *awnturs knyght*: i.e. a knight proved in adventures.

578–80 Cf. note to *King Horn* 1494.

583–4 The unemended reading (*delay*) of MS C makes no good sense; MS P reads: 'Sir Rogers body the next day / The king buryed in good array'.

655–7 These lines seem confused, and are probably corrupt. A better reading would be achieved if lines 654 and 657 were transposed, as in MS P.

687 Tryamowre wishes to prove himself a worthy warrior by shedding his blood in battle: cf. Maurice Keen, *Chivalry* (New Haven, Conn., and London, 1984), p. 88.

690 In the romances at least, the normal age for a youth to achieve knighthood is fifteen: see note to *Amis and Amiloun* 163–5.

726 This perhaps means 'And others, who had come to prove themselves'. In MS P the couplet reads: 'Princes, lords & dukes of might / Themselues for to assay'.

752 Cf. note to *King Horn* 87–8.

754 Cf. note to *Syr Launfal* 25.

801 Schmidt (*STS*, note to line 801) takes this as meaning that some of the horses had wandered off and were roaming around loose, but even if that is the correct interpretation it does not fit the context in any obvious way. The sense seems to me to be irrecoverable.

846 Cf. line 749.

848 *wyth comyns assente*: i.e. with the consent of the people, though probably with no very democratic implications; cf. line 937.

881–2 The sense appears to be that what had started as King Ardus' men coming to Tryamowre's aid had become a series of single combats.

904 Cf. note to *Amis and Amiloun* 29–30.

945 This probably means that they had achieved nothing with the princess.

955–6 Cf. lines 749, 846.

978 Cf. note to *King Horn* 1376.

983–4 Hurling large stones down on the besieging enemy was standard practice in siege warfare.

997 But cf. lines 871–9.

1043 We have not been told of any promise; but cf. line 1378.

1066–8 Such penalties were common in the Middle Ages for taking the king's game.

1089 See *Sir Gawain and the Green Knight*, ed. Tolkien and Gordon, note to line 1362; *Sir Eglamour of Artois*, ed. Frances E. Richardson, EETS, OS 256 (London, 1965), note to lines 298–300. Both cite Twiti, Edward II's huntsman: 'Quant le cerf est pris vous devez corner quatre mootz' ('When the stag is caught, you must blow four long notes on your horn').

1190–1 As an unknighted man was not technically able to lead troops in battle, there is a number of parallel historical instances of the conferring of knighthood in association with an imminent battle: see Barber, *The Knight and Chivalry*, p. 41.

1219 The precise meaning of this line is unclear, but the general sense seems to be that Tryamowre means to pay Moradas back for the blows he has received: cf. line 309.

1220–3 For the frequent recurrence in Middle English romance of the motif of a horse's being killed by a blow intended for its rider, see *Sir Beues of Hamtoun*, ed. Kölbing, note to A 1887. It is always considered shameful, though it is usually the hero who does it, accidentally. Cf. *Amis and Amiloun* 1325–6.

1231–3 Cf. *Amis and Amiloun* 1341–4.

1251 The reading *Moradas* must be wrong, since Tryamowre has just run his sword through Moradas' heart. Probably we should read *Ardus* (i.e. the emperor asks Ardus for a truce).

1325 The time taken to ride a mile: estimated at about twenty minutes.

1368 Cf. note to *Amis and Amiloun* 845.

1370 Cf. note to *Florys and Blauncheflour* 218.

1472 Cf. note to *Amis and Amiloun* 845.

1479 She does not know how strong he is, because she is unaware as yet that it is Tryamowre. In the following lines, however, Barnard is able to identify his arms.

1497 Cf. note to *Amis and Amiloun* 29–30. Meaningless tags do not abound in *Syr Tryamowre*, however, and I suspect that the line is corrupt. MS P reads 'The fought full sore indeed'.

1551 This is perhaps a grim joke: 'he tricked him out in the latest fashion'.

1556–7 The lines do not yield a satisfactory sense, but it is clear that they continue the savage humour at Burlond's expense. There has been no suggestion hitherto that Burlond is a giant.

1561–3 A similar incident occurs in the fifteenth-century ballad *Chevy Chase*: see *The Oxford Book of Ballads*, newly sel. and ed. James Kinsley (Oxford, 1969; repr. 1971), p. 505.

1576 An unusual epithet for a woman; it must refer to her political power.

1584 Cf. note to line 848.

1619 Many Middle English romances uphold the ideal of considerate treatment of messengers, irrespective of the nature of the message: see M. A. Gist, *Love and War in the Middle English Romances* (Philadelphia, 1947), pp. 171–7. Generosity to messengers is always a sign of true nobility: cf., e.g., *Sir Beues of Hamtoun*, ed. Kölbing, lines 1171–4.

1636 Cf. note to *Amis and Amiloun* 686.

Syr Launfal

4–5 *Syr Launfal* derives (via the Middle English *Sir Landevale*) from the Breton lay *Lanval* of Marie de France, the most famous exponent, if not the originator, of the genre (see p. xviii above. *Sir Landevale* itself makes no mention of its source.

8 *Kardevyle*: Cardiff (= *Kardoel* in *Lanval*). According to Zimmer (cited *SLB*, note to line 8), 'the frequent mention of Carlisle in the Breton lays may be a reminiscence of the expedition of 1092, in which Breton warriors may have taken part'.

13–22 Neither *Lanval* nor *Landevale* names these knights. Perceval (the Grail knight) and Ywain are both the heroes of Middle English romances (see *Ywain and Gawain [etc.]*, ed. Mills); Gawain, Gaheris and Agravain are the sons of Arthur's half-sister, Morgause, and of King Lot of Orkney; Kay, Arthur's stepbrother and seneschal, is usually characterized as malicious and cowardly; Lancelot, of course, is Guinevere's lover (though that fact is not mentioned in this romance: see note to lines 46–8); King Ban of Benwick (Lancelot's father) and King Bors of Gaul are Arthur's allies; *Booght* is puzzling – it may be an additional name for Ban or, more probably, a scribal corruption;

Galafre may possibly be a mistake for Galahad; Launfal himself does not appear elsewhere in Arthurian romance.

25 Bliss (*SLB*, note to line 25) quotes the definition given in *OED*: 'A young knight, not old enough, or having too few vassals, to display his own banner, and who therefore followed the banner of another; a novice in arms.'

28–30 Generosity (*largesse*) is a knightly virtue: cf., e.g., *Sir Isumbras* 25–30 (in *Six Middle English Romances*, ed. Mills, p. 125). As in *Launfal*, it is seen as being carried to excess in *Sir Amadace* 13–24 (*ibid.*, p. 169).

32 Cf. notes to *Amis and Amiloun* 191, 205–16. Launfal's duties seem to have been solely domestic, like those of the Middle English Amiloun.

37–72 Not in *Landevale* or in *Lanval*.

38 Merlin is not mentioned in *Landevale*, in *Lanval* or elsewhere in this romance.

41–2 Guinevere is usually represented, at least in later romance, as the daughter of King Leodegraunce of Camelerde: see, further, *SLB*, p. 38. The parentage ascribed to her here is peculiar to this romance.

44 The verb *liken* is usually used in an impersonal construction, such that the sense here would be that Guinevere did not like Launfal. However, lines 45–8 suggest that it is he who does not like her. Cf. note to lines 676–81.

46–8 The hostile attitude towards Guinevere in *Syr Launfal* goes back to an earlier Arthurian tradition: see *SLB*, pp. 37–8. Guinevere's love-affair with Lancelot is not mentioned in *Syr Launfal*.

50 *Wytsonday*: one of the great feasts of the Christian year. Cf. note to *King Horn* 475–6. Bliss (*SLB*, note to line 50) notes: 'Whitsunday is especially common as the occasion of the beginning of adventures in the Arthurian romances.' Cf. line 133.

58 Cf. notes to *Amis and Amiloun* 686, 1900.

82 Cf. note to *Amis and Amiloun* 1628. Sir Hugh and Sir John (see line 136) are otherwise unknown to fame, but cf. Bliss's suggestion that the names may be corruptions of Ywain and

Gawain, who were indeed Arthur's nephews (*SLB*, note to line 82).

85–216 There is no parallel in *Landevale* or in *Lanval* to this episode, which is borrowed from *Graelent*.

88 *Karlyoun*: Caerleon-upon-Usk, which Geoffrey of Monmouth describes as having become a glorious city in Arthur's time; it is therefore often identified with Camelot: see Derek Brewer, *Arthur's Britain: The Land and the Legend* (Cambridge, 1985), p. 109.

89 In *Graelent* (172–80) he is not described as a mayor.

118–20 Launfal is speaking of what it will be like for his two attendants to serve a lord of *lytyll pryse*; in line 120, *he* should be read as an impersonal 'one'.

130 The unemended reading *savargelych* shows an unusual form and suggests emendation to the more commonplace *largelych* ('generously', 'lavishly'); cf., however, the reading of *Landevale* (23), *wildely*.

133 Cf. note to line 50.

136 Cf. note to line 82.

149 *Glastyngbery*: Glastonbury, replete with Arthurian associations, and the traditional site of the island of Avalon: see Brewer, *Arthur's Britain*, pp. 60–2.

171 Cf. note to *Amis and Amiloun* 507.

181 This probably refers to Trinity Sunday, the first Sunday after Whitsun.

183 *Carlyoun*: cf. note to line 88.

185 *boriaes*: cf. note to *Florys and Blauncheflour* 155.

211 *courser*: a powerful horse of a kind used by knights in battle.

214–16 This incident is peculiar to *Syr Launfal*; but cf. *Lanval* (46), where Lanval's horse trembles so much on approaching a river that he is obliged to dismount. On the supernatural resonances of this, which Chestre has perhaps rationalized away, see *SLB*, note to line 214; Elizabeth Williams, 'Hunting the deer: some uses of a motif-complex in Middle English romance and saint's life', in *Romance in Medieval England*, ed. Mills, Fellows and Meale, pp. 187–206 (pp. 190–4).

227 To sit under the shadow of a tree invariably leads to some momentous event in the Breton lays: cf., e.g., *Sir Orfeo*, ed. A. J. Bliss, 2nd edn (Oxford, 1966), lines 69–82 (Auchinleck text). Cf. Constance Bullock-Davies, '"Ympe tre" and "nemeton"', *Notes and Queries*, n.s. 9 (1962), 6–9; John Block Friedman, 'Eurydice, Heurodis, and the noon-day demon', *Speculum*, 41 (1966), 22–9. The detail is not in *Lanval*, but it is present in *Landevale* (42).

230 Cf. note to *Amis and Amiloun* 507.

232 It is possible that *inde* here denotes the colour indigo: see *SLB*, note to line 385.

237 *grys* is specifically grey fur; *gro* simply denotes fur of some kind.

243 Cf. *Landevale* 63–4: 'Fayrer women neuer he see –/They semyd angels of hevin hie'.

247 The kerchief was a covering which might be worn to cover the head or the bosom.

255 Cf. note to *Syr Tryamowre* 452.

261 *flour*: either 'flower' or 'flour' – probably the latter.

266 Bliss (*SLB*, note to line 266), following French & Hale, notes that Saracen weaving and metalwork were much admired in the Middle Ages; probably the pavilion is an elaborately woven tent.

271–3 Cf. note to *Florys and Blauncheflour* 584.

274 Alexander, like Julius Caesar, was one of the Nine Worthies (cf. note to *Florys and Blauncheflour* 181) and was the hero of several Middle English romances. See also note to *Florys and Blauncheflour* 584.

275 Cf. *Landevale* 88–9: 'Ne Salamon yn hys honour,/Ne Charlemayn the riche kyng'.

278 *Olyroun*: *Landevale* (92) reads *Amylion*; *Lanval* (641) has *Aualun*: cf. note to line 149.

281 Avalon, and fairy lands generally (such as the Irish Tir-nan-Og), were traditionally located in the west.

292–300 Cf. note to lines 934–45.

301–6 Cf. note to *King Horn* 271–2. No criticism of Tryamour's behaviour is implied – perhaps such conduct is allowable in a fairy.

319–33 *Landevale* and *Lanval* do not specify the nature of the gifts; the details are taken from *Graelent*.

323 Cf. note to *Florys and Blauncheflour* 162.

327 Gyfre does not occur in *Landevale* or in *Lanval*. He corresponds to the unnamed attendant given to the hero in *Graelent* (351).

328–9 A *pensel* is a small pennon. Ermine is one of the 'furs' used in heraldry; but the *thre ermyns* sound more like heraldic representations of the actual animal.

336 Bliss interprets this line: 'I have never embraced a more generous [lady]': see *SLB*, note to line 336.

344 *Pyement* and *clare* are both spiced red wines; *reynysch wyn* is a white wine like modern hock.

357 Perhaps a 'mixed simile': the modern sense of 'still' accords better with the comparison to a stone, while the sense 'quiet', 'silent' fits the context better.

359 Cf. note to *Amis and Amiloun* 474.

361–5 *Syr Launfal* here agrees with *Landevale* against *Lanval* (143–50) and *Graelent* (316–18), where the lady gives the hero this warning *before* their night of love-making.

373–420 Not in *Landevale* or in *Lanval*.

385 Cf. note to line 232.

392 The phrase *yn present* may perhaps have more the sense of 'to Launfal in person': cf. *SLB*, note to line 392.

422–30 The rhetorical repetition is also a feature of *Landevale* (173–7), though there the repeated word is *Landevale*; cf. *Lanval* 209–12.

430 Romances often contain examples of generosity to minstrels – perhaps dictated by self-interest.

473 i.e. the heraldic crest surmounting the helmet.

474 See note to lines 4–5; and cf. note to *Amis and Amiloun* 27.

479 *Walssche* can also be used to mean, simply, 'foreign'.

489 *Wythout oth yswore* is a formulaic locution with the sense 'without doubt' (cf. line 456). Here, however, it may also convey the sense that Launfal's preeminence was undisputed.

505–612 The entire Valentyne episode is absent from *Landevale*, though it is paralleled in *Lanval* and in *Graelent*, as well as in a story told by Andreas Capellanus. On the relationships between these versions and the episode as it appears in *Syr Launfal*, see *SLB*, note to lines 505–612, and p. 25.

527 Cf. lines 1027–8; in the present context the words are clearly insulting.

548 Cf. note to *Amis and Amiloun* 434.

582 This is the first indication that Gyfre has the power of making himself invisible to all (but Launfal?). See *SLB*, p. 26.

606 Cf. note to *King Horn* 1494.

618 Probably the feast of St John the Baptist (24 June).

668 On the fiddle, see Page, *Voices and Instruments*, pp. 144–5; the citole was a plucked stringed instrument related to the lute.

676–81 On the inconsistency (if there is one) between these lines and lines 44 and 177–80 – an 'inconsistency' not found in *Landevale* or in *Graelent* – see *SLB*, p. 28. Cf. note to line 44.

683 Cf. *Landevale* 219–22:

> 'Madame,' he said, 'be God, nay!
> J wil be traitour neuer, parfay!
> J haue do the kyng oth & feaulté –
> He shal not be traid for me!'

689 In *Lanval* (281–2) the queen explicitly accuses the hero of homosexuality; *Landevale* (226) has exactly the same line as *Syr Launfal*.

726 Cf. note to *King Horn* 1494.

733–44 Not in *Lanval* or in *Landevale*. In *Graelent* (529–30) the hero finds that the attendant given to him by his mistress has disappeared. On possible sources for this episode, see M. Mills, 'A note on *Sir Launfal*, 733–744', *Medium Ævum*, 35 (1966), 122–4.

741 Cf. note to *Amis and Amiloun* 27.

750 Cf. note to *Amis and Amiloun* 434.

811–16 Cf. note to *Amis and Amiloun* 877–97.

831 Cf. *Landevale* 329–30, which (following *Lanval*) read: 'The kyng lett recorte tho / The sewt and the answer also' ('The king had the charge and the defence read out from the record'). The meaning of the line here, however, remains obscure. See *SLB*, note to line 831.

846 A nice irony, for Launfal will 'flee' with his mistress.

887 *Champayne*: *Landevale* (388) reads *Almayn* (Germany).

897 The line is undoubtedly corrupt. See *SLB*, note to line 897.

899 Cf. note to *Amis and Amiloun* 686.

904 Cf. *Landevale* 406–8:

> Lete dight thyn hall with honour,
> Bothe rofe and grounde & wallys
> With clothys of gold and riche pallys.

929–30 Cf. *Landevale* 428–30:

> There nesse kyng þat hath gold ne fee
> That myght by þat palfrey
> Withoute sellyng of londe awey.

934–45 The details of the lady's physical appearance (her grey eyes, golden hair and slender waist) conform to a clearly defined ideal: see D. S. Brewer, 'The ideal of feminine beauty in medieval literature . . .', *Modern Language Review*, 50 (1955), 257–69. Cf. *The Erle of Tolous* 340–57.

961 *Landevale* (447), following *Lanval*, has *sparowhauke*. According to medieval notions as to the falcons or hawks properly carried by the various ranks of society, the gerfalcon should be carried by a king (Tryamour is, of course, a king's daughter: see line 278). Sparrowhawks were usually assigned to priests, but females were often carried by ladies, and the bird was considered particularly appropriate for mixed hunting-parties of men and women: see John Cummins, *The Hound and the Hawk: The Art of Medieval Hunting* (London, 1988), pp. 188, 194.

972 Cf. *Landevale* 459–60: 'Now J haue her seyn with myn ee, / J ne reke when that J dye'.

1006–8 The blinding of Guinevere occurs only in *Syr Launfal*.

1015–17 In *Landevale* (503–28), though not in *Lanval*, the hero is upbraided by his mistress but finally secures her forgiveness. The passage in *Landevale* ends: 'Loo, howe love is lefe to wyn / Of wemen that arn of gentyll kyn!' (lines 527–8).

1023 Cf. note to line 278.

1025 In *Graelent* (735–40) the horse is heard neighing for his master, who was swept off his back in crossing a river.

1027–8 Cf. lines 526–7.

1039 We know nothing of the poet except his name, though the romances of *Octavian* and *Libeaus Desconus* have also been attributed to him: see M. Mills, 'The composition and style of the "Southern" *Octavian*, *Sir Launfal* and *Libeaus Desconus*', *Medium Ævum*, 31 (1962), 88–109.

The Erle of Tolous

1–6 Cf. note to *King Horn* 1–2.

131 A proverbial saying: see *Sir Beues of Hamtoun*, ed. Kölbing, note to E 4313[200].

149 The precise sense is unclear: perhaps 'Therefore whatever I decide to do, my decision is taken in sorrow'.

183 They would probably have been hawking for waterfowl by the river. Cf. *Syr Tryamowre* 1177.

190 The book and bell are those used in the celebration of Mass.

The oath is a common one in medieval literature, but accords well with the quasi-clerical elements in the romance: see, in particular, line 286 etc.

235 *Seynt Andrewe.* The founding of the Church of Constantinople was attributed to him in the Middle Ages, and his relics are supposed to have been translated to Scotland, whose patron saint he therefore became: see Farmer, *The Oxford Dictionary of Saints*, s.n. ANDREW.

245 Although there are good pragmatic reasons for the earl's disguise, note also that he disguises himself now as a hermit, later (lines 1058–9) as a monk; and that his crucial encounter with the empress takes place in her chapel (line 305).

256 Another common medieval oath. Christ's apocryphal Harrowing of Hell was represented in the miracle plays and, most famously, is the subject of Passus XVIII of *Piers Plowman*.

285 The stanza lacks three lines. MS A reads: 'Hit were agaynst curtesye / For to do hym vylanye / That trusteth the untyll'; MS T has a couplet only: 'For I saye the by Sayne Gyle / It ne es noghte goddis wille'; MS R reads: 'Late thou never that gentyll knyght / Also ferre forth as thou myght / Sofer no maner off ill'.

307 An oriel is a recess or antechamber with a window.

323 Cf. note to *Syr Tryamowre* 1325.

340–57 Cf. note to *Syr Launfal* 934–45.

350 Not part of the conventional description; but cf. note to line 245.

380 This must mean something by which he will be able to remember her each day.

403–4 He is referring, of course, to the empress herself: cf. line 897, where the emperor is referred to as *the kyng*.

414 Cf. note to *King Horn* 156.

430 The name *Kaym* may be a corruption of that of Cain, who, as the first murderer, typified wickedness in the Middle Ages.

540 An example of the somewhat more specialized religious language of the romance.

549 Cf. note to line 190.

572 Cf. note to *King Horn* 1494; cf. also line 585 below.

578 Cf. *Syr Tryamowre* 111.

597 Cf. note to *King Horn* 156.

606 The usual expression is 'to wed (or marry) to board and bed'. The phrase therefore has a certain appropriateness here in recalling the empress's married status.

625 A common distortion of the phrase *ord and end*, meaning 'beginning and end', 'the whole matter' (cf. *Syr Launfal* 314).

659 *myddyllerd*: cf. note to *Florys and Blauncheflour* 608.

675 A serious consideration, since the emperor would provide for the knights in return for their services. Cf. line 678.

676 A proverbial expression, heavily ironic in that it is the empress's *trewthe* that nearly brings her to the stake.

706–56 The motif of a young man's being 'framed' in order to incriminate a faithful wife occurs elsewhere in the romances: e.g. in *Octavian* 133–56 (in *Six Middle English Romances*, ed. Mills, pp. 78–9). It is unusual, however, and disturbing that he should be characterized to such an extent: Sir Antore's courtesy and consideration towards the empress, which lead to his own death, are tellingly contrasted with the two knights' ruthless pursuit of their own ends.

707 Cf. note to *King Horn* 230–4.

708 Cf. note to *King Horn* 19.

729 *Seynte Jermayne*: probably Germanus of Auxerre, who refuted the Pelagian heresy (the denial of the doctrine of Original Sin), and is supposed to have directed British forces in battle against Picts and Saxons: see Farmer, *The Oxford Dictionary of Saints, s.n.* GERMANUS OF AUXERRE.

788 The sense is unclear; perhaps it is something like 'You will be astonished at how word of this will spread'.

793 *Thy love ys lorne* may mean that her beloved is dead or that the love she allegedly gave him is therefore wasted.

805–10 Cf. note to *Amis and Amiloun* 1015–16.

857 Cf. note to *Amis and Amiloun* 886–8.

873 Cf. note to *Syr Tryamowre* 848.

880 The lady would have slept literally naked; the young man was still partially dressed. Cf. *Amis and Amiloun* 1972.

941–2 Cf. note to line 540.

966 The earl seems to be saying that he will do as the merchant wishes, but in what respect is not clear.

988 *eme*: maternal uncle. Cf. note to *Amis and Amiloun* 1628.

1018 The oath by St Paul perhaps acquires a certain irony through the saint's reputation for misogyny.

1058–9 Cf. note to line 245.

1091 Perhaps 'You will answer to us' or 'You will behave rightly towards us'.

1094 Cf. note to *Amis and Amiloun* 845.

1109 The basinet was a small, light helmet over which a larger one, resting on the shoulders, might be worn – as is clearly the case here.

1144 The intention here is surely comic – that the emperor should think a bishopric an appropriate reward for a fighting monk.

1158 Cf. note to *Amis and Amiloun* 156.

1197 Cf. note to *Amis and Amiloun* 27.

1198 Cf. notes to *Amis and Amiloun* 188, 191, 205–16.

1199 Cf. note to *Amis and Amiloun* 1508.

1214 Cf. note to *Syr Launfal* 4–5.

1216–18 Cf. note to *King Horn* 1525–32.